Yosemite Valley
Free Climbs
S U P E R T O P O S

Greg Barnes
Chris McNamara
Steve Roper
Todd Snyder

Published by
SuperTopo
2 Bradford Way
Mill Valley, CA 94941
www.supertopo.com

Topos and text by Chris McNamara, Greg Barnes, and Todd Snyder
History by Steve Roper
Managing Editor and Designer: Sarah Felchlin
Contributing Designer: David Safanda
Editors: Sarah Felchlin, Chris McNamara, and Greg Barnes
Copyeditor: "Pass the Pitons" Pete Zabrok

Front cover: Timmy O'Neill on the East Buttress of El Capitan. *Photo by Corey Rich*
Back cover: Rikke Ishoy fires Fish Crack. *Photo by Corey Rich*

Library of Congress Cataloging-in-Publication Data

Yosemite Valley free climbs : Supertopos / by Greg Barnes, Chris McNamara, Steve Roper, and Todd Snyder.-- 1st ed.
    p. cm.
  Includes index.
  ISBN 0-9672391-4-1 (pbk. : alk. paper)
  1. Rock climbing--California--Yosemite Valley--Guidebooks. 2. Yosemite Valley (Calif.)--Guidebooks. I. Barnes, Greg, 1971-
GV199.42.C22Y6799 2003
796.52'23'0979447--dc21
                    2003001292

Contents

Acknowledgements	5
Preface	9
Introduction	11
Ratings	18
Free Climbing Ratings	19
Minimize Your Impact	20
Staying Alive	22
Cam sizes by brand	32
Understanding the maps	33
Yosemite overview maps	34
Arch Rock	37
Cookie Cliff	40
Pat and Jack Pinnacle	47
Generator Station	53
New Diversions Cliff	54
Knob Hill	57
Reed's Pinnacle Area	60
Five and Dime Cliff	66
Highway Star	68
El Capitan	69
East Buttress, 5.10b	71
El Capitan Base	74
Schultz's Ridge	82
The Moratorium, 5.11b	83
Schultz's Ridge Base	84
Manure Pile Buttress	88
Camp 4 Wall	94
Swan Slab	96
Five Open Books	100
Sunnyside Bench	108
Arrowhead Arête	112
Church Bowl	116

Royal Arches Area	120
Super Slide, 5.9	120
Serenity Crack, 5.10d	125
Sons of Yesterday, 5.10a	126
Royal Arches, 5.10b or 5.7 A0	128
Arches Terrace, 5.8 R	134
North Dome	135
South Face, 5.8	136
Crest Jewel, 5.10a	138
Washington Column	140
Astroman, 5.11c	141
North Dome Gully	144
Half Dome	146
Snake Dike, 5.7 R	147
Glacier Point Apron	150
Sentinel Rock	156
Steck Salathé, 5.10b	157
Lower Cathedral Spire	161
South by Southwest, 5.11a	162
Higher Cathedral Spire	164
Regular Route, 5.9	165
Higher Cathedral Rock	168
Braille Book, 5.8	169
Northeast Buttress, 5.9	171
Middle Cathedral Rock	174
East Buttress, 5.10c or 5.9 A0	176
Kor-Beck, 5.9	179
Central Pillar of Frenzy, 5.9	180
DNB, 5.11 or 5.10 A0 R	182
Lower Cathedral Rock	186
The Rostrum	188
North Face, 5.11c	189
Appendix	
Crag Comparison Chart	193
Yosemite Topropes	194
Climbs by Rating	196
Climbs by Technique	199
Climbs by Name	202

Warning!

Climbing is an inherently dangerous sport in which severe injuries or death may occur. Relying on the information in this book may increase the danger.

When climbing you can only rely on your skill, training, experience and conditioning. **If you have any doubts as to your ability to safely climb any route in this guide, do not try it.**

This book is neither a professional climbing instructor nor a substitute for one. **It is not an instructional book. Do not use it as one.** It contains information that is nothing more than a compilation of opinions about climbing in Yosemite Valley. **These opinions are neither facts nor promises.** Treat the information as opinions and nothing more. Do not substitute these opinions for your own common sense and experience.

Assumption of Risk

There may be errors in this book resulting from the mistakes of the authors and/or the people with whom they consulted. The information was gathered from a variety of sources, which may not have been independently verified. Those who provided the information may have made mistakes in their descriptions. The authors may have made mistakes in their conveyance of the information in this book. **The authors cannot, therefore, guarantee the correctness of any of the information contained in this book.** The topographical maps, the photo-diagrams, the difficulty ratings, the protection ratings, the approach and/or descent information, the suggestions about equipment and other matters may be incorrect or misleading. Fixed protection may be absent, unreliable, or misplaced. **You must keep in mind that the information in this book may be erroneous, so use your own judgement when choosing, approaching, climbing, or descending from a route described in this book.**

DO NOT USE THIS BOOK UNLESS YOU [AND YOUR ESTATE] PROMISE NEVER TO TRY TO SUE US IF YOU GET HURT OR KILLED.

Disclaimer of Warranties

THE AUTHORS AND PUBLISHER WARN THAT THIS BOOK CONTAINS ONLY THE AUTHORS' OPINION ON THE SUBJECTS DISCUSSED. THEY MAKE NO OTHER WARRANTIES, EXPRESS OR IMPLIED, OF MERCHANTABILITY, FITNESS FOR PURPOSE, OR OTHERWISE, AND IN ANY EVENT, THEIR LIABILITY FOR BREACH OF ANY WARRANTY OR CONTRACT WITH RESPECT TO THE CONTENT OF THIS BOOK IS LIMITED TO THE PURCHASE PRICE OF THE BOOK. THEY FURTHER LIMIT TO SUCH PURCHASE PRICE THEIR LIABILITY ON ACCOUNT OF ANY KIND OF NEGLIGENT BEHAVIOR WHATSOEVER ON THEIR PART WITH RESPECT TO THE CONTENTS OF THIS BOOK.

Acknowledgements

This book is the collective work of hundreds of climbers. Listed below are those we want to acknowledge who took the time to make sure our information is as accurate as possible.

First of all, SuperTopo is not just Chris Mac. It is a team of climbers which is motivated to avoid real jobs, climb a lot, and be poor. Sarah Felchlin is the Managing Editor and is the only reason anything gets completed remotely close to schedule. Greg Barnes is our top author and rebolting god who spends the year migrating among awesome climbing areas. (Tough life, Greg!) Randy Spurrier is the brains—make that the only brain—behind the SuperTopo web site. Steve Roper is the SuperTopo historian who also gives gentle writing advice to Chris such as, "This is shit, man!" David Safanda keeps SuperTopo looking slick.

Next, we need to thank all the folks with inside local knowledge who provided either topos or detailed beta: Jerry Anderson, Karl Baba, Bruce Bindner, Mark Kroese, Erik Sloan, Tom Frost, and Todd Snyder.

Also, thank you to the many people who provided feedback: Joel Ager, Mark Anderson, Justin Bastien, Robert Behrens, Eric Beck, Tresa Black, Andy Bourne, Dave Buchanan, Chongo, Coiler, Clint Cummins, John Dill, Dick Duane, Lincoln Else, David Emrich, Steve Fettke, Mark Fincher, Hans and Jacqueline Florine, Simon Foley, Doug Fulford, Marilyn Geninatti, Brad Goya, Mark Gosselin, Ted Hansen, Jason Hassing, Jakob Henriksen, Em Holland, James C. Holmes, Sean Jones, Brian Ketron, Bryan Law, Melissa Michelitsch, Tom McMillan, Andrew McMullin, Kristin Tara McNamara, Kay and Steve McNamara, Mark Melvin, Mark Miller, Russell Mitrovich, Pam Neal-Townley, Mike Nelson, Herwig Nosko, Todd Offenbacher, Ron Olsen, Mike Ousley, Steven Piper, Al Ramadan, Ron Renspie, Brian Reynolds, Bernie Rivadeneyra, Karen Roseme, Mick Ryan, Theresa Saunders, James Selvidge, Jason "Singer" Smith, Bill Swerbinski, Robin Weber, Mark Whaling, Jim Wilson, Cedar Wright, Ken Yager, and "Pass the Pitons" Pete Zabrok.

Thank you to Corey Rich for the fantastic photographs throughout the book and to Dan and Janine Patittuci for the Rostrum photo.

Not mentioned individually here are all the first ascensionists who established these wonderful routes, past guidebook authors, Yosemite historians, online forums, emails, and conversation in The Café. In addition, we acknowledge the hard work the following organizations do to improve and preserve the Yosemite climbing experience: Climb For Yosemite, American Alpine Club, American Safe Climbing Association, and the Access Fund. Please support them!

ACCESS: It's every climber's concern

The Access Fund, a national, non-profit climbers' organization, works to keep climbing areas open and to conserve the climbing environment. Need help with closures? Land acquisition? Legal or land management issues? Funding for trails and other projects? Starting a local climbers' group? CALL US!

Climbers can help preserve access by being committed to leaving the environment in its natural state. Here are some simple guidelines:

• **ASPIRE TO CLIMB WITHOUT LEAVING A TRACE,** especially in environmentally sensitive areas like caves. Chalk can make a significant impact on dark and porous rock—don't use it around historic rock art. Pick up litter, and leave trees and plants intact.

• **DISPOSE OF HUMAN WASTE PROPERLY.** Use toilets whenever possible. If toilets are not available, dig a "cat hole" at least six inches deep and 200 feet from any water, trails, campsites, or the base of climbs. *Always pack out toilet paper.* On big wall routes, use a "poop tube" and carry waste up and off with you (the old "bag toss" is now illegal in many areas).

• **USE EXISTING TRAILS.** Cutting across switchbacks causes erosion. When walking off-trail, tread lightly, especially in the desert where cryptogamic soils (usually a dark crust) take thousands of years to form and are easily damaged. Be aware that "rim ecologies" (the clifftop) are often highly sensitive to disturbance.

• **BE DISCREET WITH FIXED ANCHORS.** *Bolts are controversial and are not a convenience—don't place them unless they are really necessary.* Camouflage all anchors. Remove unsightly slings from rappel stations (better to use steel chain or welded cold shuts). Bolts sometimes can be used proactively to protect fragile resources—consult with your local land manager.

• **RESPECT THE RULES** and speak up when other climbers don't. Expect restrictions in designated wilderness areas, rock art sites, caves, and in sensitive wildlife areas such as nesting sites for birds of prey. *Power drills are illegal in wilderness areas and all national parks.*

• **PARK AND CAMP IN DESIGNATED AREAS.** Some climbing areas require a permit for overnight camping.

• **MAINTAIN A LOW PROFILE.** Leave the boom box and day-glo clothing at home. The less climbers are seen and heard, the better.

• **RESPECT PRIVATE PROPERTY.** Be courteous to land owners. Don't climb where you're not wanted.

• **JOIN THE ACCESS FUND.** To become a member, make a tax-deductible donation of $25.

THE ACCESS FUND
Keeping climbing areas open and conserving the climbing environment
P.O. Box 17010
Boulder, CO 80308

A deadly bolt more than 20 years old ... one of several
thousand on popular climbs throughout the United States.

A new bolt rated to over 5,000 pounds. The ASCA
wants to replace the bad bolt above with one of these.

Bad Bolts Kill

We need YOUR help. The American Safe Climbing Association has helped replace more than 3,000 bolts throughout the country and over 1,300 in Yosemite Valley alone. We estimate that there are more than 20,000 bad bolts remaining on popular climbs today. Your $50 donation will make at least one route safe . . . and that one route could be the next one you climb. The ASCA would like to get there before you do.

Does your crag need re-bolting? Please contact us.

American Safe Climbing Association

❏ $25 Supporter   ❏ $50 Contributor   ❏ $100 Advocate   ❏ $500 Lifer

Name _____

Address _____

E-Mail/Phone _____

All contributors receive the ASCA newsletter.
Make checks payable to: ASCA, 2 Bradford Way, Mill Valley, CA 94941
Phone 650-843-1473 www.safeclimbing.org

The American Safe Climbing Association is a 501(c)3 organization and contributions are tax-deductible.

Preface

When Tom Frost talks, most people listen. As I was writing the first SuperTopo book, *Yosemite Big Walls*, I ran into Tom in the Yosemite Lodge Cafeteria. We talked a bit and as I was leaving I asked, "Do you think I should put first ascent stories in the book?" Just as I hoped he wouldn't say, Tom shot back a resounding "Yes!"

Damn. My nearly completed book would be delayed for months as I made almost a hundred phone calls to interview first ascensionists. But Tom was right—the book was vastly improved, and history has now become an essential component of all subsequent SuperTopo books. This time around we are fortunate to have preeminent Yosemite historian Steve Roper telling the fascinating stories behind the climbs as well as contributing profiles of some of the major players.

For this next major SuperTopo print book, I again consulted Tom. He believed that guidebooks had recently become geared toward elite free climbers. He longed for the old guides that were filled with more moderate routes, and included information on when you could get through a tough spot by pulling on gear. According to Tom, "In the 1960s we used to climb everything because the guidebook was friendly and because we always had the aid slings handy to pull through the hard sections. For us, climbing wasn't just about numbers. Instead, doing the classic routes up Yosemite's more-than-awesome walls was the adventure. Surviving it, and doing something we could free, was the icing on the cake."

Heeding Tom's advice, in this book we aim to make it clear when it's possible to pull through a crux on gear. We also scoured the Valley for obscure but quality climbs in the 5.4 to 5.9 range. By bringing to light many of these lesser known routes we hope to provide more ways to avoid crowds.

Like *Yosemite Big Walls*, this is a select guidebook. We chose the climbs using basically one guideline: Would you recommend this climb to a friend? We also skewed the route selection to well-protected routes in the 5.4 to 5.11 range. Using our standard procedure of climbing every route ourselves to make sure the information is accurate, we focused on routes that the greatest number of people could enjoy. In future editions we will include more 5.10 to 5.12 routes (as well as any additional 5.5 to 5.9 routes that we come across).

We hope this book inspires many climbing adventures. Please let us know how the book helped your climbing trip and then, gently, please tell us how it can be improved. A guidebook is always a work-in-progress. We will continually work to make *Yosemite Valley Free Climbs* the best resource possible with which to enjoy the magic of Yosemite.

Chris McNamara
Chris@SuperTopo.com

Introduction

by Chris McNamara

Yosemite is much more than a valley with 3000-foot rock walls and incredible climbing. It is an outlet for the energies of the world's most passionate and adventurous people. Yosemite inspires the souls of climbers and non-climbers to reach for something beyond themselves and to travel to a place—physical and mental—where they have never been before. Few climbers can resist Yosemite; nearly every climber who has the opportunity to get to Yosemite manages to make the trip.

The first visit to Yosemite is overwhelming—there's so much rock on an incomparable scale. First, the big walls dominate your view: El Capitan, Half Dome, and Sentinel. They seem too massive to be of this world, let alone climbable. Next, you look at all the small cliffs between their giant neighbors. Wait a minute . . . those "small" cliffs are more than 500 feet high! Is this place real? It's all a bit hard to comprehend at first. There is little to which you can compare Yosemite's walls other than tall buildings, which isn't much of a comparison. All this rock of such unfathomable size fills you with both fear and anticipation. Yet as daunting as the rock faces in Yosemite appear to be, they scream to be climbed. And that's why you've come here.

Yosemite Climbing Skills

At first, Yosemite climbs feel weird and insecure. They demand strength and technique not easily acquired at your local gym or crag. The slick, glacier-polished rock has few handholds. Instead, you jam your hands and feet in cracks and smear your feet on, well, sometimes on nothing. There is more balance and subtlety involved

Tommy Caldwell on Pitch 6 (5.12c) of Lurking Fear. (Corey Rich)

than brute strength. When your natural instinct is to grab and pull, often you need to relax and balance.

At first, don't be surprised if you find yourself yelling down to your partner, "This 5.9 feels like 5.11!" The good news is that Yosemite climbs are within your grasp—they just take extra patience and resolve. Take solace in the fact that all new Yosemite climbers get humbled at some point but they eventually develop the subtle skills necessary to move up Yosemite granite. The more time you spend on the rock and the more technique you build, the more climbing opens up to you. Suddenly the thousand-foot-tall walls shrink a little and don't seem as intimidating. Before too long you're planning your ascent of The Nose of El Cap.

Unfortunately, there are few easy climbs to introduce you to Yosemite climbing. We searched the Park for every easy and moderate route worth climbing and put them in this book. However, there still isn't much at the lower end of the spectrum. If you're looking for 5.7 and easier climbs, be prepared to bunch up on a few crowded routes. It's not until you climb 5.8 and harder that your options start opening up in Yosemite. If you cannot lead 5.8 or harder, it's a good idea to climb with someone who is familiar with the area and can give you pointers, set up topropes, and lead you up multi-pitch routes.

Most climbing in Yosemite is traditional climbing where you climb cracks and place your own gear. But the crack technique here is difficult, and it's not an ideal place to learn. It is best to have your gear-placing, anchor-setting, and rope-managing skills dialed before visiting. Your best bet is to start toproping the very lowest grades of cracks. Once familiar with the rock, try out some one-pitch leads and then move on to the multi-pitch climbs.

Overall, Yosemite is not a great sport climbing destination, but we highlight about 40 well-bolted climbs, mostly in the 5.10 and 5.11 range. In general, most bolted climbs easier than 5.10 are runout except for about ten well-bolted 5.8 and 5.9 routes in this book.

Equipment

It's hard to climb in Yosemite without a full trad rack of cams from .5-4"and two sets of stoppers. For the bigger cracks (1-4") almost any brand of cam will do. For the thin pin-scarred cracks, Aliens work best. On most climbs you will also want about eight quickdraws and eight slings to reduce rope drag because many pitches wander. A cordalette is useful for equalizing gear in a natural belay.

Most pitches in Yosemite are 90 to 130 feet long so a 50m rope works fine. However, a 10mm x 60m rope has become the Yosemite standard because it allows you to link pitches and it gives you more options for setting up topropes at the crags. For some crags and most multi-pitch routes where you must descend by rappel, you will need a second rope to get down. (8mm is a good diameter).

On long routes, avoid the hassle of climbing with a pack by using a Camelback and clipping your lightweight hiking shoes to your harness. The Camelback holds enough water for most long climbs as well as space for a few essentials such as food, a small LED headlamp, super-compact rain shell, sunscreen, and cell phone.

Corey Rich

Anchor Conditions

Since 1997, the American Safe Climbing Association has replaced more than 1,300 bolts in Yosemite Valley. While most popular climbs now have safe bolts, be aware that some bad bolts remain. View which routes the ASCA has replaced at the ASCA web site, www.safeclimbing.org and please make a tax-deductible donation. Even a mere five dollars will replace at least one bolt. And that bad bolt could be the one that blows on somebody!

Essential Yosemite Beta

Below we list some fundamental information for planning a trip to Yosemite. However, for more updated and extensive information you should visit the Yosemite Beta Page on the SuperTopo web site: www.supertopo.com/climbingareas/yosemite.html

Getting There

Air Travel

The closest major international airports are Oakland International (3.5-hour drive) and San Francisco International (4-hour drive). Of the two, Oakland is preferred because it's less chaotic and 30 minutes closer to Yosemite. Sacramento International is also a 4-hour drive from Yosemite but has fewer connecting flights. Fresno Yosemite International is only a 3-hour drive but offers the fewest flights. Since all of these airports are about the same distance from Yosemite, shop around for the best fares. Some climbers fly into Los Angeles International, which is a 7-hour drive to Yosemite.

Train Travel

The train is not the fastest way to Yosemite but it's a cool way to travel. From Emeryville (a 20-minute bus ride from San Francisco) take Amtrak to Merced and board the Via Bus to Yosemite. There are three runs from Merced in the morning and one at 5:25 P.M. The cost is $20 round trip from Merced to Yosemite. From Los Angeles, Amtrak has a bus to Bakersfield that connects with a train to Merced. From there take the Via Bus to Yosemite.

Bus Travel

Short of having a car, the bus is the best
way to get from a major airport to
Yosemite. From Oakland, San Francisco, or
Los Angeles take the Greyhound Bus to
Merced and then the Via Bus to Yosemite.
Plan a full day of travel if riding the bus.
From June to November you can only reach
Yosemite from Mammoth by the YARTS bus.

Car Travel

There are four state highways that access
Yosemite: 120 from the west, 120 from the
east, 140 from the west, and 41 from the
southwest. The fastest access from the San
Francisco Bay Area is 120. Highway 140 is
the best option if coming from Los Angeles
or Fresno. Highway 140 is also the lowest
elevation road and offers the best winter
access if 120 and 41 have chain controls
(chains are rarely required on 140).
Highway 120 from the east (aka The Tioga
Pass Road) offers the best summertime
access from Bishop, Utah, Nevada, and
eastern states. However, this road closes
after the first major winter storm (usually
in November) and doesn't open until the
snow melts (usually late May). To access
Yosemite from the east in winter, you must
get to the west side access roads by driving
north through Tahoe or south through
Bakersfield.

Rent a car at any airport or major city.
International climbers who stay in the
United States for more than a month often
buy a used car in San Francisco or Los
Angeles and sell it (or scrap it) at the end of
their trip. To find a cheap car, look in the
local papers or on www.craigslist.org.

Many people stay in Yosemite without a
car. Renting a car is expensive and it's
possible to reach most climbs by the free
park shuttle bus. However, the shuttle does
not serve areas west of Camp 4, including
El Capitan, Leaning Tower, Cookie Cliff,
and Reeds Pinnacle. To reach these areas
without a car, hitchhike or ride a bike.

NOTE: Major changes are planned for
Yosemite that will greatly affect
transportation inside the Valley. Check the
SuperTopo web site for the most current
information on changing car restrictions
and bus routes.

Driving times and distances to Yosemite Valley

From	Time (hours)	Distance (miles)
Boulder, CO*	20:00	1,254
Fresno, CA	2:20	90
Truckee, CA	4:00	240
Los Angeles, CA	6:00	311
Mammoth, CA*	2:30	95
Oakland, CA	4:00	172
Sacramento, CA	4:00	174
Salt Lake City, UT*	12:00	707
San Francisco, CA	4:00	192
Tuolumne Meadows	1:30	60

*Driving times are 2 to 4 hours longer when Tioga pass is
closed, usually from November to May.

When to Climb

Yosemite has some of the best weather of
any climbing area in the United States, but
nasty storms occur throughout the year.
Because the climbs start from elevations
between 2,800 and 7,500 feet, there is
usually some place with good climbing
temperatures most of the year. Spring and
fall have the best climbing weather. Summer
cragging is usually uncomfortably hot but
the longer and higher routes can be cool
enough. Winter can have good climbing
weather but can also have months of severe
Sierra storms. A dry November is our
favorite time in Yosemite—perfect temps in
the sun and no crowds. For current road
and weather conditions call 209-372-0200
AND check the many online forecasts.

Seasons

November–March The Valley empties of
climbers and tourists, which creates a more
pristine setting and unspoiled feel in the
Valley. During this time there is usually an
equal number of clear and stormy days.
Most of the long routes at higher elevations
are too wet or cold, but there are many
sunny and dry cragging areas, mainly west
of the Highway 140/120 junction in Lower
Merced Canyon. When bad weather rolls in,
things get nasty very quickly. Pacific storms
usually bring three days of heavy snow or

rain but can last up to a week or longer. Usually it only takes a day for most sunny crags to dry out after a storm. If a two-week storm system rolls in, it's time to ski or snowboard at Badger Pass in Yosemite or head to Joshua Tree. If camping in the Valley during the winter, prepare for long cold nights.

April–May 15 Walls and the Valley are still uncrowded. It's warmer, but there is the same 50/50 chance of getting either good or miserable weather. If you are traveling from far away this is a risky time to visit, especially if you only have a week or less of vacation. Most of the long climbs are still too wet or cold, but the crags are dry.

May 15–June Perfect weather and big crowds of both tourists and climbers. Long days make this a great time to do a lengthy multi-pitch route.

July–August The Valley is still crowded with tourists, but the climbs are uncrowded as most people head to Tuolumne for cooler weather. While Valley floor temperatures are often in the 90s and 100s, temperatures on the walls 500 feet above the Valley are usually comfortable in the 70s and low 80s. Prepare for the heat with plenty of extra water.

September–October The Valley is crowded with tourists and climbers. The weather is generally perfect except for the occasional lingering heat wave. The first winter storm usually arrives in late October or early November.

Staying in the Park

Yosemite Valley is a small tourist town filled with buildings, roads, cars, and people. The bad news is that the restaurants, stores, and motel-like rooms take away from the natural beauty of the park. The good news is that these same things make the Valley quite accommodating. You will find pizza, burgers, groceries, climbing gear, a medical clinic, motels, swimming pools, rafts, bike rentals, and if you find yourself in an unfortunate situation, a jail.

Month	Average precipitation	Max/min temp in degrees F
January	6.35"	47/25
February	6.64"	55/26
March	5.87"	58/30
April	3.29"	65/34
May	1.48"	71/39
June	.51"	80/46
July	.29"	89/50
August	.06"	89/50
September	.55"	82/48
October	1.68"	72/39
November	3.49"	57/30
December	7.10"	49/26

Camping

Camp 4 is the historic center of American climbing. It is also Yosemite's only walk-in campground and the cheapest place to stay. No reservations are required, but during peak season (May–October) expect a long wait to secure a campsite. The cost is $5 per person per night with a 14-day limit on your stay. Each six-person site is a twenty-foot-square patch of dirt with fire pit and picnic table. If there are fewer than six people in your group you will share the site with others. There is a bathroom and a sink in the middle of Camp 4, but no warm water or showers. A bulletin board next to the Ranger Kiosk offers the chance to find climbing partners, friends, and used climbing gear. All other Yosemite campgrounds require reservations during peak season. Call 800-436-PARK to make reservations or go online to: http://reservations.nps.gov

There are a variety of places to camp outside the park boundary on Forest Service Land. Check out the Forest Service web site for more info: www.r5.fs.fed.us

Lodges and Cabins

In addition to campsites, there are more plush accommodations available in Yosemite. If you are ready to pay the big bucks, you can stay at the lovely Ahwahnee

Hotel, or for a more modest price you can crash in a motel-like room at the Yosemite Lodge or a canvas-topped cabin in Curry Village. Also, vacation homes are located just minutes out of the Valley in Foresta (with views of the summit of El Capitan and Half Dome). Check out the awesome cabins at www.4yosemite.com or call 800-723-4112 and ask about the climbers' specials. In the summertime your best bet is to make reservations well in advance of your visit. Spaces fill up early for lodges and cabins in the tourist season of June–September.

Food
Groceries are available in the Valley at the Village Store, Curry Village Store, or Lodge Store, but it is much cheaper to buy groceries in Oakdale, Merced, or Oakhurst on the drive to Yosemite.

There are a variety of restaurants in the Valley that serve everything from pizza and deli sandwiches to the spendy stuff at the Ahwahnee Hotel. Here is a quick listing of some of the Valley restaurants by location:

Yosemite Lodge: "The Cafe" (cafeteria), Mountain Room Bar and Grill.

Yosemite Village: Degnan's Deli, The Loft (pizza and pasta), burger stand.

Curry Village: Pizza Deck (with bar), cafeteria, taco shop, all-you-can-eat buffet.

Showers and Laundry
Showers cost $2 (towel included) and are available at Housekeeping or Curry Village. Laundry is available at Housekeeping.

Climbing Gear and Climbing Guides
The Mountain Shop (209-372-8396), located in Curry Village, is one of the premiere climbing shops in The West. From bouldering pads to haulbags to the latest route beta, they have it all.

You can get climbing instruction, arrange for a guide, and also rent gear from the Yosemite Mountaineering School and Guide Service. There are also a variety of climbing shops in the San Francisco Bay Area where you can purchase gear. In San Francisco: Mission Cliffs and The North Face. In Berkeley: REI, Wilderness Exchange, Berkeley Ironworks, and Marmot Mountain Works.

If you are coming from the east side of the Sierra, then visit Wilson's Eastside Sports in Bishop or Mammoth Mountaineering Supply in Mammoth—both have an extensive selection of rock climbing and mountaineering gear.

Bears

Bears have damaged cars for as little as a stick of gum or an empty soda can. If you want what's yours to remain yours, remember three things: bears are hungry, smart, and strong. Bears are responsible for close to a thousand car break-ins every year in Yosemite, as all the shattered glass in the parking lots will tell you.

When bears smell food, even if it's locked in your trunk or glove compartment, they shift into high gear. They get turned on by odors of containers that used to contain food, and for toothpaste and sunscreen. Bears don't even need to smell food; they see something like a grocery bag or an ice chest, and associate it with food. In fact, they don't need to see that much. If a bear notices clutter inside a car, he'll think, "I wonder what's under all that stuff?" and go to work.

Breaking into a car is a trivial exercise for a bear. He inserts his claws at the top of the door frame and pulls down. Then he climbs in and trashes the car. You can't outsmart or out-muscle a bear. Stash your food in one of the bear-proof storage lockers provided by the Park Service at all campgrounds and throughout the Valley. Proper food storage is essential to protecting your property and more importantly the life of the bear. When a bear starts to endanger people it may be killed by the Park Service. Visit www.nps.gov/yose/bears.htm for more info.

Poison Oak

Poison Oak grows sporadically throughout the Valley, especially in the Lower Merced Canyon west of the 120/140 junction. Find someone to show you what it looks like and be especially careful in the winter when poison oak loses its leaves and is difficult to see.

Cell Phones

Should you or your partner get hurt while climbing, cell phones shorten the rescue response time. However, cell phones in the outdoors are annoying so keep them put away except for in emergencies. Cell phone coverage in Yosemite is spotty. There is generally decent reception between El Cap Meadow and Curry Village. As you gain elevation on a climb, the reception often improves. West of El Capitan the coverage deteriorates quickly. A good number to have programmed on your phone is the road and weather report: 209-372-0200.

Rest Days

What do you do when Valley temperatures hit the 90s? Head for the water. Rent rafts from Curry Village and float down the Merced River, or just dip into the water next to El Capitan Meadow. There are two great swimming holes 40 minutes outside of the Park boundaries. About 10 miles west of the Highway 120 entrance station, take a left immediately after a large bridge.

Here you will have your choice of jumping off 15- to 25-foot cliffs or just kicking back next to the water. West of the Highway 140 entrance station is the Octagon, which features a rope swing, sketchy cliff and tree jumps, and great spots to kick back and have a BBQ. The directions to this place are more devious so you will have to hunt down a local Yosemite climber for information. In winter, when the Valley is too snowy, go ice skating at Curry Village or head to Badger Pass for some skiing or snowboarding. There are also a number of interesting exhibits in the Valley such as the Indian Museum, Visitors Center, and the Ansel Adams Gallery.

Don't forget the many great Yosemite hikes. Here's our favorite: park at El Cap Meadow and hike to the base of The Nose. Next, skirt the base right for about 30 minutes all the way to the edge of the Southeast Face around Zodiac. Look for booty (dropped gear from El Cap climbers) and bring a bag to pick up trash.

Justin Bailie

SuperTopo Mission

- Help climbers ascend and descend routes quickly, efficiently, and safely by creating the most accurate and informative climbing topos ever published.

- Capture the mystery, adventure, and humor of climbing by publishing the histories, anecdotes, and outrageous stories of each route.

- Promote clean climbing by publishing the most up-to-date rack info as well as hammerless ratings for each pitch.

- Stress the importance of low impact climbing and promote stewardship of the environment.

Visit www.SuperTopo.com before each climb

There is much more beta available for free on the SuperTopo web site: www.supertopo.com. Visit the web site before your climb to be sure you have the latest information.

The web site offers additional free beta for each climb:
- photo galleries
- trip reports
- route condition updates
- closures and rockfall warnings
- sign up for "route beta email alerts"

The web site is packed with general Yosemite info:
- free downloadable color topos
- road and weather conditions
- everything you need to know about staying in Yosemite
- good routes for first time Yosemite climbers
- general trip planning info

Ratings

Rating climbs is never easy, especially in a place like Yosemite with a tradition of sandbagging. In the past, even though a climb might have 5.11 moves by modern standards it could be kept at 5.10 "just because it has always been that way." In this book we toss the sandbagged ratings in favor of accurate ones. After all, if ratings don't accurately compare climbs, and if some 5.10s are harder than 5.11s, what is the point of a rating system? As a result, about 5 percent of the climbs in this book have been bumped up in rating from past guides. For instance, Waverly Wafer was 5.10c and now it's 5.11a. The Steck-Salathé was 5.9 and now it's 5.10b. This move will no doubt be controversial to some but we feel the majority of climbers will appreciate more accurate comparisons of climbs. That said, ratings are decided by discussion and consensus, so we would like to hear your criticism and feedback. Please send a note to chris@supertopo.com or post a message on our forum at www.supertopo.com.

Keep in mind the subjective nature of rating cracks. Everyone has different sized hands and feet so a 5.9 hand crack to someone with big hands might be a 5.10 fist crack for someone with small hands.

Ratings of offwidths and chimneys will seem much different than those for face routes and finger cracks. Because offwidths and chimneys are initially so foreign and unpleasant, few people dedicate the necessary time to learn the techniques. As a result, it's no surprise that when a 5.11 sport climber jumps on his first 5.9 offwidth it usually feels like 5.12! The key point here is that it took many months and probably years to develop face climbing technique. It will take at least that long to develop offwidth technique to the point where you can climb as hard on offwidths as you can on face climbs.

Also, because some routes with the same rating are harder or easier than other routes at that same rating, we've listed all the climbs in order of overall difficulty in the Appendix. For example, both Commitment and Arrowhead Arête are rated 5.9, but the latter is a much longer and more demanding climb, which is reflected by its position in the Climbs by Rating list in the Appendix.

Some climbs have an optional "A0" rating. A0 means a section you can get through by pulling on bolts or making a pendulum. For example, on Royal Arches (5.10b or 5.7 A0) the 5.10b section can be avoided with a pendulum.

Free Climbing Ratings

USA Yosemite Decimal System	UIAA	France	UK	Australia
5.1	I	1		4
5.2	II	2	M	6
5.3	III	2+	D	8
5.4	III+	3-	3A/3B VD	
5.5	IV	3	3B/3C HVD	10
5.6	IV+	3+	3C/4A S	12
5.7	V-	4	4A/4B HS	
5.8	V	4+	4A/4C VS	14
5.9	V+	5		16
5.10a	VI-	5+	4C/5B HVS	18
5.10b	VI	6A	5A/5C E1	19
5.10c	VI+	6A+	5B/6A E2	20
5.10d	VII-	6B	5C/6A E3	21
5.11a	VII	6B+		22
5.11b	VII+	6C	6A/6B E4	23
5.11c	VIII-	6C+		24
5.11d	VIII	7A		25
5.12a	VIII+	7A+	6A/6C E5	26
5.12b	IX-	7B		27
5.12c	IX	7B+	6B/6C E6	28
5.12d		7C		29
5.13a	IX+	7C+	6C/7A E7	30
5.13b	X-	8A		31
5.13c	X	8A+	6C/7A E8	32
5.13d		8B	7A/7B E9	33
5.14a	X+	8B+		34
5.14b	XI-	8C	7A/7B E10	35
5.14c	XI	8C+		36
5.14d	XI+	9A		
5.15a		9A+		

Minimize Your Impact

by Mark Fincher and Lincoln Else

The National Park Service is responsible for ensuring that Yosemite's beauty and ecological health remain unimpaired for future generations. Congress heightened this duty when it designated the walls of Yosemite Valley as Wilderness in 1984. Wilderness is defined as a place that retains "its primeval character and influence, without permanent improvements or human habitation, which is protected and managed so as to preserve its natural conditions." This means that, somehow, the park is to remain natural despite hundreds of thousands of people hiking and climbing in it each year. This won't happen without your help. Climbers, like other visitors to Yosemite's wilderness, need to minimize their impact if we are to fulfill our obligation to future generations.

How you can help

- **Stay informed.** Check the climbing bulletin boards at Camp 4 for the latest information: rules, closures, upcoming events, and other climbing news.

- **Spread the word.** Talk to other climbers about ways to climb smart and limit your impact. If you see someone acting in a way you think is inappropriate, let them know how you feel.

- **Get involved.** Help with local clean-ups, trail projects, and other climbing community events. When you're out on your own do your part to pick up trash, clean anchors, and minimize what impacts you leave behind.

Approach and descent trails

Some of the worst climbing impacts in Yosemite result from people approaching and descending from climbs. Many of the approach trails in Yosemite are on steep terrain, and even a small amount of use in these areas can quickly destroy vegetation and cause erosion. Some approach trails in Yosemite have eroded more than three vertical feet in just 20 years. In other areas multiple trails leading to the same climb compound the problem.

What you can do:

- Take a minute to look for a well used and established trail before starting off. In some popular areas the Park Service has marked one established trail to keep others from forming (look for a carabiner symbol on a post).

- If there is no obvious trail try to walk on rock whenever possible.

- Slow down on the descent. Two people running down a loose slope can erode as much soil as twenty people walking.

- If you found a good trail on the approach, take the time to find it again on the way down instead of taking a shortcut.

- When you're giving out beta for the climb, do so for the approach as well.

Litter

No one admits to littering, yet in a four year period Park Rangers and volunteers removed 75 large garbage bags full of trash from the summit of El Cap.

What you can do:

- Don't litter, and carry out any trash you find.

- Don't stuff trash into cracks. The rock is not a landfill.

- Clean fixed gear when you can, and replace old anchor slings with earth-toned webbing. For bolt anchors, use "quick links" instead of webbing.

- Try to minimize your use of chalk, especially near trails and other high profile areas.

Peregrines and other animals

Yosemite's walls are home to many animals. Some live elsewhere in the park, but some such as peregrine falcons, swallows, swifts, and some bat species, nest or feed primarily on or near the cliffs. Climbing near these animals can cause serious negative impacts.

What you can do:
- Check the climbing information boards or the park's wilderness website for current peregrine closures. These closures usually run from January 31st to August 31st but may be adjusted to fit the birds' nesting schedule. When these closures are in place, respect them and tell others to do the same.

- Leave your dog at home. Dogs harass wildlife and even the smell of a leashed dog at the base of a wall can alter the behavior of other animals. Dogs are not allowed away from paved trails, roads, and bikepaths.

Human waste

Improperly buried human waste is a problem near parking areas, at the base of climbs, and on the summit.

What you can do:
- Take the time to dig a deep hole (at least 6 inches) in the soil to bury your waste and pack out the toilet paper.

Vegetation (Gardening)

National Parks like Yosemite were created in part to protect plants and animals. Plants on frequently climbed routes often die from repeated trampling, while those on less popular routes may be able to survive if the first ascensionists didn't kill them and subsequent climbers tread lightly. Gardening (an ironic euphemism for the deliberate destruction of plants), cutting trees and shrubs, and using a wire brush to remove lichen from holds are all illegal.

What you can do:
- Plants have a chance to survive on less popular routes if you tread lightly. If you must pull or step on a plant or tree, do so in a way that causes the least harm.

- Never place a rappel rope directly around a tree—use an earth-toned sling instead.

Camping

Impacts from climbers camping at the base of long routes are becoming far too common: fire rings, soot scars on the walls, tent platforms, constructed windbreaks, litter, and habituated wildlife. Two large wildfires have been caused by climbers' bivy fires. Camping is not allowed anywhere in the Valley except in designated campgrounds, and a wilderness permit is required for all camping in Yosemite's backcountry.

What you can do:
- Stay in a designated campground in the Valley. Wherever you camp, leave the area looking exactly the same as when you arrived.

- If you top out after dark and have to bivy, find a natural, sheltered campsite instead of excavating a platform and building a windbreak. If you need a fire to make it through the night, find an existing fire ring (there are numerous rings at the top of climbs where people commonly bivy: Royal Arches, Middle Cathedral, etc.) and remove the combustible materials around it.

Making climbing history

Yosemite is viewed around the world as one of rock climbing's true gems, and people will climb here long after we are gone. As a final piece of advice for how you can help protect the future of Yosemite, learn its past. The history of climbing in this park is a tale replete with determination, adventure, and desire to preserve true wilderness. It is our job to preserve that wilderness so that others who come after us can experience it as it ought to be.

Staying Alive

by John Dill, NPS Search and Rescue

Most climbers do a good job coping with the hazards of their sport, yet more than a hundred climbing accidents occur in the Park every year. What factors contribute to them? What, if anything, can climbers do to avoid them? And just how dangerous is climbing, anyway? With these questions in mind, the National Park Service (NPS) examined most of the serious accidents that occurred in the park from 1970 through 1990. The conclusions provide interesting reading for those who wish to stay alive.

Fifty-one climbers died from traumatic injuries in that period. A dozen more, critically hurt, would have died without rapid transport and medical treatment. In addition, there were many serious but survivable injuries, from fractured skulls to broken legs (at least 50 fractures per year), and a much larger number of cuts, bruises, and sprains.

Not surprisingly, most injuries occurred during leader falls and involved feet, ankles, or lower legs; for many, these are the accepted risks of climbing. However, leader falls accounted for only 25 percent of the fatal and near-fatal traumatic injuries; roughly 10 percent were from rockfall, 25 percent from being deliberately unroped, and 40 percent from simple mistakes with gear. Many cases are not clear cut; several factors may share the credit, and it is sometimes hard to quantify the weird adventures climbers have.

Not to be overlooked in the body count are environmental injuries. Inadequately equipped for the weather, four climbers died of hypothermia and perhaps 45 more would have died of the cold or the heat if not rescued.

Fifteen to 25 parties require an NPS rescue each year. Sixty more climbers stagger into Yosemite's medical clinic on their own, and an unknown number escape statistical immortality by seeking treatment outside the park (or at the Mountain Room Bar).

Most Yosemite victims are experienced climbers: 60 percent have been climbing for three years or more, lead at least 5.10, are in good condition, and climb frequently. Short climbs and big walls, easy routes and desperate ones—they all get their share of the accidents.

The NPS keeps no statistics on how many climbers use the park, but 25,000 to 50,000 climber-days annually is a fair estimate. With this in mind, a few serious injuries and 2.5 deaths per year may seem a pretty low rate. It's much too high, however, if your climbing career is cut short by a broken hip, or worse. It's also too high when you consider that at least 80 percent of the fatalities, and many of the injuries, were easily preventable. In case after case, ignorance, a casual attitude, and/or some form of distraction proved to be contributing factors to the accidents.

As the saying goes, "good judgment comes from bad experience." Condensed in the following pages are 21 years of bad experience—the situations Yosemite climbers faced, the mistakes they made, and some recommendations for avoiding bad experiences of your own. This information comes in many cases from the victims' own analysis or from those of their peers.

Environmental Dangers

On October 11, 1983, a climber on El Cap collapsed from heat exhaustion. On October 11, 1984, a party on Washington Column was immobilized by hypothermia. You can expect this range of weather year-round.

Heat

No Yosemite climber has died from the heat, but a half-dozen parties have come close. Too exhausted to move, they survived only because death by drying-up is a relatively slow process, allowing rescuers to reach them. Temperatures on the sunny walls often exceed 100° F, but even in cool weather, climbing all day requires a lot of water. The generally accepted minimum, two quarts per person per day, is just that, a minimum. It may not replace what you use, so don't let the desire for a light pack be an overriding concern, and take extra for unanticipated delays.

If you find yourself rationing water, remember that dehydration will seriously sap your strength, slowing you even further. It's not uncommon to go from mere thirst to a complete standstill in a single day. Continuing up may be the right choice but several climbers have said, "I should have gone down while I could."

Storms

We still hear climbers say, "It never rains in Yosemite." In fact, there are serious storms year-round. Four climbers have died of hypothermia and almost 50 have been rescued, most of whom would not have survived otherwise. Several were very experienced, with winter alpine routes, Yosemite walls, and stormy bivouacs to their credit—experts, by most measures. In many cases they took sub-standard gear, added another mistake or two, and couldn't deal with the water.

Mountain thunderstorms are common in spring, summer, and fall. They may appear suddenly out of a clear blue sky and rapidly shift position, their approach concealed by the route you are on. A few minutes warning may be all that you get. Thunderstorms may last only a couple of hours, but they are very intense, with huge amounts of near-freezing water often mixed with hail, strong winds, and lightning. The runoff can be a foot deep and fast enough to cause rockfall. A common result is a panicky retreat, a jammed rope, and cries for help.

No climber has died thus far in such a storm because rescuers were able to respond. No climbers have died from lightning either, but there have been several near misses, and hikers on Half Dome and elsewhere have been killed. Get out of the way of a thunderstorm as fast as you can, and avoid summits and projections.

The big Pacific storm systems have proven more dangerous. They sweep through the Sierra at any time of year, most frequently from September through May. They are unpredictable, often appearing back-to-back after several weeks of gorgeous, mind-numbing weather. It may rain on Half Dome in January and snow there in July. These storms are dangerous because they are usually warm enough to be wet, even in winter, yet always cold enough to kill an unprotected climber.

With no soil to absorb it, rain on the walls quickly collects into streams and waterfalls, pouring off overhangs and down the corner you're trying to climb up. Wind blows the water in all directions, including straight up.

Once cold and wet, you are in trouble and your options run out. Even with good gear, water runs down your sleeve every time you reach up. As your body temperature drops, you begin making dumb mistakes, such as clipping in wrong or dropping your rack. Once you become seriously hypothermic, you will just hang there, no longer caring. It happens quickly. In two separate incidents, climbers on the last pitch of The Nose left what protection they had to make a run for the top. They all died on that pitch.

Staying put may be no better. If you need help, no one may see you or hear you, and reaching you may take days. Don't forget your cell phone! Survivors say they had no idea how helpless they'd be until it happened to them. To find out for yourself, stand in the spray of a garden hose on a cold windy night. How long will you last?

How to Prepare for Bad Weather

- Check the forecast just before you start up but don't rely on it. For several parties it provided no warning whatsoever.

- Evaluate ahead of time the problems of retreat from any point on the route.

- If it's starting to rain, think twice about climbing "just one more pitch"—once wet you won't dry out.

All such hints and tricks aside, the bottom line is your ability to sit out the storm. Your first priority is to keep the wind and outside water away. Second is to be insulated enough to stay warm, even though you are wet from your own condensation.

- Stick with high quality gear in good condition, and don't leave key items behind to travel lighter. Don't go up with a poorly equipped partner; it will be your neck as well.

- For insulation, never rely on cotton or down (even if it's covered with one of the waterproof/breathable fabrics). Even nylon absorbs water. Wool, polypropylene, and polyester insulators stay relatively warm when wet, and the synthetics dry fastest. Take along warm pants, long underwear, sweater, jacket, balaclava/hat, gloves, sleeping bag, insulating pad, extra socks or booties, and plenty of food and water— dehydration hastens hypothermia.

WARNING: Several climbers have blamed the waterproof/breathable fabrics for their close calls. They claim that no version of it can take the punishment of a storm on the walls. Whether true or not, you must be the judge; test all of your gear ahead of time under miserable conditions, but where your exit is an easy one.

Unplanned Bivouacs

Getting caught by darkness is common, especially on the longer one-day climbs and descent routes, e.g., Royal Arches and Cathedral Rocks. It happens easily—a late start, a slow partner, getting off-route, a jammed or dropped rope, or a sprained ankle. Usually it's nothing to get upset about, but if you are unprepared, even a cold wind or a mild storm becomes serious. One death and several close calls occurred this way. To avoid becoming a statistic:

- Consider the following gear for each person's day pack: long underwear, gloves, balaclava, rain jacket, and pants (which double as wind protection). In warmer weather, all can be of the lightweight variety. If that's too heavy for you, at least take one of those disposable plastic rain-quilts or tube tents that occupy virtually no space. Take more warm clothes in colder weather. A head lamp with spare bulb and new batteries is very important for finding safe anchors, signaling for help, or avoiding that bivy altogether. Matches and heat-tabs will light wet wood. Food and water increase your safety after a night of shivering.

- Keep your survival gear with you whenever practical, not with your partner—climbers get separated from their gear, and each other, in imaginative ways, sometimes with serious consequences.

- Standing in slings on poor anchors is not the way to spend a night. If a bivy is inevitable, don't climb until the last moment—find a safe, sheltered, and/or comfortable spot while you've got enough light.

Descents

Consult the guidebook and your friends, but be wary of advice that the way down is obvious; look the route over ahead of time. If you carry a topo of the way up, consider one for the way down, or a photograph. Your ultimate protection is routefinding ability, and that takes experience. Some trouble spots: North Dome Gully, the Kat Walk, Michael's Ledge.

Many rappel epics are born when an easy descent, often a walk-off, is missed. Search for it thoroughly before you commit to a big drop—it may be well worth the effort.

Conversely, footprints and rappel anchors often lead nowhere—they were someone else's mistake. Be willing and able to retrace your steps and remember that the crux may not be at the top.

Any time you can't see anchors all the way to the ground, take the gear to set your own. This includes established descents.

Consider taking a second (7-9mm) rope, even for one-rope descents and walk-offs.

You'll save time, depend on fewer anchors, leave less gear, and more easily reverse the climbing route in an emergency. This is one advantage of leading on double ropes. But don't forget that thinner ropes are more vulnerable to sharp edges.

Friction from wet or twisted ropes, slings, ledges, cracks, and flakes may jam your rope. Plan ahead when you rig the anchor and be willing to leave gear behind to avoid friction. You can retrieve the gear later.

Rappelling through trees? Consider short rappels from tree to tree. It's slow but avoids irretrievable snarls.

Is your rope jammed? You can go back up and rerig if you still have both ends, so keep them until you're sure it will pull or you have to let go. If you do have to climb that rope, be careful that it isn't jammed by a sharp edge. Don't forget to untie the knots in the ends before you pull.

Loose Rock
There's plenty of it in Yosemite. Ten percent of all injuries are associated with rockfall, including six deaths and one permanent disability to date. In several other deaths, loose rock was implicated but not confirmed, e.g. possible broken handholds and failed placements. Spontaneous rockfall is not the problem—all the fatal and serious accidents were triggered by the victim, the rope, or by climbers above.

Rocks lying on ledges and in steep gullies are obviously dangerous. Not so obvious is that old reliable mantel block, five times your weight, wedged in place, and worn smooth by previous climbers. Yet with distressing regularity, "bombproof" blocks, flakes, and even ledges collapse under body weight, spit out cams, or fracture from the pressure of a piton. The forces placed on anchors and protection, even from rappelling, may be far higher than you generate in a test. Handholds may pass your scrutiny, then fail in mid-move. The rock you pull off can break your leg after falling only a couple of feet. Finally, watch out for rotten rock, responsible for at least two of these fatalities. It's common on the last couple of pitches of climbs that go to the rim of the Valley (e.g. Yosemite Point

Buttress and Washington Column).

The East Buttress of Middle Cathedral Rock is a well-known bowling alley and the site of many rockfall injuries. The Northwest Face of Half Dome is another, with the added excitement of tourist "firing squads" on the summit. But the most dangerous, surprisingly, may be El Cap; on rock so steep, loose blocks balance precariously and big flakes wait for an unlucky hand to trigger the final fracture.

Some rockfall accidents may not be preventable, but being alert to the hazard and following a few guidelines will cut the injury rate:

- Wear a helmet. (See "Helmets")

- Throw in an occasional piece on long, easy runouts as insurance against the unpredictability of the medium.

- Avoid rotten rock as protection, even if you can back it up. When it fails it endangers everyone below you.

- Ropes launch almost as many missiles as climbers do. Watch where you run your lead rope. Use directionals to keep it away from loose and sharp stuff, and check it frequently. Keep in mind that your bag or pack, when hauled, may dislodge everything in its path. When you pull your rappel ropes, stand to one side, look up, and watch out for delayed rockfall.

- You have no control over a party above you, and by being below you accept the risk. If you are catching up, don't crowd them—ask for permission to pass. You can probably get by them safely, but remember that climbers have been killed or hurt by rocks dislodged by parties above, including those they allowed to pass. The party you want to pass may have gotten an early start to avoid that risk, and they have no obligation to let you by. When you are above someone else, including your partner, put yourself in their shoes. Slow down and watch your feet and the rope.

Climbing Unroped

Everybody does it to some extent. There's no reason to stop, but good reason to be cautious: fourteen climbers were killed and two critically injured while deliberately unroped. At least eight climbed 5.10 or better. Most, if not all, of those accidents were avoidable. You may find yourself unroped in several situations—on 3rd class terrain, spontaneously on 5th class, and while deliberately free-soloing a route.

Third class terrain may be easy, but add a bit of sand, loose or wet rock, darkness, plus a moment of distraction, and the rating becomes meaningless. Four climbers have died this way, typically on approach and descent routes such as North Dome Gully, all in spots that did not demand a rope.

Sometimes you lose the way on the approach, or unrope at what you thought was the top of the climb, only to find a few feet of "easy" 5th class blocking your way. Your rope is tucked away in your pack, and you're in a hurry. Before you go on, remember that you didn't plan to free-solo an unknown quantity today. Four died this way, falling from 5th class terrain that they were climbing on the spur of the moment.

Seven of the 14 killed were rappelling or otherwise tied in. They unroped while still on 5th class rock, for various reasons of convenience, without clipping into a nearby anchor. Three slipped off their stances, a ledge collapsed under another, one decided to downclimb the last few feet, and two tried to climb their rappel ropes hand-over-hand to attend to some problem. Like the previous group, they all went unroped onto 5th class terrain on the spur of the moment. In addition, they all had a belay immediately available. Did its nearness give them a false sense of security?

Only one true free-soloer has been killed, although another one, critically hurt, survived only by the speed of his rescue. Is the free-soloer more alert to the task, having planned it in advance, than those who unroped on the spur of the moment? Were the unlucky fourteen still relaxed in their minds, not quite attuned to their new situation? We can only speculate.

Keep these cases and the hidden hazards in mind as you travel through any steep terrain. Be aware of what is underfoot, and in hand, at each moment. Be patient enough to retrace your steps to find the easy way.

Leading

Nine climbers died and six were critically injured in leader-fall accidents involving inadequate protection. Most fell simply because the moves were hard, and several were victims of broken holds. They were all injured because they hit something before their protection stopped them. Either they did not place enough protection (one-third of the cases) or it failed under the force of the fall (the remaining two-thirds). In every case, their injuries were serious because they fell headfirst or on their sides—the head, neck, or trunk took a lethal blow. Half fell 50 feet or less, the climber falling the shortest distance (25 feet) died, and the longest (270 feet!) survived.

Were these catastrophes avoidable? It's sometimes hard to tell, but the answer is often yes. Here are a few lessons frequently learned the hard way:

- Climbers frequently describe the belaying habits they see on Yosemite routes as "frightening." Before you start up, how frightening is your belay? Can the anchor withstand pulls in all directions? Is there more than one piece, with the load shared? Is the tie-in snug and in line with the fall force? Is your belayer experienced with that belay gadget and in position to operate it effectively when you fall? (You'd be surprised.) Will you clip through a bombproof directional as you start up, even on an easy pitch?

- Don't cheat on your ground fall calculations. (A good belayer will keep you honest.) With rope stretch and slack in the system, you may fall twice as far below your last protection as you are above it—if it holds.

- Nuts want to fall out. One that self-cleans below you may turn a comfortable lead into a ground-fall situation. Or, during a fall, the top piece may hold just long enough for the rope to yank the lower nuts out sideways, and then also fail. For more reliable placements, set those nuts with a tug and sling them generously. A tug on a marginal nut however, is worthless as a test. Be especially cautious about placements you can't see. Back them up.

- Camming devices "fail" regularly, but it's seldom the fault of the device. It's more likely due to haste, coupled with undeserved faith in technology. As with nuts, a blind placement—often in a lieback crack—may feel solid but be worthless.

- Fixed pitons loosen from freeze-thaw cycles and repeated use. They may not have been installed well to begin with. A hammer is the only reliable way to test and reset them, but you don't see many hammers on free routes these days. You don't see them on rappel routes, either, but you may find yourself hanging from anchors that belong in a museum. If you don't test pitons properly, do not depend on them—routinely back them up.

- There is no reliable way to test bolts but plenty of reasons to want to. For example, the common 3/8 split-shaft type was not designed or intended for life support, let alone for rock climbing. Their quality varies; several have broken under body weight, and others like them await you. Reliability also depends on the quality of the rock and the skill of the bolter. Add years of weathering and mistreatment by climbers and the result is many bolts that are easily pulled out by fingers or a sharp yank with a sling. Several bolt hangers have cracked as well, with one fatal accident so far.

- Never test a bolt with a hammer. Instead, examine the surrounding rock, the bolt, and the hanger for cracks, and hope they are large enough to see. Is the bolt tight and fully seated in the hole? Is the nut snug?

- Back up all untested fixed protection. Leave gear, even cams, before rappelling off of antique pieces. Is your life worth a cam?

Okay. So you know this stuff. You're a little shaky on the lead right now and you've had some trouble getting your pro to stick, but the book said this was 5.10a. It's only 20 feet more and one of those pieces is bound to hold. Think for a minute. Are you willing to free-solo this pitch? Keep your answer in mind as you climb, because poorly placed protection amounts to just that—you may not be deliberately unroped, but you might as well be.

About Falling

There's an art to falling safely—like a cat. Bouldering helps build the alertness required. Controlling your fall may be out of the question on those 200-foot screamers, but it will reduce the risk of injury from routine falls. Whenever possible, land on your feet—even if you break your leg, absorbing the shock this way may save your life. Liebacks and underclings hold special risks in this regard—you are already leaning back, and if you lose your grip the friction of your feet on the rock may rotate you into a headfirst—and backward—dive.

Pendulum falls are particularly dangerous. If you swing into a corner from 20 feet to one side of your protection, you will hit with the same bone-breaking speed as when striking a ledge in a 20-foot vertical fall. The crucial difference is, you are "landing" on your side, exposing vital organs to the impact. Two climbers died this way and others suffered serious injuries. Even small projections are dangerous: a 20-foot swing on Glacier Point Apron fractured a skull, and another smashed a pelvis. In a pendulum there is no difference between a leader and a follower fall; don't forget to protect your second from this fate as you lead a hard traverse.

Learning to Lead

Four of the 15 killed or critically injured in leader falls were good climbers on well-defined routes, but the majority were intermediates, often off-route. There may be a couple of lessons in that.

- Don't get cocky because you just led your first 5.8 or your protection held on your first fall. Experienced climbers have died from errors "only a beginner would make," so you have plenty of time left in your career to screw up.

- Climbing and protecting are separate skills but both keep you alive. Don't challenge yourself in both at the same time—you may not have the skill and presence of mind to get out of a tight spot. If you're out to push your limits, pick a route that's well defined and easy to protect, place extra pieces for practice, and be willing and equipped to back off.

- Routefinding is another survival skill. A mistake here can quickly put you over your head in climbing, protecting, or both. Learn to look ahead and recognize what you want to avoid. Climb it mentally before you climb it physically.

- Some "easy" terrain in the valley is actually pretty dangerous. Low angle gullies are often full of loose blocks cemented together with moss. Opportunities for protection may be scarce and routefinding subtle. These are not usually cataloged routes. Three or four climbers have been killed, or nearly so, on such terrain while looking for easy routes to climb.

The Belay Chain

Whether you are climbing, rappelling, or just sitting on a ledge, the belay chain is what connects you to the rock. There are many links, and mistakes with almost every one have killed 22 climbers, 40 percent of all Yosemite climbing fatalities. In every case the cause was human error. In every case the death was completely preventable, not by the subtle skills of placing protection on the lead, but by some simple precaution to keep the belay chain intact. Experienced climbers outnumbered the inexperienced in this category two to one. Mistakes with the belay chain can occur at any time. Make one and you'll fall to the end of the rope . . . or farther. Minor injuries are rare. Here are some key points to remember:

- Before you commit yourself to a system, always apply a few pounds of tension in the directions in which it will be loaded, analyzing it like an engineer—what if this happens . . . or that? Check every link, from the buckle of your harness to the rock around your anchor. You would be amazed at the inadequate systems often used by experienced climbers, even though it takes only a few seconds to run a proper check. Both lives depend on that system, so go through it with your partner. Nine climbers have died in multi-victim accidents.

- Check the system periodically while you're using it. Forces may change direction (two died when their anchors failed for this reason), ropes and slings can wear through (serious injuries and one death) and gear can come undone (two died when a wiggling bolt hanger unscrewed its nut—they were relying on a single bolt).

- Are you about to rappel? Stay clipped to the anchor for a few seconds. Check both the anchor and your brake system, as above. If one anchor point fails, will you remain attached to others? Are the knots in your rappel slings secure? Did you check every inch of those fixed slings for damage? Skipping these precautions cost eight lives plus serious injuries, from poorly tied slings, partially dismantled anchors (a simple misunderstanding), relying on single carabiners, and other reasons. The next accident may be caused by something new, but it will have been preventable by double-checking.

- Two climbers died by rappelling off the ends of their ropes, even though both had tied knots in the ends as a safety measure. In one case the knots pulled through the brake. In the second, the victim forgot to double-check the ropes after a knot had been untied to deal with a problem. Knots are still a recommended safety procedure, but do not take anything for granted. Tie both strands into one knot or knot each separately—there are pros and cons to each method.

- When rappelling in unpredictable circumstances—darkness, wind, poor communications, unknown anchors below—consider a Prusik Hitch or a mechanical ascender as a safety. If improperly handled, neither one may stop you if you fall—they are primarily for quickly but deliberately stopping yourself to deal with other emergencies. Both of those who rappelled off their ropes would have survived with safeties.

- Self-belayers should also tie in short—one died when his Prusik belay melted during a fall (a Prusik cord too large for the rope). At least two were treated to close calls when other types of self-belay systems jammed open.

- Clip into a new belay point before unclipping from the old one. During those few, vulnerable seconds, pitons have pulled, hero loops have broken, rocks have struck, and feet have slipped.

- Three climbers were killed and one critically injured by "failures" of single-carabiner tie-ins and rappel anchors. Be careful of relying on a single non-locking carabiner for any link in the chain. The rope or sling may flip over the gate and unclip itself, especially if it is slack, or shock loaded. Even if you watch it carefully and/or it is "safely" under tension, you may become distracted. One climber died when his Figure Eight descender unclipped while he was busy passing a knot on rappel. (He should have tied in short.) For those critical points, use either two non-locking carabiners with gates opposed and reversed, or a locking carabiner. Don't forget to lock it! For many applications the two-carabiner method is safer and faster to operate.

- Ropes have been cut in three fatal accidents. They did not break, but were stressed over sharp edges, a condition never intended by the manufacturer. Two of these accidents were avoidable: one climber should have tied in short to prevent a 100 foot fall that cut the rope; the other should have protected a fixed rope from a well-defined sharp edge. Ascending a rope produces a weighted, see-sawing action that can destroy it, even over a rounded, moderately rough, edge.

- As with ropes, most gear failure falls into the misuse category. Failure from a design or manufacturing flaw is rare. It was the initiating factor in one fatal accident—three climbers died when a bolt hanger broke at a two-bolt rappel anchor. The tragic outcome would have been avoided, however, had the climbers noticed they were not properly backed up to the second bolt.

These cases illustrate one of the rules most commonly overlooked: BACK YOURSELF UP. No matter what initially pulled, broke, slipped, jammed, or cut, the incident became an accident because the climber did not carefully ask himself, "What if . . .?" By leaving yourself open, you are betting against a variety of unpredictable events. You don't lose very often, but when you do, you may lose very big.

Beginners

From your first day on the rock, you have the right to inspect, and ask questions about, any system to which you're committing your life. It's a good way to learn, and a good way to stay alive. If your partner or instructor is offended, find someone else to climb with. Never change the system or the plan, however, without your partner's knowledge.

Helmets

While we can never know for certain, helmets might have made a difference in roughly 25 percent of the fatal and critical trauma cases. They would have significantly increased—but not guaranteed—the survival chances for five of those fatalities. Furthermore, helmets would have offered excellent protection against less serious fractures, concussions, and lacerations. There are no compelling reasons not to wear a helmet on any Yosemite climb and many reasons why you should.

States of Mind

This is the key to safety. It's impossible to know how many climbers were killed by haste or overconfidence, but many survivors will tell you that they somehow lost their good judgment long enough to get hurt. It's a complex subject and sometimes a touchy one. Nevertheless, at least three states of mind frequently contribute to accidents: ignorance, casualness, and distraction.

Ignorance
There is always more to learn, and even the most conscientious climber can get into trouble if unaware of the danger ("I thought it never rained . . . ") Here are some ways to fight ignorance:

Look in the mirror. Are you the stubborn type? Do you resist suggestions? Could you be a bit overconfident? (Ask your friends.) Several partners have said of a dead friend, "I wanted to give him advice, but he always got mad when I did that. I didn't realize he was about to die."

Read. The climbing magazines are full of good recommendations. Case histories in the American Alpine Club's Accidents in North American Mountaineering, a yearly compilation of accident reports, will show you how subtle factors may combine to catch you unaware. Such accounts are the next best (or worst?) thing to being there.

Practice. Reading may make you aware but not competent. In fact, you can be dangerously misled by what you read, including this report—important details are often left out, the advice may be incorrect, and in the long run you must think and act for yourself. Several climbers, for example, waited to learn how to prusik until it was dark, raining, overhanging and they were actually in trouble. They had read about it, but they had to be rescued despite having the gear to improvise their own solutions. Book-learning alone gave them a complacency that could have proved fatal.

Casualness
"I just didn't take it seriously," is a common lament. It's often correct, but it's more a symptom than a cause—there may be deeper reasons for underestimating your risk. Ignorance is one, and here are some more:

Habit reinforcement. The more often you get away with risky business the more entrenched your lazy habits become. Have you unconsciously dropped items from your safety checklists since you were a chickenhearted (or hare-brained) beginner? Your attitudes and habits can be reinforced by the experiences (and states of mind) of others. The sense of awe and commitment of the 1960s is gone from the big wall trade routes, and young aspirants with no Grade VIs, or even Vs, to their credit speak casually about them. Even for experts, most accidents on El Cap occur on the easier pitches, where their guard is down.

Memory Decay. "I'm not going up again without raingear—I thought I would die!" A week later this climber had forgotten how scared he had been in that thunderstorm. Raingear was now too heavy and besides, he was sure he'd be able to rap off the next time. Many of us tend to forget the bad parts. We have to be hit again.

Civilization. With fixed anchors marking the way up and ghetto blasters echoing behind, it may be hard to realize that the potential for trouble is as high in Yosemite as anywhere. Some say the possibility of fast rescue added to their casualness. Maybe, but who wants a broken leg, or worse, in the first place?

Distraction

It is caused by whatever takes your mind off your work—anxiety, sore feet, skinny-dippers below—the list is endless. Being in a hurry is one of the most common causes. Here are two ways it has happened:

- Experienced climbers were often hurt after making "beginner errors" (their words) to get somewhere quickly. There was no emergency or panic, but their minds were elsewhere—on a cold beer, a good bivy—or just sick of being on that route for a week. (It's often called "summit fever.") Their mistakes were usually shortcuts in protecting easy pitches, on both walls and shorter climbs. As one put it, "We were climbing as though we were on top."

- Darkness had caught two day-climbers for the first time. Unprepared, upset, and off route, they rushed to get down, arguing with each other about what to do. After several errors, which they knew how to avoid, one died rappelling off the end of his rope.

Rescue

Despite the best of attitudes, an accident can happen to anyone. Self-rescue is often the fastest and safest way out, but whether it's the wise course of action depends on the injury and how well prepared you are. Combining with a nearby party will often give you the margin of safety you need, but do not risk aggravating an injury or getting yourself into a more serious predicament —ask for help if you need it. (Sometimes a bit of advice, delivered by loudspeaker, is all that's required.) In making your decision, keep an eye on weather and darkness—call for help early.

If you don't have formal first aid training (which is strongly recommended), at least know how to keep an unconscious patient's airway open, how to protect a possible broken neck or back, and how to deal with external bleeding and serious blood loss.

These procedures are lifesaving, do not require fancy gear, and are easy to learn.

Head injury victims, even when unconscious, may try to untie themselves. If you have to leave one alone, make escape impossible.

Risk and Responsibility

The NPS has no regulations specifying how you must climb. There is a regulation, however, requiring that all park users act responsibly. This applies to climbers, in that the consequences of your actions put rescue and other climbers at risk. One rescuer has been killed in the park so far. Thus, if your own negligence got you into trouble, you may be charged with "creating a hazardous condition" for others. As an example, a climber was fined because he became stranded by a hailstorm while attempting to free-solo the Steck-Salathé on Sentinel Rock. Storms had been predicted and his rescue should not have been necessary.

Even avoidable accidents are understandable, thus legal charges are not frequently filed. Of all park users, however, climbers should be particularly aware— they know that their sport is dangerous, that safety lies in education and training, and that there is an information network available. So take what you'll need with you on the climb, or have competent friends ready to back you up.

Climbing will always be risky. It should be clear, however, that a reduced accident rate is possible without seriously restricting the sport. You have a right to choose your own climbing style and level of risk, but you owe it to yourself and everyone else to make that choice with your eyes wide open.

Accident/Hazard Reporting

If you know of dangerous route conditions such as loose rock, consider posting the information on the bulletin board at Camp 4 or at www.supertopo.com. If you know of bad anchors, email the ASCA at badbolt@safeclimbing.org. Your information will help other climbers.

Cam Sizes by Brand

Ref Size*	BD Camalots	CCH Aliens	Metolius Cams	Trango Big Bros	Wild Country Friends
0.4"	.1 red	.33 black	00 gray		
0.5"	.2 yellow	.375 blue	0 purple		0 red
0.6"	.3 purple	.5 green	1 blue		.5 orange
0.75"	.4 gray	.75 yellow	2 yellow		1 yellow
1"	.5 pink	1 red	3 orange		1.25 brown
1.25"	.75 green	1.5 orange	4 red		1.5 sky
1.5"	1 red	2 purple	5 black		2 pink
1.75"	1 red	2.5 gray	6 green		2.5 royal
2"	2 yellow	2.5 gray	7 blue		3 navy
2.5"	2 yellow		8 purple		3.5 purple
3"	3 blue		9 burgundy		4 black
3.5"	3.5 gray		10 dark blue		4 black
3.5-4.5"	4 purple			1 red	5 silver
4.5-5.5"	4.5 red			2	
5.5-7"	5 green			3 green	6 plum
7-8"				3 green	
8-12"				4 blue	

"Ref size" is the optimal crack width for a given camming unit. It is not the range given by the manufacturer.

Understanding the maps

Topo Symbols

Right-facing corner		Roof		Bolt	x
Left-facing corner		Ledge		Rappel anchor	
		Slab	///		
Straight-in crack		Belay station	❶	Face climbing	
Groove		Pitch length	130'●	Pine Tree	
Arete				Oak-like Tree	
Flake		Optional belay	○	Bush	
				Knob	o
Chimney		False belay	⊘	Hole	●

Notes on Rack

– "nuts" refers to any nut, stopper, or chock. "micro"= #1, 2; "sml"= #3-5; "med"= #6-8; "lrg"= #9-13
– for cams, "2 ea .75-1.5" means bring two sets of all sizes between .75" and 1.5". Check the cam size chart to see which cam corresponds to which crack size.

Notes on Topo

– "belay takes .6-1" means, while leading the pitch, save enough .6-1" cams and nuts to build a natural anchor.
– a number next to a tree is its height.

Topo abbreviations

ow = offwidth
lb = lieback
p = fixed piton
R = runout (dangerous fall)

Metric system conversions

1 inch = 2.54 centimeters
1 foot = 0.305 meters
100 feet = 30.5 meter
50 yards = 45.7 meters

Overview graphics

Low-clearance dirt road · · · · · · · · · · ·

High-clearance dirt road

Road or State Route

Federal Highway

Hikers' trail

Climbers' trail – – – – – – – – –

Cross-country travel · · · · · · · · · · · · ·

Star Ratings

★★★★★ - undisputed classic
★★★★ - excellent climb
★★★ - good climb
★★ - okay climb
★ - barely included in this book

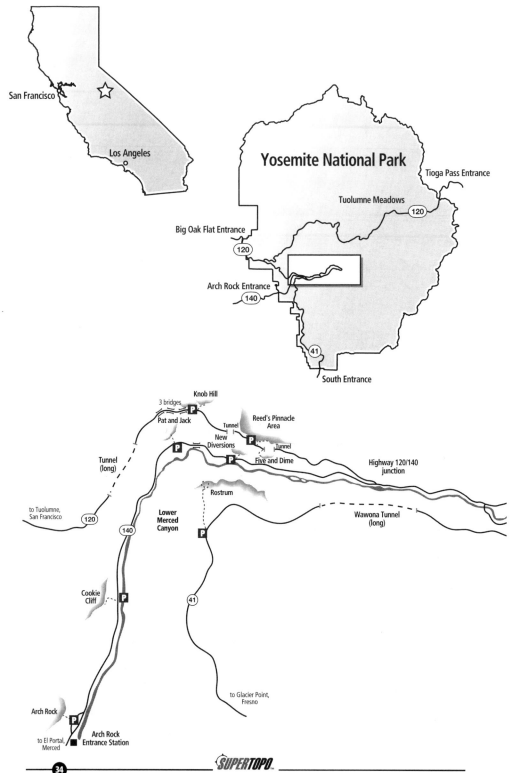

Yosemite National Park

Tioga Pass Entrance

Tuolumne Meadows

120

Big Oak Flat Entrance

120

Arch Rock Entrance

140

41

South Entrance

San Francisco

Los Angeles

Knob Hill

3 bridges

Pat and Jack

Reed's Pinnacle Area

Tunnel

New Diversions

Tunnel

Five and Dime

Highway 120/140 junction

Tunnel (long)

Rostrum

to Tuolumne, San Francisco

120

140

Lower Merced Canyon

Wawona Tunnel (long)

Cookie Cliff

41

to Glacier Point, Fresno

Arch Rock

Arch Rock Entrance Station

to El Portal, Merced

Legend

Road or State Route ———(10)———

Federal Highway ———(10)———

Hikers' trail

Climbers' trail

Cross-country travel

Yosemite Falls
Lost Arrow Spire
Arrowhead Arête
Sunnyside Bench
Five Open Books
Yosemite Falls Trail
Yosemite Village
Swan Slabs
P
Camp 4 Wall
Yosemite Lodge
Camp 4
to Tamarack Flat
to Yosemite Falls Trail and Camp 4
Three Brothers
one way
one way
East Ledges descent
raps
El Capitan
Manure Pile Buttress
Merced River
P
Four Mile Trail
Southwest Face
Southeast Face
Zodiac talus
Schultz's Ridge
Sentinel Rock
standard approach
P   P   P
one way
El Capitan Meadow
P
P
one way
Bridalveil Fall
Lower Cathedral Rock
Middle Cathedral Rock
Lower Cathedral Spire
Higher Cathedral Spire
Highway 41
Leaning Tower
Higher Cathedral Rock

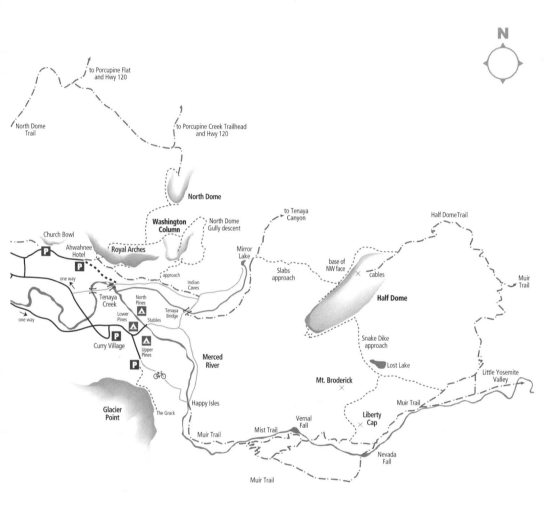

N

to Porcupine Flat
and Hwy 120

North Dome
Trail

to Porcupine Creek Trailhead
and Hwy 120

North Dome

Half Dome Trail

Washington
Column

North Dome
Gully descent

to Tenaya
Canyon

Church Bowl

Ahwahnee
Hotel

Royal Arches

Mirror
Lake

base of
NW face

cables

Muir
Trail

P

P

one way

approach

Slabs
approach

Half Dome

Indian
Caves

Tenaya
Creek

North
Pines

Tenaya
Bridge

one way

Lower
Pines

Stables

Snake Dike
approach

Curry Village

Upper
Pines

Lost Lake

Little Yosemite
Valley

P

Merced
River

Mt. Broderick

Muir Trail

Glacier
Point

Happy Isles

The Grack

Vernal
Fall

Liberty
Cap

Muir Trail

Mist Trail

Muir Trail

Nevada
Fall

Muir Trail

Arch Rock

Approach time: **15 minutes**

Sun exposure: **morning to afternoon**

Height of routes: **300'**

Arch Rock rivals the Cookie Cliff in quality and difficulty. Packed with 5.10 and 5.11 cracks, it is Yosemite's training ground to perfect burly cracks. Because it faces south and is at a low elevation, temperatures are ideal on cool spring or fall days and in the winter. Summer is typically too hot.

Chris McNamara

1	Anticipation	5	Leanie Meanie
2	Entrance Exam	6	Gripper
3	English Breakfast Crack	7	New Dimensions
4	Midterm		

Approach

If driving west from the Valley, Highway 140 splits 200 yards before the Arch Rock Entrance Station. Just after the split, park in a dirt pullout on the right in front of some power equipment. If driving from the east into Yosemite, park at the lot on the right just after the entrance station and walk up the left road (against traffic) to the dirt pullout in front of the power equipment.

From the dirt pullout, hike up the talus directly toward the cliff.

Descent

Rappel most climbs with two 50m or 60m ropes. Another option is the loose, technical, and poison oak-covered walk-off from the top. Follow a trail through trees and eventually scramble down steep sections above the midpoint of the crag. Go west and down a loose section to the back around eastward to Anticipation.

History

One day in the summer of 1964, while paying his fee at the Arch Rock Entrance Station, Chuck Pratt happened to look up at the rather nondescript wall to the north. It sure wasn't another El Cap, but the lower part, mostly obscured by the foreground forest, showed a few gleaming faces and dihedrals. Worth a look, he decided.

Pratt and Tom Frost hiked up to the base and discovered a wealth of cracks and

chimneys. The pair chose an obvious line and climbed it free, onsight, and the result was one of the hardest Valley climbs yet. A thin 10b crack near the bottom formed the crux, but a 10a fist crack higher up proved more strenuous. Midterm, the modest pair named their route, knowing they hadn't yet reached their potential (an easier Pratt route just to the left later became Entrance Exam, and a non-Pratt 10d route at the base of Half Dome later became Final Exam).

In 1970 another Valley crackmaster appeared on the scene: Jim Bridwell. In May he established New Dimensions with protégé Mark Klemens. The first three pitches of this severe thin crack route to the right of Midterm were all in the lower 5.10 range, but then the climbing got tough. A bit of 11a led to a place that had even Bridwell stymied, so he made a pendulum to the right to reach easier ground. Two years later the brilliant climbers Steve Wunsch and Barry Bates climbed the upper pitch free.

A few months after climbing New Dimensions, Bridwell was responsible for yet another classic in this area: Gripper, a 10b route done with Klemens and Bruce Kumph. This marvelous climb featured lots of hand jamming, some straightforward, but some hard enough that the leader was "gripped."

Jim Donini, later to become one of the world's finest all-around climbers, was just beginning his career in 1972 when he, Mark Chapman, and Rob Carrington put up a clean, classic line they named Leanie Meanie. This 11b ever-widening crack, as one might guess, leaned to one side for much of its length—and as any crack climber knows, this poses problems. Two years later, Donini and Chapman established Anticipation, another sterling crack climb, this one involving fingerlocks at the 11b crux.

Punchline, the most controversial—and hardest—climb in the Arch Rock area was established in 1988 by Ron Kauk, who had done the unthinkable by placing the protection bolts from above, while on rappel. Trad climber John Bachar soon chopped these, resulting in an incident back in Camp 4 where Bachar was sucker-punched by Chapman, Kauk's sidekick. Mike Kennedy, editor of *Climbing* magazine, facetiously suggested that Kauk and Bachar "duel to the death so the rest of us can get back to actually climbing rather than arguing about it." The name, of course, stems from this affair.

- Steve Roper

A. Anticipation 5.11b★★★★
FA: Mark Chapman and Jim Donini, 1974.

The next step after New Dimensions. Pitch 2 is the business—steep hand jams lead to even steeper finger jams followed by an awkward flare (look for a no-hands rest). Thin finger jams lead to the anchor.

B. Supplication 5.10c★★★
FA: Barry Bates and Bev Johnson, 1971.

The dirty start soon transforms into high-quality steep and technical finger jamming and liebacking. Good preparation for the finale of New Dimensions. A dirty 5.9 pitch leads to the top (not recommended).

C. Entrance Exam 5.9★★★
FA: Chuck Pratt, Chris Fredericks, Larry Marshik, and Jim Bridwell, 8/65.

This feels like 5.10 and is good Steck Salathé training. Awkward moves around blocks

occasionally interrupt classic chimney climbing. You may want extra wide gear for the chimney runouts.

D. Goldilocks 5.12a★★★
FA: James Lombard and Sean Jones, 11/97.

Short but excellent steep fingertip liebacking. Set up a toprope while rappelling English Breakfast Crack.

E. The Principle 5.12b/c★★★★
FA: James Lombard and Brian Ketron, 11/97.

Follows a beautiful line up a steep flake that is well-protected. Set up a toprope while rappelling English Breakfast Crack.

F. English Breakfast Crack 5.10c★★★★★
FA: Chris Fredericks and Kim Schmitz, 7/66.

This route requires every Yosemite Valley technique—exposed and technical liebacking, steep finger jams, offwidth climbing, and chimneying. The next step after Midterm.

G. Midterm 5.10b★★★★★
FA: Chuck Pratt and Tom Frost, 8/64.

The most classic route at Arch Rock. The striking and unrelenting line gradually widens from fingers jams to a notoriously polished chimney. A full body workout.

H. Leanie Meanie 5.11b★★★★
FA: Jim Donini, Rob Carrington, and Mark Chapman, 1972.

A perfect corner with lean and mean liebacking and steep finger jams. The second pitch is not recommended.

I. Gripper 5.10b★★★★★
FA: Jim Bridwell, Bruce Kumph, and Mark Klemens, 8/70.

Steep and committing chimneys and awkward and technical moves. This is a step up in difficulty from Midterm.

J. New Dimensions 5.11a★★★★★
FA: Jim Bridwell and Mark Klemens, 5/70.
FFA: Barry Bates and Steve Wunsch, 1972.

Yosemite's first 5.11 and first 5.11 solo (made by John Bachar in 1976). With continuously physical and steep jams, the route remains a testpiece today. To descend, walk off or rappel Gripper.

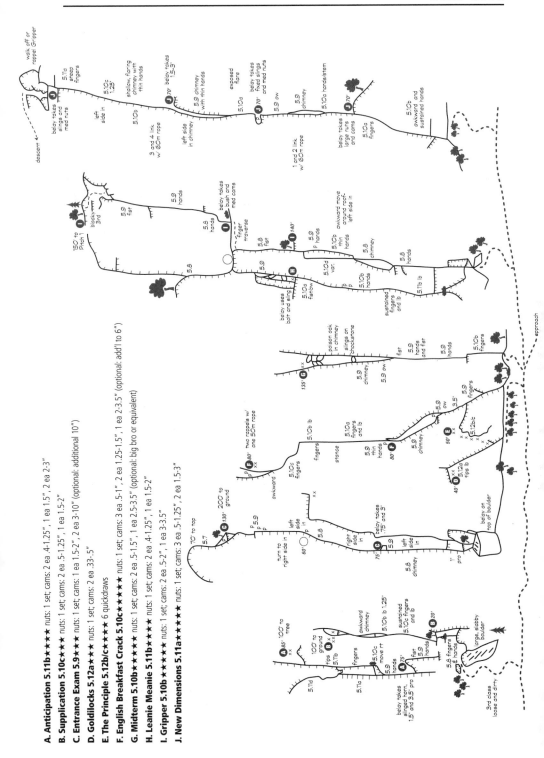

A. Anticipation 5.11b ★★★★ nuts: 1 set; cams: 2 ea .4-1.25", 1 ea 1.5", 2 ea 2-3"

B. Supplication 5.10c ★★★ nuts: 1 set; cams: 2 ea .5-1.25", 1 ea 1.5-2"

C. Entrance Exam 5.9 ★★★ nuts: 1 set; cams: 1 ea 1.5-2", 2 ea 3-10" (optional: additional 10")

D. Goldilocks 5.12a ★★★ nuts: 1 set; cams: 2 ea .33-.5"

E. The Principle 5.12b/c ★★★ 6 quickdraws

F. English Breakfast Crack 5.10c ★★★★ nuts: 1 set; cams: 3 ea .5-1", 2 ea 1.25-1.5", 1 ea 2-3.5" (optional: add'l to 6")

G. Midterm 5.10b ★★★★ nuts: 1 set; cams: 2 ea .5-1.5", 1 ea 2.5-3.5" (optional: big bro or equivalent)

H. Leanie Meanie 5.11b ★★★★ nuts: 1 set; cams: 2 ea 4-1.25", 1 ea 1.5-2"

I. Gripper 5.10b ★★★★★ nuts: 1 set; cams: 2 ea .5-2", 1 ea 3-3.5"

J. New Dimensions 5.11a ★★★★★ nuts: 1 set; cams: 3 ea .5-1.25", 2 ea 1.5-3"

Cookie Cliff

Approach time: **10 minutes**

Sun exposure: **morning to afternoon**

Height of routes: **60-350'**

The Cookie Cliff offers the best hard crag climbing in Yosemite. It features perfectly cut cracks mostly one to two pitches long. It played a significant role in the free climbing renaissance of the 1970s. If you wanted to test yourself against some of the hardest crack climbs in the world, then you went straight to the Cookie.

Because of its lower elevation, the Cookie Cliff is a good winter destination, but too hot in the summer until the late afternoon when it's shaded. Most routes are steep and short with more textured rock than is typical for Yosemite. Expect crowds.

Approach

From the Highway 120/140 junction, drive west 2.2 miles on 140 and park at the second of two large paved pullouts on the left. Locate a climbers' trail to the left of a large, white talus field and hike a few minutes to the old road and the right side of the Cookie Cliff. For routes on the left side, follow the road until you locate the appropriate climbers' trail heading up.

Descent

It is almost always best to rappel instead of walking down. If you do top out, contour left (west) and skirt down steep dirt to the left (west) edge of the cliff.

History

This small cliff, opposite Elephant Rock on Highway 140, is a crack climber's paradise. Home to more than 40 routes, the steep wall is replete with giant dihedrals, jamcracks, chimneys, and "Yosemite pinnacles"—dramatic exfoliation slabs lying against the face.

Todd Snyder

1	Hardd	5	Waverly Wafer
2	Crack A-Go-Go	6	Butterballs
3	Meat Grinder	7	Wheat Thin
4	Beverly's Tower	8	The Cookie, Right

It's no accident that this region was discovered by the master crack climber Chuck Pratt. While most climbers were content to stay within the Valley itself, on his way back to the city Pratt would look for spectacular formations outside the Valley. And in September 1958 he actually persuaded someone into accompanying him to one such area, now known as the Cookie Cliff. With Wally Reed, Pratt climbed a prominent cleft that they named, naturally, The Cleft. Around the same time, he and Dick Sykes did the upper left side of a slab they named The Cookie (Cookie Calderwood, a strikingly beautiful woman climber, was coveted by all of us in Camp 4, but unfortunately she was married).

Little new climbing took place at the Cookie Cliff during the next seven years, but 1965 saw a resurgence. The highlight of that year was the incredibly bold Twilight Zone, led by Pratt. A 5.10d offwidth high on the route had very poor protection. Even with camming devices, the route is still feared today. In this same year Pratt, feeling a little guilty for using four aid pitons on the Cleft in 1958, returned with Chris Fredericks to make a free variation at 5.9.

Also in 1965, Jim Bridwell put up the first of his many new routes on the cliff when he climbed the 5.8 Elevator Shaft with Phil Bircheff.

More years went by with little action, but another resurgence took place in the early 1970s. Bridwell got serious in 1970, liebacking Waverly Wafer, the first pitch of the steep face above the Cookie in the general region soon named the Nabisco Wall. The next year Bridwell returned to the same area, and with Peter Haan continued up the Nabisco Wall to establish Wheat Thin, another lieback route. Days later Bridwell and Charley Jones climbed the upper pitch of Nabisco, the horrendously difficult Butterfingers. In 1973, the immensely talented eastern climber Henry Barber put up Butterballs, a pitch just left of Wheat Thin. The three-pitch Nabisco Wall combination was quite likely North America's hardest crack climb. The Cookie Cliff had become famous!

– *Steve Roper*

A. Hardd — 5.11b★★★★

FA: Henry Barber, Ron Kauk, and Steve Wunsch, 5/75.

A challenging combination of wide crack moves and finger jams. Wear pants to protect yourself on the lower wide section. Up high, a few well-placed hand jams let you recover before the crux. The second pitch delivers increasingly steep fingerlocks followed by fist jams.

B. Crack A-Go-Go — 5.11c★★★★★

FA: Harvey Carter and Pete Pederson, 5/67.
FFA: Pete Livesy and Ron Fawcett, 1974.

Maybe the most classic fingertip crack in Yosemite. Tiny edging and technical moves lead to a stance for placing the first piece of protection—a scary 15 feet above the ground. Next you'll encounter delicate stemming between fingertip liebacks past thin, hard-to-place protection for the next 15-20 feet. Higher, the crack appears easy but packs several tricky cruxes to an easier finale of hands and liebacking.

C. Outer Limits — 5.11a★★★★★

FA: Jim Bridwell and Jim Orey, 1971.

Every 5.11 climber must do the first pitch of this route. The classic book *Yosemite Climber* called Outer Limits "perhaps the most sought after two-pitch climb in Yosemite." The route starts with what appears to be a lieback flake, but is actually a pumpy hand and fist crack. Down low is the technical crux, but it is the steep and pumpy jams up high that stymie most people. It is hard to resist setting a toprope on the first pitch and doing multiple laps. The second pitch is very polished and tricky and ia usually avoided.

D. Elevator Shaft — 5.8 R★★

FA: Jim Bridwell and Phil Bircheff, 6/65.

This adventurous outing offers an alternative if the other climbs in the area are crowded. Gear is sparse at times. The last pitch is rarely climbed.

Jack Hoeflich delicately placing gear at the crux of Crack-A-Go-Go.

E. Cookie Monster (Pitch 1)   5.12a★★★★

FA: Bill Price, et al., 1979;
FFA: Kurt Smith and Scott Cosgrove, 1987.

The first free ascensionists boldly led this route on RPs and nuts and rated it 5.12c. The climb was downgraded to 5.12a after it was bolted. With bolts, the route changed from a seldom-repeated trad lead to the most popular 5.12 sport climb in Yosemite.

Move fast through the start and conserve energy for the tips lieback crux. The second pitch is 5.13b.

F. Twilight Zone   5.10d★★★

FA: Chuck Pratt and Chris Fredericks, 9/65.

This is the most classic offwidth climb in Yosemite. Not only was it one of the first 5.10s, Chuck Pratt led the crux pitch with only three poor pieces of gear. Imagine a 5.13 put up onsight with a potential death fall and you will understand how significant this climb was in the mid-60s when 5.10 was the limit. Today few people climb this route because it is just too darn hard. The crux can either be climbed by hand stacking or with wild stem moves. Avoid the last pitch.

G. Red Zinger   5.11d★★★★

FA: Ray Jardine and Dave Altman, 9/79.

Steep, clean, and beautiful, Red Zinger has a surprisingly moderate first half. Then a desperate thin finger section leads to the endurance-testing top half. A great route with good protection.

H. Meat Grinder   5.10c★★★

FA: Royal Robbins and TM Herbert, 3/68.

This route is so sustained at 5.9 that it's rated 5.10. The first pitch features a mixture of hand and chimney moves that provides a preview of challenges to come. The second pitch is burly and sustained, the two ingredients of a classic Yosemite crack, and involves a variety of strenuous stems and jams with wide protection. The last pitch is seldom climbed.

I. Beverly's Tower   5.10a★★★

FA: Gerry Czamanske and Warren Harding, 1959.
FFA: Roger Breedlove and Alan Bard, 5/73.

The scene of one death, the first 20 feet of this stout 5.10a are difficult to protect. Climb the arête past thin protection and move right into the right-facing corner. Lieback and stem the corner to an interesting overhanging stem box. Hand and thin hand jamming past the overhang leads to the bolted anchor. Continue above and right to gain the Wheat Thin belay ledge.

J. Aftershock   5.11b★★★

FA: Tony Yaniro and Max Jones, 1981.

Start with a fingertip traverse and steep edging moves right along the crack. A thin mantel gains the shallow left-facing corner then lieback moves and edging continue to reach the overhang. Get your right hand high then reach up and over the bulge for a left finger lock.

K. Waverly Wafer   5.11a★★★★

FA: Jim Bridwell, Barry Bates and Beverly Johnson, 10/70.

Long considered the most challenging 5.10c in Yosemite, this is in all honesty a 5.11. The challenge is a very difficult offwidth pod leading to an endless off-finger lieback. Begin up the steep corner with perfect hand jams and great edges for your feet. The off-fingers crux section takes pumpy straight-in ring locks, but is usually liebacked.

L. Butterballs   5.11c★★★★

FA: Henry Barber, et al., 5/73.

In the 1970s, Henry Barber would show up in the Valley for a few weeks and snatch a handful of classic, cutting-edge routes from the astonished locals. Butterballs was one of Barber's many prized picks. It ascends steep fingerlocks with occasional good edges for your feet. Move quickly and stay close to the wall using precise footwork. A wide finger section with poor footholds proves especially challenging to those with thin fingers. You'll find flaring thin hands in the pod more difficult than you expected and the finish is steep with secure liebacking.

Most climbers toprope this climb before feeling solid enough to hang around and place protection on lead.

M. Butterfingers 5.11a★★★★

FA: Jim Bridwell and Charlie Jones, 8/71.

This crack requires more face moves than jams. It starts with thin fingerlocks and tiny edges for your feet. Steep and technical edging leads to the right crack with secure hand jams.

N. Wheat Thin 5.10c★★★★

FA: Peter Haan and Jim Bridwell, 8/71.

This amazing flake which you'll wish goes on forever is also the first rap-bolted climb in Yosemite. While later rap-bolted routes created a bolt chopping war among locals, Wheat Thin escaped controversy because the bolts were placed on rappel in order to preserve the fragile flake. The crux involves gear-protected off-balanced moves to reach the bolt-protected lieback flake. From the top of this climb it is easy to set up a toprope on Butterballs.

O. The Cookie, Right Side 5.9★★★★

FA: Royal Robbins and Loyd Price, 2/68.

This is one of the few good 5.9 climbs at the Cookie. On the first pitch, climb the short technical thin crack in the left-facing corner to a ledge. Continue up a beautiful chimney to a large ledge inside. On the second pitch, climb out to the edge of the chimney with right side in to a flake. Protect here and continue up the sustained and incredible chimney to the top of the giant flake with slings around it. From this point, perfect hand jams lead to the top of the pillar.

P. Catchy 5.10d★★★★★

FA: Jim Pettigrew, Jim Bridwell and Mark Klemens, 10/71.

Steep with predominantly thin hand jams, Catchy is a great climb to push your 5.10 level. Using good technique and stems, you reach a one-move crux to a jug at the top.

Q. Catchy Corner 5.11a★★★★★

FA: Jim Bridwell and Dale Bard, 1974.

A blocky and bushy start past hand jams leads to a gorgeous right-facing corner containing good finger and toe jams. Focus on good footwork and steady movement through steep liebacking to the large ledge on the left for a stem rest. Fire through the crux lieback at the small discontinuity in the corner and take advantage of great fingerlocks to the bolt anchor. Many climbers get their ropes stuck when rappelling.

R. The Enema 5.11b★★★★★

FA: Jim Donini and John Bragg, 1974.

Approach the first pitch via a quality 5.7 chimney that climbs past the old bolts below the squeeze section. The second pitch is the business: begin up an awkward flaring crack to sharp and secure hand jams. Big, steep moves lead to the diorite jugs and then a large knob for a no-hands rest. Steep and flaring hands finish the last 20 feet of the route.

Greg Barnes

Hugo Rivera leading Catchy (5.10d).

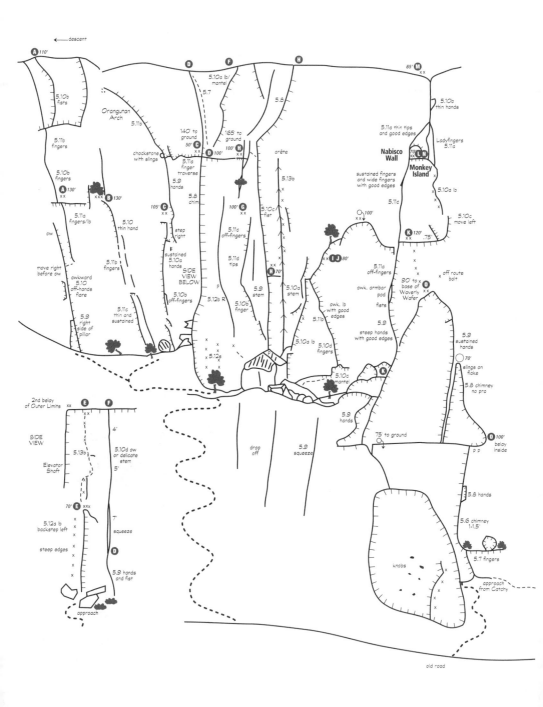

←── descent

A 110'

5.10b
fists

Orangutan
Arch

5.11b
fingers

5.11b

5.10b
fingers

5.11a
fingers/lb

A 130'
xx

B 130'
xxx

5.10
thin hand

ow

move right
before ow

awkward
5.10
off-hands
flare

5.11b
fingers

5.9
right
side of
pillar

5.11c
thin and
sustained

chockstone
with slings

140' to
ground
50'
C xx
100'

105'
C xx

step
right

sustained
5.10a
hands

5.10b
off-fingers

5.11a
finger
traverse

5.9
hands

5.8
chim

SIDE
VIEW
BELOW

5.10b
off-fingers

5.12b R

D 165' to
ground
100'
D 100'

5.7

D xx

5.11c
off-fingers

5.11d
tips

G 100'
xx

5.10c
fist

p

5.12s
x x x
x x x

5.9
stem

F 5.10a lb/
mantel

arête

5.13b

5.8

5.10c

H 70'
xx

5.9
stem

5.10a
stem

5.10b
finger

5.10a lb

5.10d
fingers

5.10c
mantel

H

M 65'
xx

5.10b
thin hands

5.11a thin tips
and good edges

Ladyfingers
5.11a

**Nabisco
Wall**

L M 70'
xx

**Monkey
Island**

sustained fingers
and wide fingers
with good edges

5.11c

5.10a lb

5.10c
move left

K 120'
xx .75'

5.11a
off-fingers

x

x

x

awk. armbar
pod

fists

awk. lb
with good
edges

5.11b

5.9
steep hands
with good edges

O 100'
xx

I J 80'

90' to x
base of
Waverly
Wafer

x off route
bolt

O xx

5.9
sustained
hands

O 70'
slings on
flake

5.8 chimney
no pro

5.9
hands

K

75' to ground

O 100'
belay
inside
p p

5.8 hands

5.6 chimney
1-1.5'

5.7 fingers

knobs

approach
from Catchy

old road

SIDE VIEW (lower left):

2nd belay
of Outer Limits
xx

E xx
xx

F

SIDE
VIEW

Elevator
Shaft

5.13b

4'

5.10d ow
or delicate
stem

5'

E 70'
xxx

5.12a lb
backstep left

steep edges

7'
squeeze

D

5.9 hands
and fist

approach

drop
off

5.9
squeeze

A. Hardd 5.11b nuts: 1 set; cams: 3ea .6-1.5", 2 ea 1.75-2.5"

B. Crack A-Go-Go 5.11c nuts: 1 ea micro, 1 set; cams: 2 ea .5-2"

C. Outer Limits 5.11a nuts: 1 set; cams: 2 ea .6-3", extra 2-2.5"

D. Elevator Shaft 5.8 R nuts: 1 set; cams: 2 ea .6-3"

E. Cookie Monster (Pitch 1) 5.12a 7 quickdraws

F. Twilight Zone 5.10d nuts: 1 set; cams: 2 ea 1-7"

G. Red Zinger 5.11d nuts: 2 sets; cams: 2 ea .6-2", 3 ea 2.5-4"

H. Meat Grinder 5.10c nuts: 1 set; cams: 2 ea .6-4.5"

I. Beverly's Tower 5.10a nuts: 2 sets; cams: 2 ea .4-2"

J. Aftershock 5.11b nuts: 1 set; cams: 2 ea .4-2"

K. Waverly Wafer 5.11a nuts: 1 set; cams: 2 ea .5-3"

L. Butterballs 5.11c nuts: 1 set; cams: 3 ea .6-1", 2 ea 1.25-2"

M. Butterfingers 5.11a nuts: 1 set; cams: 2 ea .6-1.5"

N. Wheat Thin 5.10c nuts: 1 set; cams: 2 ea .6-.75", 1 ea 1-2"

O. The Cookie, Right Side 5.9 nuts: 1 set; cams: 2 ea .6-3"

P. Catchy 5.10d nuts: 2 sets; cams: 2 ea .4-2"

Q. Catchy Corner 5.11a nuts: 1 set; cams: 2 ea .4-2.5"

R. The Enema 5.11b nuts: 1 set; cams: 2 ea .5-3.5"

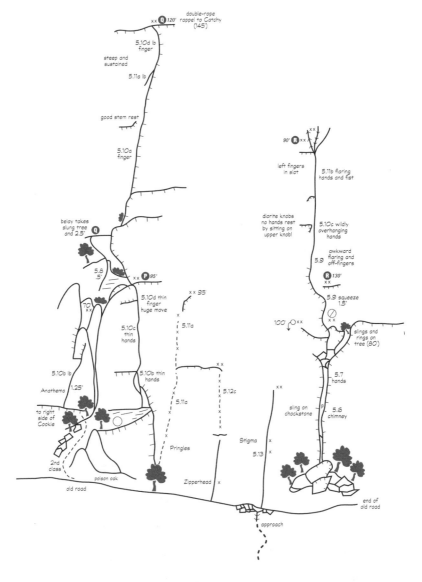

Pat and Jack Pinnacle

Approach time: **2-3 minutes**

Sun exposure: **morning to afternoon**

Height of routes: **180'**

Giant knobs on unusual rock give the climbing here a different feeling than at most Yosemite crags and allow for very steep routes at moderate grades. Long reaches and challenging mantels are often the name of the game. A few splitter cracks without knobs also grace the rock.

This crag is a popular winter destination, although it doesn't dry out as quickly as the nearby Cookie Cliff. Spring and fall are perfect. Summer tends to be too hot at these lower elevation crags, but on cooler days in the afternoon the short approach makes this a great end of the day crag. Beware of poison oak, especially in the winter when it loses its leaves and is hard to see.

Approach

From the Highway 120/140 junction, drive 1.8 miles west on 140 to just past the Cascade Creek bridge. Park in the large paved lot on the south side of the road. From the west end of the parking lot, cross the road and pick up a climbers' trail which eventually meets the cliff at Knuckleheads.

Descent

Descend all routes by rappelling. Occasionally you need two ropes.

A. Sherrie's Crack   5.10c★★★

FA: Kevin Worrall and George Meyers, 1976.

A splitter, widening finger crack leads to a nice 5.9 hands corner. While the finger crack is short, its fierce and powerful moves defeat many 5.10 climbers. This is a great climb to do laps on. Easily access the anchor by traversing left from Nurdle's first pitch anchors.

Chris McNamara

1	Sherrie's Crack	5	Knuckleheads
2	Nurdle	6	Skinheads
3	Knob Job	7	The Tube
4	G-Man		

B. Nurdle   5.8★★★★

FA: Bob Ashworth and George Meyers, 1973.

One of the steepest 5.8s in Yosemite. Link this route with the second pitch of Knob Job using a 60m rope and you get one incredible 5.8 pitch. You can climb around the short offwidth pod on the first pitch, but it is easy and a good place to introduce yourself to this mandatory Yosemite skill. The second pitch has beautiful, steep crack climbing with a mantel. By setting up a two-rope toprope you can access awesome 5.10 terrain below the top pitch anchor.

C. Knob Job   5.10b★★★

FA: Kevin Worrall and George Meyers, 1976.

Fun hand cracks and huge jugs. The crux can be done three ways: insecure and delicate climbing in the flared finger crack, the usual technique of liebacking the (hard to spot) right crack, or perhaps the easiest way, by transferring entirely into the right crack and cranking to the jugs. No matter how you do it, the pro is great and the jugs only a few feet out of reach. Pitch 2 offers great 5.8 hands, fingers, and a mantel.

Beth Rodden cranks on The Phoenix (5.13a). (Corey Rich)

D. Book 'em, Dano 5.10d★★★★

FA: Dimitri Barton and Dave Neilson.

This route normally starts at the first belay on Nurdle, but a great alternate way is to start by climbing Knob Job, then continue up the thinning crack where Knob Job walks left on knobs. Huge knobs, mantels, delicate liebacking on a steep wall and finally a long reach and crank at the crux (much harder if you are under 6 feet tall). This route is a scary and runout lead, so toproping after climbing Nurdle is recommended.

E. G-Man 5.11b R★★

FA: Steve Grossman, mid-1980s.

Another runout lead or fun toprope from the top anchor of Nurdle. Easy, big knobs to short blank sections.

F. Trough of Justice 5.10b★★

FA: Chris Cantwell et al, 1980.

A wandering route through huge knobs, this is rarely done since the classic arête route Knuckleheads was established.

G. Knuckleheads 5.10b★★★★

FA: Dan and Sue McDevitt, 1991.

Excellent and extremely technical, Knuckleheads has stymied more than its share of 5.12 gym climbers. The mantel past the third bolt is tricky and has scored many sprained ankles. Generally well-protected, there is still a runout section near the top that is reasonable, but may be scary for those used to more tightly bolted routes.

H. Skinheads 5.10d★★★

FA: Dan and Sue McDevitt, 1991.

Forty feet of well-protected, sustained, and technical face leads to a runout on positive holds. A midway anchor allows lowering off and toproping of Underclingon, but continue to the top for the full experience.

I. Underclingon 5.12a★★★

FA: Ron Skelton and Dan McDevitt, 3/88.

Killer technical underclinging to face climbing. A great toprope.

J. The Tube 5.11a★★★★

FA: Jim Bridwell, Kevin Worrall, Dale Bard, and George Meyers, 1974.

"Tubing" is a stemming technique which involves pressing on the wall behind your lower back with the palm of your outside arm, fingers pointed downward. It's tricky to protect the crux and the fall is not clean, so this is only for confident 5.11 leaders. Easy to toprope after climbing Polymastia. Good practice for the crux of Moratorium.

K. Polymastia 5.10d★★★★

FA: Anderson Family, 2/94.

This juggy route starts up The Tube then makes a challenging traverse right. Place gear to clip the bolt then clean it to reduce rope drag (you essentially do the crux on toprope). Stay low at the crux. Above the difficulties ease, but there are a few more 5.10 moves between good rests.

L. Babble On 5.10a★★

FA: Jim Beyer, Mike Sawyer, and Bob Sullivan, 1978.

A fun lieback or jamming problem. Start with either wide climbing or a pumpy lieback with big gear for protection. The crux roof traverse is a little polished and usually underclinged but sometimes jammed, especially if you have big hands. The standard finish is the bay tree up and left but it's more fun to traverse right to Boneheads. It's also easier to set a toprope from the Boneheads anchor.

M. Boneheads 5.10b★★★★

FA: Anderson Family and Dan and Sue McDevitt, 1999.

A wild and fun journey on big knobs. The crux comes low and is followed by steep and mostly moderate moves on basketball-sized knobs. From the anchor, consider toproping Babble On.

N. Makayla's Climb 5.9★★

FA: Dan McDevitt, Jerry and Sigrid Anderson, spring 2001.

A good, short warm-up. Bolts are placed just far enough apart that fledgling 5.9 leaders should be careful.

O. Suds   5.9★★★

FA: Dan McDevitt, spring 2001.

The perfect first 5.9 lead. You'll find many good stances to place pro at each crux where you are usually going for a good hold. Climb with one 70m rope or bring a second rope to rappel.

P. Golden Needles   5.8★★★

FA. Jim Beyer and Janice Linhares, 1979.

Warm up with sustained hand jams in a clean corner. The second pitch takes a steep double crack to some fierce bulges. Stem and use the feet out right when possible. There is usually a big hold just when things look bleak. Don't stop at the weakened tree and instead head up to the larger tree on the big ledge. Rappel three times with one 60m rope or twice with two ropes.

Greg Barnes

Andrew McMullin leads Knob Job.

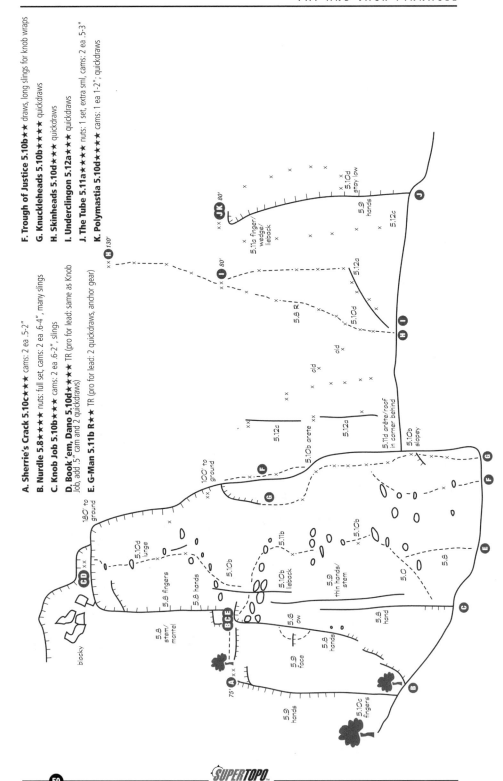

A. Sherrie's Crack 5.10c ★★★ cams: 2 ea .5-2"

B. Nurdle 5.8 ★★★★ nuts: full set, cams: 2 ea .6-4", many slings

C. Knob Job 5.10b ★★★ cams: 2 ea .6-2", slings

D. Book 'em, Dano 5.10d ★★★★ TR (pro for lead: same as Knob Job, add .5" cam and 2 quickdraws)

E. G-Man 5.11b R ★★ TR (pro for lead: 2 quickdraws, anchor gear)

F. Trough of Justice 5.10b ★★ draws, long slings for knob wraps

G. Knuckleheads 5.10b ★★★★ quickdraws

H. Skinheads 5.10d ★★★ quickdraws

I. Underclingon 5.12a ★★★ quickdraws

J. The Tube 5.11a ★★★★ nuts: 1 set, extra sml, cams: 2 ea .5-3"

K. Polymastia 5.10d ★★★ cams: 1 ea 1-2", quickdraws

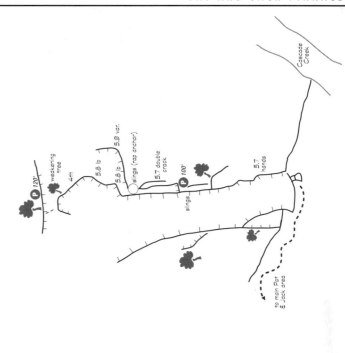

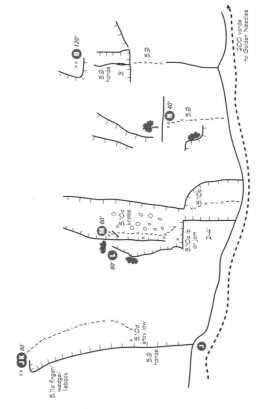

L. Babble On 5.10a★★ cams: 1 ea .5-1", 2 ea 1.25-4.5"

M. Boneheads 5.10b★★★★ quickdraws

N. Makayla's Climb 5.9★★ quickdraws

O. Suds 5.9★★★ nuts: 1 set; cams: 1-2 ea .6-3.5"

P. Golden Needles 5.8★★★ nuts: 1 set; cams: 1-2 ea .6-3"

Generator Station

Approach time: **45 seconds**

Sun exposure: **mostly tree shaded**

Height of routes: **60'**

These strenuous climbs are next to the road and easy to toprope. They are ideal if you want to build hard crack climbing technique or only a few hours of daylight remain. Although usually shaded, their low elevation means hot temperatures in the summer. Fall, winter, and spring offer the best climbing conditions.

Approach

From the Highway 140/120 junction, drive west 1.2 miles on 140 and park on the left paved pullout just after the generator station (marked by a gated access road and "do not enter" sign). Walk back to the gated access road. Generator Crack is on the large boulder on the south side of the road (scramble up 3rd class next to the gate to set a toprope). For Conductor Crack, cross the road and follow a climbers' trail for 100 feet to the obvious crack (walk around left to set a toprope).

Generator Crack   5.10c★★★★

This burly offwidth is easily toproped and seldom led. The crux comes just a few feet off the ground but the climbing remains physical and sustained to the top. Some advanced offwidth climbers use the "leavittation" technique but most climbers just throw in a knee, make a chicken wing, and struggle. Wear long sleeves and pants and you may want to tape your hands and ankles. Climb this route in cooler temperatures—even if it is near freezing the strenuous moves will keep you warm. Don't be discouraged if it takes you multiple visits to this climb to finally get it. Once you do,

Looking up at Generator Crack.

you'll be ready to tackle most 5.10 and easier offwidths and squeeze chimneys in Yosemite.

Conductor Crack   5.10d★★

A great toprope or lead to hone your finger crack and tight hand techniques. This is a hard and technical 5.10d. To set a toprope, bring a 20-foot piece of webbing to sling a nearby tree and equalize with the bolt. This climb can be wet and mossy in winter.

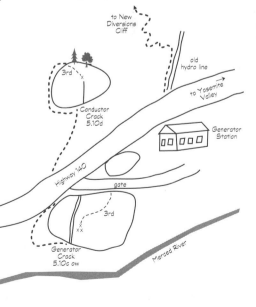

Sue McDevitt working up the 5.9 squeeze finish of Generator Crack. (Corey Rich)

New Diversions Cliff

Approach time: **10 minutes**

Sun exposure: **morning to early afternoon**

Height of routes: **200'**

This cliff is home to amazing basketball-sized knobs and features wild free climbing moves more typical of the gym than of Yosemite. It's a great place for confident 5.9 and 5.10 leaders and most routes offer opportunities to toprope even more challenging climbs. This is a low-elevation cliff that faces south and gets sun most of the day. Spring and fall are best, but during warm trends you should climb early in the morning or late in the afternoon when the climbs are shaded. Winter can offer great climbing conditions if the rock is dry. Summer is generally too hot.

A good circuit is to warm up on Chicken Pie (5.9) then climb New Diversions (5.10a) and toprope Burst of Brilliance (5.11b). Next climb New Deviations (5.9) and toprope Highlander (5.12c).

Approach

From the Highway 140/120 junction, drive west 1.2 miles on 140 and park on the left paved pullout just after the generator station (marked by a gated access road and "do not enter" sign). Walk back to the gated access road and continue east on the road for another 100 yards and look for the old hydro line ditch running up the hill. Walk up this for 100 feet and locate the climbers' trail on the left. Hike this trail for a few hundred yards to the base of New Diversions.

Descent

Rappel most climbs with two 50m or 60m ropes except where noted in the topo. If you top out, scramble down to the west.

A. Highlander   5.12c★★

FA: Dave Schultz, 1988.

Sustained, very thin edges give way to bigger holds and eventually a juggy roof move to the anchors. Set a toprope while rappelling New Deviations.

B. New Deviations   5.9★★★★

FA: Jack Johnson and Mike Whawski, 1992.

This fun route is a considerable step down in difficulty from New Diversions yet also contains unusual large knobs. Continue up the offwidth to juggy knobs that traverse left to a bolted anchor. Rappel to the Highlander anchors where you can set up a toprope or continue to the ground.

C. New Diversions   5.10a★★★★★

FA: Rick Sylvester, Claude Wreford-Brown, and Jerry Coe, 6/71.

One of the harder and more classic 5.10a climbs anywhere. The climb is sustained from bottom to top and involves truly wild and committing moves. At the crux, tie off and wrestle large spaced-out knobs. They're positive but it's not obvious how to use them. This climb definitely favors the taller leader. The anchor is slightly sketchy slings wrapped around the base of a block. Save a 4" piece to back them up. Most climbers rappel from here with one 60m rope to the Burst of Brilliance anchors or with two 50m ropes to the ground.

D. Burst of Brilliance   5.11b★★★

FA: Eric Kohl, 1990

This stout 5.11 is unrelenting for the first 40 feet. It requires a mixture of balancy face moves and tenuous liebacking. Great for developing delicate crack technique. This climb is well-protected with bolts for the first 20 feet, after that you may want a few small pieces.

E. Chicken Pie   5.9★★★★

FA: Jerry Coe and Rick Sylvester, 4/71.

This climb looks much harder than it is. Start in an ever-steepening open book with a finger crack in the back and face holds on the left. The roof at the top pulls easily to the left. Above, climb either the face or a combination of face and chimney to the anchor. At present there is a bolt anchor, which permits a rap with a 60m rope. If this is gone, continue up the face to a tree and a double-rope rappel.

A. Highlander 5.12c★★★ 8 quickdraws

B. New Deviations 5.9★★★★ cams: 2 ea .75-3.5"; 5 quickdraws

C. New Diversions 5.10a★★★★★ nuts: 1 set; cams: 2 ea .6-4.5"

D. Burst of Brilliance 5.11b★★★ cams 1 ea .6-1"; 5 quickdraws

E. Chicken Pie 5.9★★★★ nuts: 1 set; cams: 2 ea .6-4"

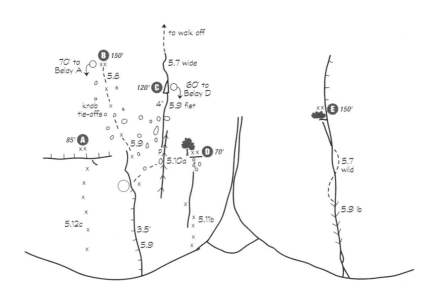

Knob Hill

Approach time: 2 minutes

Sun exposure: mid-morning to afternoon

Height of routes: 60-200'

Knob Hill is a convenient introduction to longer Yosemite 5.7 and 5.8 pitches. The climbs are generally low angle and offer a mixture of straight-in cracks and wild face climbing on giant knobs. On most climbs, the cruxes come down low and are well-protected. If it is your first time in Yosemite, you may want to stop at Swan Slab to get a feel for the rock and then head to Knob Hill to get in some longer moderate pitches. All the anchors use bolts or trees. The south-facing cliffs receive sun all day and are scorching in the summer, but often temperate during the winter.

Just for Starters, Sloth Wall, and Anti Ego Crack use the same tree anchor, which may cause problems if multiple parties are on the wall. Be prepared to wait for teams to finish or build intermediate anchors below and right of the tree. It is possible but impractical to toprope these climbs because they are so long. To set a toprope you will need to tie two ropes together and use numerous directionals. One toprope will tie up all three routes so be considerate of other climbers at the crag.

Approach

From Camp 4, drive west to the Highway 120/140 junction. Turn right onto Highway 120 and drive 1.8 miles and park in the eastern-most paved pullout before the first Cascade Bridge over Cascade Creek. If that pullout is full, park in the larger paved pullout between the two bridges. From the east end of the eastern-most bridge, follow a climbers' trail up and right for two minutes to the base of the crags.

Descent

Descend Just for Starters, Sloth Wall, and Anti Ego Crack by rappelling from the tree

Justin Bastien on Blotto, aka Axis (5.10d) at Arch Rock. (Corey Rich)

Chris McNamara

with one 50m or 60m rope. Be sure to angle west toward the gully and be extra careful not to rappel off the end of the rope. If the tree anchor is in use by other parties, move left into the gully, belay off a tree, and then descend by scrambling down the gully.

To descend the other climbs, walk off from the last anchor.

History

I first saw Knob Hill from directly beneath when I was working for the NPS Road Crew. One day during a lunch break, I walked to the base and realized there were a couple of good climbs to do. I returned on my next days off with a guy from the east coast named Steve Miller and my late first wife Elsie.

We did the "Anti Ego Crack" first and named it because it was hard to have an ego trip over a climb with 20 feet of 5.7 right off the ground and then a big jug haul on a slab. Remember that this was a time when people like Jim Bridwell were really pushing into unheard realms of difficulty and this climb went in the opposite direction.

The "Sloth Wall" was named because there were so many jugs you could climb hand over hand like a monkey. With climbers being more indolent in their habits and lifestyles, "Sloth Wall" seemed more appropriate.

We named "Just For Starters" because it looked like a fun little introductory route. Unfortunately, somebody pulled off the initial holds since we climbed it, so instead of a well-protected 5.8 move it is a well-protected 5.10a move. I imagine many people just french free past that move to get to the easier climbing above.

- Jerry Anderson

A. Unnamed   5.9★★

FA: Kevin Worrall and George Meyers, 1976.

A good climb to enhance your finger jamming and footwork techniques. While the crack takes decent protection, it is tricky to place and therefore the route is seldom led. As you climb higher, the moves get harder as the locks and footholds are less positive. The crux bulge involves thin fingerlocks and sparse face holds over a bulge. To focus more on face technique, climb the 5.9 starting variation to the left.

B. Pot Belly   5.8★★★

FA: Bill Griffin and Bruce Price, 4/73.

Start your day on this climb, which offers great straight-in hand jamming. The first 10 feet are committing and technical—you'll want a spot if leading. The undercling roof starting variation may feel easier depending on your granite face climbing experience. Either start is unprotected at the bottom and is usually avoided by scrambling to the bolt anchors and setting a toprope. Above the tricky start, a splitter 5.7 hand crack offers sustained and enjoyable jamming. Once comfortable on Pot Belly, try toproping the unnamed 5.9 to the left.

C. Just for Starters   5.10a★★★

FA: The Anderson Family, 1992.

After a bouldery start, the climbing dramatically eases as large knobs appear. Because the crux is the first move, this is an easy way to break into the 5.10a realm. By Yosemite standards, this climb is well-protected at all the hard sections and runout once the climbing eases to 5.4.

Chris McNamara

D. Sloth Wall   5.7★★★★

FA: Steve Miller, Jerry Anderson, and Elsie Anderson, 10/72.

This climb takes you through moderate knob climbing paradise. A 5.7 crux down low is followed by enormous and comfortable chickenheads more reminiscent of the climbing gym than Yosemite. To make things even better, cracks appear frequently to offer ample protection. Be sure to use many long slings down low to reduce rope drag.

E. Anti Ego Crack   5.7★★★

FA: Steve Miller and Jerry Anderson, 10/72.

A strenuous start leads to low-angle wandering on big holds. At the start, lieback or fist jam as quickly and efficiently as possible. After 20 feet, the wide crack narrows and the climbing becomes dramatically easier. Almost all climbers avoid the optional second pitch because of the mediocre climbing and lame descent.

F. Turkey Pie (aka Chicken Pie)   5.7★★

FA: Jerry Anderson, 7/73.

This is a great way to break into 5.7 wide crack climbing. A leaning lieback corner is followed by a gradually widening straight-in crack. Hand jams, fist jams, and a little offwidth technique are required. You can set a toprope with one 60m rope, but leave many directionals to protect a follower from a huge swing.

A. Unnamed 5.9★★ nuts: 1 set; cams: 1 ea .4-2"

B. Pot Belly 5.8★★★ nuts: 1 set; cams: 1 ea .5-2.5"

C. Just for Starters 5.10a★★★ 7 quickdraws

D. Sloth Wall 5.7★★★★ nuts: 1 set; cams: 1 ea .5-3"

E. Anti Ego Crack 5.7★★★ nuts: 1 set; cams: 1 ea .4-1.5", 2 ea 1.75-3.5"

F. Turkey Pie (aka Chicken Pie) 5.7★★ nuts: 1 set; cams: 1 ea .5-1.5", 2 ea 1.75-4"

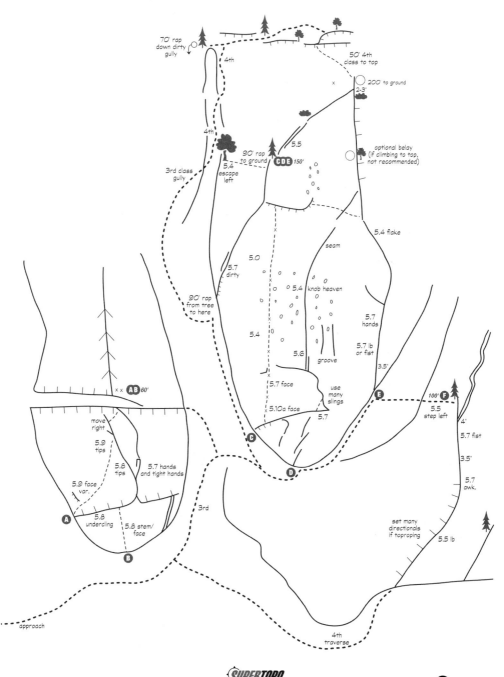

Reed's Pinnacle Area

Approach time: **5 minutes**

Sun exposure: **mid-morning to sunset**

Height of routes: **80-300'**

Chris McNamara

1	Direct Route	**4**	Stone Groove
2	Regular Route	**5**	Ejesta
3	Lunatic Fringe		

Reed's Pinnacle Area is known for its steep and intimidating cracks. The crag starts almost a thousand feet above the Valley floor, with spectacular views of The Rostrum and the narrow river-carved lower Merced Canyon. Although the popular climbs rise to only 250 feet above the ground, as soon as you are above the tree line it feels as though you are much higher.

Start early to avoid crowds or climb in the off-season (November-April) when much of the Valley is soggy but Reed's is in great condition. Summer temperatures are hot.

Approach

If driving from inside the Valley, take Highway 120 west and park at the large turnout on the left just past the first tunnel. (If the pullout is full, the cliff is probably crowded.) Unless there's no traffic and your vehicle has a tight turning radius, the only safe way to park in the turnout is to drive another mile and turn around at one of the two small parking lots flanking the Cascade Falls bridge.

If driving on Highway 120 from outside Yosemite Valley, park at the large turnout on the right located about one mile past the end of the first long tunnel.

Hike up the road for a hundred feet or so, looking for a vague path going up the steep dirt and rock embankment that is marked with a carabiner post. Watch for a spot where the trees and roots come near the road and be EXTREMELY careful not to knock any rocks down onto the road. Once into the trees, a trail leads up to the start of Lunatic Fringe. Contour left along the base for Reed's Pinnacle routes or right to get to Stone Groove and Ejesta.

Descent

Descend all routes by rappelling, usually with 50m ropes. Find the correct trail back to the road by going to the base of Lunatic Fringe and then carefully following the slightly right-trending trail down. Attempting to get down other spots will likely drop rocks onto the road, and if you slip you could find yourself in the grill of a tour bus.

Rappelling Beta for Reed's Pinnacle routes

From the summit of Reed's Pinnacle, rappel 70 feet. From here, there are three options: 1) Walk to the west end of the ledge and carefully traverse out to chain anchors. One rappel with two 60m ropes reaches the ground. 2) Walk over to the east end of the large ledge and make one rappel with two 50m ropes. 3) To rappel with just one 60m rope, walk to the east end of the ledge and make one rappel to a big ledge. Then, staying on rappel, walk out the exposed backside of the Reed's Regular Route chimney to bolts on the inside of the chimney. From here, make one more rappel with one 60m rope.

Here's a good strategy to avoid trailing a second rope while climbing: Climb with just one 60m rope and then, on the descent at the second belay, have the first person rappel on a single line. Once he reaches the ground, attach the second 60m rope. The second person pulls up the second rope and then makes a double rope rappel.

History

If ever a climbing area deserves to be named for an individual, this is it. During the eight-year period from 1956 to 1964, the immensely talented Wally Reed was involved in every first ascent in the region that now bears his name. Since he was the most modest fellow I've ever met, I could never elicit information from him, except "nice climb" or "not really too hard" or "you'll have no trouble," the last two of which were usually wrong. This quiet fellow wasn't a climbing bum like the rest of us; on the contrary, he was a desk clerk for many years at Yosemite Lodge.

He discovered his fine cliff in 1956 not long after he began climbing. First on his tick list was the Iota, an easy chimney climb behind a 150-foot slab. A year later he and Herb Swedlund, another excellent, unheralded climber, did the devious line now known as the Regular Route on Reed's Pinnacle, a route that involved tunneling behind the entire upper slab to reach easier terrain. In 1960 the same pair did the now-popular Remnant, and in 1962 Reed climbed the left side of his namesake slab, a strenuous crack route with a short stretch of aid midway up. In 1964 came his biggest coup: Reed's Direct, a marvelous jamcrack.

Reed's Direct has a unique history in that its three pitches were climbed in the "wrong" order. In 1957 Reed and Swedlund had shunned the final vertical dihedral of the right side of the slab in favor of the tunnel. This steep 10a offwidth was done in 1964 by Reed (of course), Frank Sacherer, Mark Powell, Gary Colliver, and Andy Lichtman. A month later Reed, having noticed an extraordinary crack on the 80-degree wall below them, returned with Sacherer and Chris Fredericks to make the first ascent of this long hand/fist crack. So now the middle pitch was done. Royal Robbins heard about this splendid line and came along in 1966 with Gordie Webster to

"finish" the route—a short 5.9 crack at the very bottom. They continued to the top and thus made the first complete ascent.

The present-day climber might keep in mind that all these early routes involved inserting pitons for protection, an act perhaps not much appreciated in this day of instant cams. One had to choose the right-sized piton, wedge it in place so it wouldn't spring out with the first blow, withdraw the hammer from its holster, whop the piton eight or ten blows, test with downward smashes, pound some more, test again, pretend the thing was okay, sheath the hammer, attach a carabiner and then clip it—all this time (maybe two minutes) hanging from a hand jam. Resting on this pin was taboo, of course, as was hangdogging, a word and concept yet to be invented. No wonder these guys didn't stop often to place pro!

Chingando came next, and Wally Reed must have been on desk duty this day, for it was Chuck Pratt who in 1965 led this fiendish offwidth on the outer face of the Iota. Allen Steck and I can attest to its difficulty, for a few years later Pratt lured us to his route with a promise to teach us how to climb offwidths. He led the thing with nary a grunt and we relaxed. Our turn came and neither of us got more than 15 feet up. The usually gentle Pratt grumbled a bit since he had to leave two pitons to rappel from. We, of course, blamed him for not teaching us properly!

Two classic routes were established in 1971, both involving finger cracks. Back then a narrow crack on a steep wall was a good candidate for nailing, but a new breed of strong and daring climbers thought otherwise. Barry Bates (yet another unheralded cragrat) and that early female star Bev Johnson climbed Lunatic Fringe, a short 10c line to the right of Reed's Pinnacle. Two similarly powerful climbers, Jim Bridwell and Galen Rowell, did Stone Groove, a short gem at 10b.

– Steve Roper

A. Direct Route   5.10a★★★★★

FA: Wally Reed, Frank Sacherer, Mark Powell, Gary Colliver, Andy Lichtman, 1964.

Clean, sheer, and physically demanding, Reed's Pinnacle Direct Route is a 5.10 testpiece respected by many 5.12 climbers. The first pitch is straightforward. The second pitch grabs your attention with a draining test of power, endurance, and technique. It requires careful strategy in order to not run out of gear. The crack is wavy, rapidly jutting back and forth between 1 and 4 inches, which makes it perfect for hexes. Save larger cams for the upper part of the pitch, including a 4 inch cam for the short offwidth just after the rest ledge near the top (or avoid this with the 5.8 left variation). All moves on the first two pitches can be pulled through on gear.

Most climbers avoid the Direct Route finish by climbing the last two pitches of Reed's Pinnacle Regular Route. The testpiece flared offwidth final pitch of the Direct Route requires big cams and a few long runouts. If you reach the top of Reed's Pinnacle by the Regular Route finish, you can toprope the Direct Route's finish, which lies on the single-rope rappel route.

If you still have juice after the Direct Route, try Lunatic Fringe and Stone Groove. While harder, they each have excellent protection and outstanding climbing.

B. Regular Route   5.9★★★★

FA: Herb Swedlund and Wally Reed, 1957.

Overshadowed by its famous neighbor, Reed's Pinnacle Regular Route is a fun wandering climb that sees little traffic. The first pitch climbs flakes and ramps in an interesting chimney/corner. The second pitch follows discontinuous cracks and face to the large ledge. The third pitch follows a wild tunnel-through behind Reed's Pinnacle. This is exciting and fun, but scary and even dangerous for those not accustomed to chimneys. The eerie chimney slowly contracts below your toes

so that if you fall you slide a short stretch before becoming jammed (be aware that the third pitch is an icebox in the winter.) The recommended variation on the fourth pitch takes a fun 5.9 hand and finger crack to an exposed 5.6 traverse around easy blocks.

The finish of the Regular Route is the preferred finish to the Direct Route.

C. Bongs Away, Left   5.8★★★

FA: Jim Bridwell, 1970.

Somewhat obscure, Bongs Away, Left is an unusual and excellent chimney/hand/offwidth/lieback experience. A featured flake is recessed in a tight chimney with each side 1 to 4 inches wide, so the climbing is intriguing and well-protected. Seldom does Yosemite let you practice such needed offwidth and chimney climbing skills at a moderate level with bomber protection. Right off the belay, the best idea is usually to face straight into the chimney and move directly into some of the above mentioned techniques. After exiting the chimney, fun liebacking and cool knobs lead to a bolted anchor. Bomber chickenheads appear now and again and serve as excellent footholds. Rappel 90 feet back to the large ledge, carefully staying left.

D. Lunatic Fringe   5.10c★★★★★

FA: Barry Bates and Bev Johnson, 1971.

Varied, steep, and clean, Lunatic Fringe is one of the best 5.10 cracks in Yosemite. This amazing pitch requires every technique from fingers and thin hands to liebacking and face. With many merciful rests the climb's difficulty lies more in its diverse requisite crack climbing skills than on power and endurance. It is difficult to name a crux, since with so much variety, each climber finds a different section to be the hardest. Depending on how frequently you place protection, a large rack of thin to hand-sized pro is needed. Two ropes are needed to rappel.

E. Stone Groove   5.10b★★★★

FA: Jim Bridwell and Galen Rowell, 1971.

Stone Groove is a short but fierce climb.
The first section of right-leaning crack
beneath a small roof, with desperate
jamming and liebacking to a difficult crux,
is quite memorable. While rated easier than
Lunatic Fringe, Stone Groove is much
harder right off the ground. The crux
comes at the top of the first section—when
you're tired. Above, the easy-looking hand
crack gets hard near the finish, but savior
jugs appear on the right just in time. For
toproping, make sure to leave several good
directionals. Rap the route with one 50m
rope.

F. Center Route (Pitch 1)   5.7★★

This fun pitch climbs great steep knobs into
a long section of low-angle wide cracks.
This is a perfect pitch to build chimney
skills as the wide sections are never harder
than 5.6. The crux comes midway at a
tricky but well-protected 5.7 bulge.
Climbing this route is a great way to get
away from the crowds. The second and
third pitches are also good and rated 5.10d
and 5.8 respectively.

G. Ejesta   5.8★★★

FA: Charlie Porter, Bob Ashworth and Jeff Stubbs, 1/74.

The first pitch is of decent quality with one
powerful 5.8 section. The second pitch is
better with splitter double cracks that
gradually widen from tight hands to hands
to fist. The pitch finishes with a dramatic
and airy traverse on crumbling grains to a
great belay perch. This is an ideal climb to
learn how to hand jam.

Greg Barnes

Chris McNamara climbing Ejesta with The Rostrum in the
background.

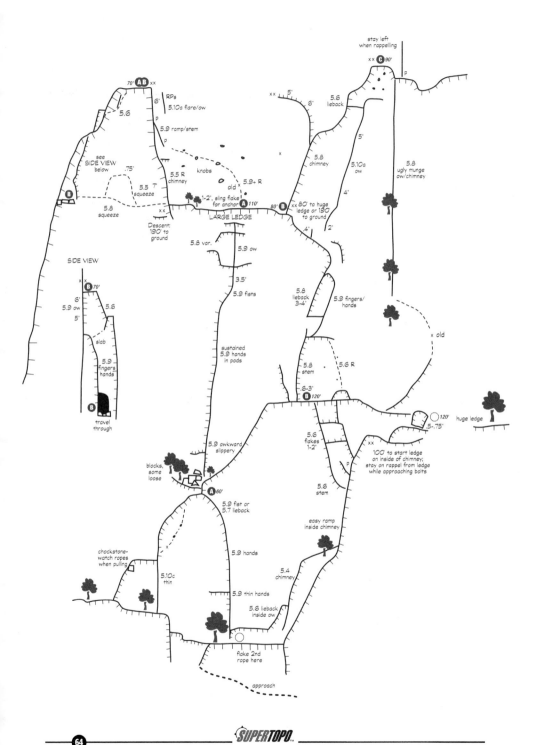

stay left
when rappelling

xx **C** 90'

70' **A B** xx

RPs
6'
5.10a flare/ow
p
5.6
5.9 ramp/stem
p

xx 5'
6'
5.6
lieback

5'

see
SIDE VIEW
below

.75'

5.5 R
chimney

knobs

5.3 7'
squeeze

old

5.9+ R

1-2', sling flake
for anchor **A** 110'

5.8
squeeze

xx

Descent:
190' to
ground

LARGE LEDGE

80' 5' **B** xx 80' to huge
ledge or 190'
to ground

x
5.8
chimney

5.10a
ow

5.8
ugly munge
ow/chimney

4'

4'

2'

5.8 var.

5.9 ow

3.5'

5.9 fists

5.8
lieback
3-4'

5.9 fingers/
hands

SIDE VIEW

x x
B 70'

6'
5.9 ow
5'

5.6

slab

5.9
fingers
hands

B

travel
through

sustained
5.9 hands
in pods

5.8
stem

5.6 R

6-3'
B 120'

x old

5.9 awkward
slippery

blocks,
some
loose

A 60'

5.9 fist or
5.7 lieback

chockstone-
watch ropes
when pulling

x

5.10c
thin

5.9 hands

5.6
flakes
1-2'

120'
5-.75'

huge ledge

100' to start ledge
on inside of chimney;
stay on rappel from ledge
while approaching bolts

p

5.6
stem

easy ramp
inside chimney

5.4
chimney

5.9 thin hands

5.6 lieback
inside ow

flake 2nd
rope here

approach

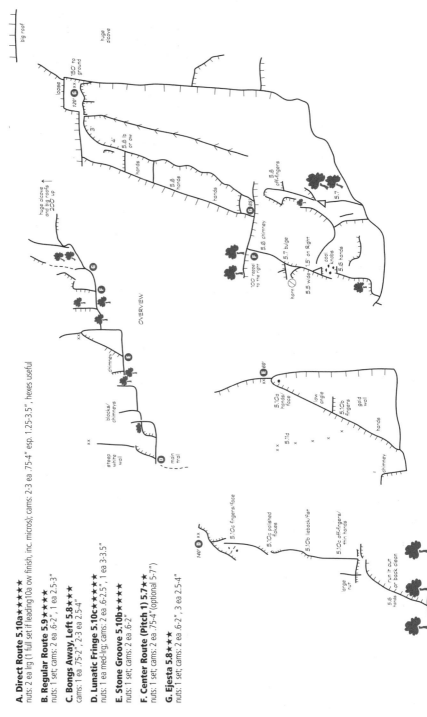

A. Direct Route 5.10a★★★★★
nuts: 2 ea lrg (1 full set if leading 10a ow finish, inc. micros); cams: 2-3 ea .75-4" esp. 1.25-3.5", hexes useful

B. Regular Route 5.9★★★★
nuts: 1 set; cams: 2 ea .6-2", 1 ea 2.5-3"

C. Bongs Away, Left 5.8★★★
cams: 1 ea .75-2", 2-3 ea 2.5-4"

D. Lunatic Fringe 5.10c★★★★★
nuts: 1 ea med-lrg; cams: 2 ea .6-2.5", 1 ea 3-3.5"

E. Stone Groove 5.10b★★★★
nuts: 1 set; cams: 2 ea .6-2"

F. Center Route (Pitch 1) 5.7★★
nuts: 1 set; cams: 2 ea .75-4"(optional 5-7")

G. Ejesta 5.8★★★
nuts: 1 set; cams: 2 ea .6-2", 3 ea 2.5-4"

Five and Dime Cliff

Approach time: **5 minutes**

Sun exposure: **morning to afternoon**

Height of routes: **50-100'**

This convenient and sunny crag offers mostly hard trad and bolted climbs with a couple of moderates here and there. It's easy to walk to the top of all climbs but making the natural toprope anchors can be intricate. Bring 30-foot slings and maybe even an extra rope to build anchors off of manzanita and oak trees. The crag is ideal in the spring, fall, and winter but usually too hot in the summer. Watch out for poison oak.

Approach

If driving from inside Yosemite Valley, take Highway 120 west and park at the large turnout on the left just past the first tunnel.

If driving from outside Yosemite Valley on Highway 120, park at the large turnout on the right located about one mile past the end of the first long tunnel.

From the east end of the turnout, walk along the stone wall until you can drop down a climbers' trail, just before the tunnel. Scramble down steep switchbacks for 200 feet to the base of the crag.

Descent

Walk off all climbs.

A. Nickel Bag   5.11d★★

FA: Sean Jones and Blair Dixon, mid-90s.

Reachy and powerful sport climb with a distinct crux at the second bolt. You can walk to the bolt anchor and set a toprope.

B. Bijou   5.10c★★★

FA: Heather Baer and Jeff Schoen, 1992.

Steep and wild face moves. You can walk to the bolt anchor and set a toprope.

C. Mockery   5.8★★★★

FA: Jeff Emshoff and Sean Jones, mid-90s.

This is a hard 5.8 but is well-protected—a Yosemite rarity for a climb of this difficulty. The steep crux is just a few moves on

Chris McNamara

positive holds before the anchor. To set a toprope, you must rappel 20 feet off a tree to reach the anchor.

D. Keystone Corner   5.8★★★

FA: Don Reid and Jay Fiske, 10/75.

Once in the corner you have many options—from chimney and stemming, to hand cracks—all in the 5.7 to 5.8 range.

E. Copper Penny   5.10a★★★

FA: Charlie Porter et al, 1971.

This offwidth is more psychological than technical. After the crux entry move, the pro becomes sparse. An inside edge offers some relief for long-armed folks but then disappears, forcing you back to chicken-wings and arm bars.

F. Five and Dime   5.10d★★★★★

FA: Barry Bates et al, 1971.

A climb so good they named a whole cliff after it. This stout 5.10d tests your jamming ability at a variety of sizes. The crux is hanging around to place gear on the steep wall. If you can lead this, you have mastered Valley 5.10.

G. Whack and Dangle   5.11b★★★

FA: Ajax Greene and Don Peterson, 4/76.

Sustained liebacking and underclinging.

A. Nickel Bag 5.11d★★ 5 quickdraws

B. Bijou 5.10c★★★ 6 quickdraws

C. Mockery 5.8★★★★ 9 quickdraws

D. Keystone Corner 5.8★★★ nuts: 1 set; cams: 1-2 ea .6-3"

E. Copper Penny 5.10a★★★ nuts: 1 set; cams: 1-2 ea .6-7"

F. Five and Dime 5.10d★★★★★ nuts: 1 set; cams: 1-2 ea .6-3.5"

G. Whack and Dangle 5.11b★★★ nuts: 1 set; cams: 2 ea .6-2"

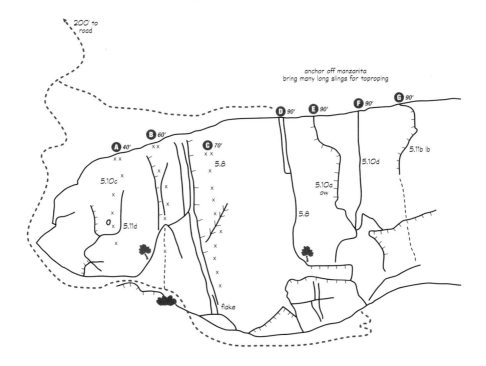

Highway Star

Approach time: **5 minutes**

Sun exposure: **late morning to early afternoon**

Height of routes: **60'**

Chris McNamara

Highway Star   5.10a★★★★

FA: Chris Falkenstein, Don Reid, and Edd Kuropat, 1975.

This is a great toprope or lead to build hand and finger crack skills. The rock is steep, high quality, and excellent for doing laps. A toprope is easy to establish by walking up the backside. Bring extra long slings for the tree anchor. If leading you will need: cams: 1 ea .6-3", 2 ea .75", 3 ea 2".

Approach

From the 120/140 junction, drive east and park in the first pullout on the right. From the west end of the pullout, pick up a faint climbers' trail next to a square-cut rock that almost pokes into the road. Walk north for 100 yards on a climbers' trail and through some boulders to the climb.

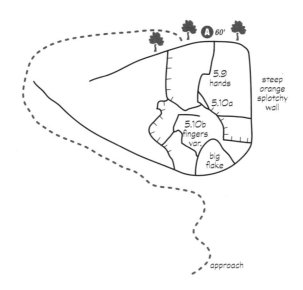

El Capitan, East Buttress

Chris McNamara

As Denali, Mt. Rainier, and the Grand Canyon dominate and define their respective national parks, so does El Capitan loom, tower, and rule over the entrance to Yosemite Valley. You can pick any synonym for "dominate" and it will still work. Overshadow. Domineer. Intimidate. Overwhelm. Not enough such words exist in our language to properly describe the effect this cliff exerts on climbers and tourists alike.

– Steve Roper

Approach

This approach takes an hour and gains 800 feet in elevation primarily on talus. From Camp 4, drive west about 2 miles and park in the large "Zodiac pullout" (200 yards before El Cap Meadow). From the east end of the pullout, locate a well-worn trail and walk east (parallel to the road) for about 100 feet and then cut left into the trees on a climbers' trail. (If you miss this trail just walk directly toward the wall and the big, open, white talus field.) After 300 feet, the climbers' trail merges into the talus field that leads to the base of Zodiac on the Southeast Face of El Capitan. From the base, walk 200 yards right (east) to the toe of the East Buttress and the start of the route. The route starts 30 feet before a huge drop-off.

A longer but less strenuous approach starts at the base of The Nose and skirts the base on a climbers' trail.

Descent

The East Ledges is the fastest and most convenient way to descend El Cap. It takes 2-3 hours, requires rappelling, and ends at the Manure Pile Buttress parking area, about one mile from El Cap Meadow.

From the top of the East Buttress, hike 50 feet away from the edge, pick up a climbers' trail and head right (east). The climbers' trail eventually parallels a wall on the left all the way to the end of the bushy terrain. (Parties that do not find the wall on their left will end up doing low-angle rappels and 5th class slabs to the start of the main rappels.) From the end of the bushy terrain, scramble down 3rd class for about 100 feet to a ledge that is roughly perpendicular to "The Wild Dikes." For rap routes A, B, and C, move down 15 feet of 4th class and then cut right (south) across a 20-foot-wide drainage gully (dangerous when wet). Walk/slide down the right side of the gully for 30-50 feet and then exit onto the right (south) shoulder and cruise down 40 feet to a ledge. For rap route A, continue toward the edge and down a 20-foot 4th class section to a tree wrapped with slings. For rap routes B and C, head left and down 30 feet of scree then right onto exposed 4th class. Work right, through a bush, to a 4-foot by 6-foot ledge with a small tree.

From the base of the rappels head east down multiple 3rd class sections joined by faint trails. Eventually a defined climbers' trail emerges. Follow it down to a wide drainage and cross to a trail that parallels the east side of the drainage for 300 feet before breaking off into the trees to the Manure Pile Buttress parking lot.

If you summit late and are unfamiliar with the East Ledges descent, bivy on top. The Falls Trail descent, which starts from El Cap's summit, is another option but takes 3-5 hours, is tedious, and the start is hard to find at night.

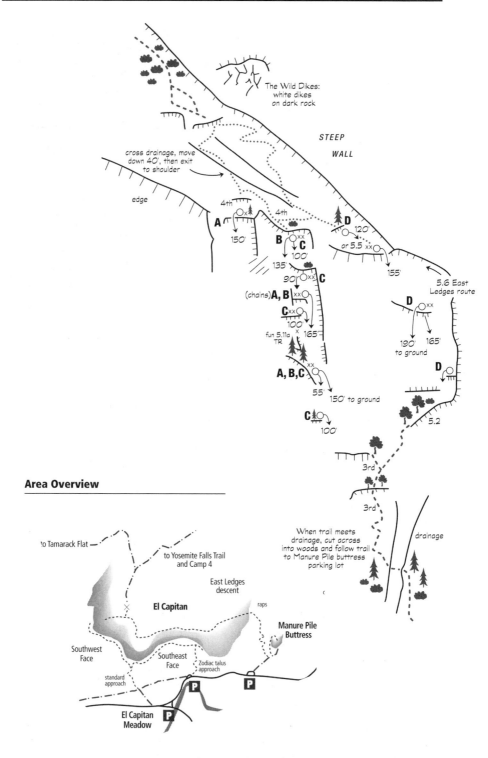

The Wild Dikes:
white dikes
on dark rock

STEEP

WALL

cross drainage, move
down 40', then exit
to shoulder

edge

4th   4th

A   B C   D
150'   100'   120'
         135'   or 5.5 xx
                            155'
         90   C
(chains) A, B xx   5.6 East
         C xx   Ledges route
         100'   D xx
fun 5.11a   190'   165'
TR   to ground
A, B, C
         55'   D
         150' to ground

C
100'   5.2

Area Overview

to Tamarack Flat

to Yosemite Falls Trail
and Camp 4

East Ledges
descent

El Capitan   raps
                            3rd
Southwest
Face   3rd
         Southeast
         Face   Zodiac talus
                approach   When trail meets
standard   drainage, cut across   drainage
approach   into woods and follow trail
El Capitan P   to Manure Pile buttress
Meadow   parking lot

Manure Pile
Buttress

East Buttress 5.10b ★★★★★

Time to climb route:	**8-10 hours**
Approach time:	**45 minutes-1 hour**
Descent time:	**2-3 hours**
Sun exposure:	**sunrise to afternoon**
Height of route:	**1400'**

This is one of the best long 5.10s in Yosemite. The climbing varies between low angle 4th class to steep 5.10 with everything from squeeze chimney to steep face. This climb is a classic distinguished by golden rock and knobs where you least expect them. And naturally, there's the thrill of just being on (or near, as the case may be) the Captain. This is a good step up in difficulty from the East Buttress of Middle Cathedral. Most of the cruxes are hard to pull through on gear.

History

On one side of the earth Hillary and Tenzing approached the summit of Everest. In London a princess approached the historic throne where shortly she would walk away a queen. In Yosemite three men approached a rounded non-summit, an event garnering no banner headlines, unlike the other two. But in climbing the East Buttress they would be the first ever to climb El Capitan. That week—the last days of May 1953 and the first days of June—was indeed a memorable time.

One can argue that the East Buttress is not really an El Cap climb. It's certainly not a "big wall" El Cap climb. The first ascensionists, in fact, never regarded their line as "climbing El Cap," knowing that the real challenge began just a few yards left of their route. But most climbers feel it certainly merits an El Cap designation, though few bragging rights adhere.

Exhilarated by his Sentinel and Yosemite Point Buttress first ascents, Berkeley climber Allen Steck soon turned to yet another project, this one in the El Cap area. The main face of the monolith was out of the question—too enormous and steep. But the beautiful black-and-gold buttress on the far eastern flank showed distinct cracks and chimneys on its lower section. Higher, the prospective route blended smoothly into the wall, but here also the rock looked broken and perhaps climbable. In late October 1952, Steck teamed up with three old buddies, Bill Dunmire and the two Long brothers, Bill and Dick. Dunmire led off on mixed free and aid, but about 50 feet up an aid pin popped and Dunmire plunged. To everyone's horror, the next few pitons popped: it was Yosemite's first "zipper" fall. The lowest pin held, however, and this saved Dunmire's life, for he had fallen upside down, stopping just as he lightly hit the ground, which was covered with big blocks. Covered with blood and unconscious, he came to a few minutes later. Steck recalls the scene: "He had no idea where he was or what he was doing. Lost a good bit of blood, too." Dunmire soon descended with the help of his friends and spent the night in the Valley hospital, suffering only from a bad concussion and bruised shoulder.

On the next attempt, Steck and Willi Unsoeld (of later Everest fame) got much higher but a nearby waterfall began to spray them in the afternoon and Willi, in the lead, decided to come down. Steck vividly remembers what happened next: "He was about 60 feet above me, at a piton. He fiddled around with something up there and then shouted for me to lower him. I did, but at the moment he arrived the rope broke loose from above and the entire 120-foot rope fell around our feet. It turned out that Willi had attached several strands of

East Buttress		Pitch 1	2	3	4	5	6	7	8	9	10	11	12	13
Free difficulty	≥5.10	●												
	5.9	●						●	●					
	5.8				●	●					●			
	5.7											●		
	5.6		●	●										●
	≤5.5				●					●				

eighth-inch parachute cord to the piton and naturally the rope had sawed through the cord. This would have been disastrous if the cord had broken earlier, but Willi was amazingly calm, telling me with his sly grin that he had planned all this out so that we wouldn't have to pull the rope down hand over hand."

Steck went back with Unsoeld, Bill Long, and a new companion, Will Siri. Bivouacking twice on the route, and using lots of aid, the quartet suffered the indignity of a gentle rain the last two days. But basically it was an uneventful climb, and they reached the top on June 1, 1953.

In July of 1964 came that now-legendary figure, Frank Sacherer, one of the boldest and finest free climbers of the mid-1960s. He and Wally Reed freed the entire route with hardly a pause.

– *Steve Roper*

Strategy

Start early as this is a long and popular climb. Luckily, several ledges allow passing. With only the slightest wind, the route is soaked by Horsetail Fall from December through May. In summer, the climb is okay if temps are below 80 degrees. Fall is ideal up until Horsetail Fall starts running.

Pitch 1 contains the only mandatory chimney. Belay at the bottom of the chimney for minimum rope drag on the pumpy 5.9 top of the pitch.

Pitch 2 starts with a steep and thin face crux. Trust your feet on the small edges to more secure finger and hand jams. Getting the few micro nuts up high and left is tricky and the only way to tension through the moves if they shut you down.

Pitch 8 has a tricky and exposed crux. As the arête ends, move left and slightly down past the fixed pin. Look for foot smears and edges low. This crack slants diagonally such that your feet are edging and smearing while your hands are in the crack.

For an especially long and challenging day, combine this with Moratorium—one of the best quality link-ups in Yosemite!

Retreat

It's easy to retreat with one 60m rope from Pitch 3. Above that there are few fixed anchors and you will have to leave gear. Carrying two ropes means leaving less gear.

Chris McNamara

Rack

nuts: 1 set, including micro
cams: 1 ea .3-.5"
       2 ea .6-2.5"
       1 ea 3"
       1 ea .6-.75" (optional)
other: several long slings, cordalette

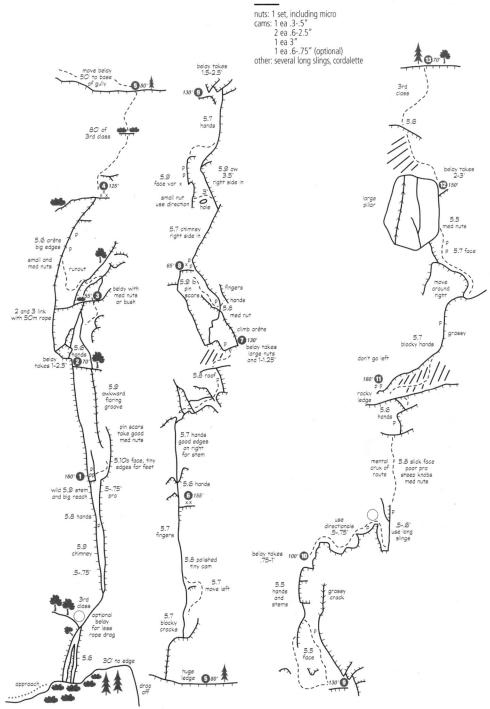

move belay 50' to base of gully
⑤ 80'

80' of 3rd class

④ 125'
X X

5.6 arête big edges

small and med nuts
runout
P
P

2 and 3 link with 50m rope

⑤ 55'
belay with med nuts or bush

5.6 hands
② 70'
belay takes 1-2.5'

5.9 awkward flaring groove

pin scars take good med nuts

5.10b face, tiny edges for feet

160' ①
P PP

wild 5.9 stem and big reach

5.8 hands
P

5.9 chimney

.5-.75'

3rd class

optional belay for less rope drag

5.6
30' to edge

approach
drop off

belay takes 1.5-2.5'

130' ⑨

5.7 hands

5.9 ow 3.5' right side in

5.9 face var x

small nut use direction
hole

5.7 chimney right side in

65' ⑧
P X

5.9 lb pin scars
fingers
hands
5.8 med nut

climb arête
⑦ 130'
belay takes large nuts and 1-1.25'

5.8 roof
P

5.7 hands good edges on right for stem

5.6 hands
⑥ 155'
X X

5.7 fingers

5.8 polished tiny cam

5.7 move left

5.7 blocky cracks

huge ledge
⑤ 80'

⑬ 70'

3rd class

5.6

belay takes 2-3'
⑫ 150'

large pillar

5.5 med nuts

5.7 face
P

move around right

grassy
5.7 blocky hands
P

don't go left

160' ⑪
P P
rocky ledge

5.6 hands
P

mental crux of route

5.8 slick face poor pro steep knobs med nuts

use directionals 5-.75'
P

.5-.6' use long slings

belay takes .75-1'
100' ⑩

5.5 hands and stems

grassy crack

P

5.5 face

130' ⑨

El Capitan Base

Approach time: **10 minutes**

Sun exposure: **late morning to afternoon**

Height of routes: **80-160'**

There are some excellent free climbs along the base of the Southwest Face. While these climbs are not long, the immense 3000-foot wall towering above sets it apart from the average crag. Because aid routes are above and sometimes start on the free climbs, there is a greatly increased danger of rockfall and dropped gear, so it is unwise to ever be at the base without wearing a helmet. The free routes along the southwest base are known for slick rock and pure cracks requiring good technique.

The southwest base of El Cap gets very hot in the summer and is best as a spring and fall destination. Even winter temperatures can be good, but frequent icefall makes winter climbing extremely dangerous. Several of the routes are very popular so prepare for a wait.

Approach

From the triangle at El Cap Meadow, pick up the trail that starts 50 feet west of the sign directing drivers to Highways 120, 140, and 41. Follow the trail a few hundred yards to a large dirt clearing. When facing the wall, walk at 10 o'clock and pick up the distinct climbers' trail that eventually leads to a point 200 feet in front of the toe of the Southeast Buttress and the start of The Nose. From here, the trail diverges to skirt either the base of the Southeast Face or the Southwest Face. Take the subtle left fork that leads to the base routes of the Southwest Face.

It is about a 0.25 mile and a 10- to 15-minute walk from the road to the toe of the Southeast Buttress and the start of The Nose.

Descent

Reverse the approach.

Chris McNamara

1	Sacherer Cracker	4	Moby Dick, Center
2	La Cosita, Right	5	Salathé Wall (Pitch 1)
3	Little John, Right	6	Pine Line

History

Not many people hiked up to the base of El Cap back in the olden days. Why do it? The cliff was obviously not climbable, so why waste your energy? All this changed in 1958 after the first ascent of The Nose. Many climbers wandered up to gaze at the lower part of Harding's route and stroke the now-famous cliff.

A striking chimney route called The Slack was established even as Harding labored on the cliff above. Charlie Raymond, one of the first ascensionists and now a renowned glaciologist, told me recently that he had forgotten the origin of the name. "I think that my head has been filled up with too much science to remember anything important like climbing! There is definitely a story behind the name of The Slack, but for the life of me I cannot remember it. I do not think that it is as simple as slot combined with crack." Within a few years this had become a popular route, and naturally, climbers soon saw other cracks and dihedrals leading to the top of minor slabs along the base of the great southwest flank of the monolith.

1962 was the breakthrough year. The weather was horrible during the spring, and long routes were out of the question. The base of El Cap, with its short approach and ultra-clean rock that dried quickly, became a favorite locale during breaks in the storms. April and May saw numerous first ascents, with perhaps the best being La Escuela, a four-pitch aid route up leaning dihedrals. This was the work of Yvon Chouinard and TM Herbert, who saw the route as ideal for beginning aid climbers (hence the name, which means "The School" in Spanish). Days later, Herbert and I did a fine, slippery lieback on tiny La Cosita, continuing the Spanish naming pattern—a trend that basically died with this route. Herb Swedlund and Penny Carr put up the spectacular Moby Dick using a few aid pins—eliminated by Frank Sacherer within days. Three routes appeared on Delectable Pinnacle. Royal Robbins got into the act also; he and Jack Turner established a complex and classic route on the right side of Little John. The spring of 1962 was quite a time!

Within a few years all the various "pinnacles" at the base of the face had been climbed, usually by three different routes: left side, center (often an aid route involving hairline cracks), and right side. Variations soon sprung up, an important one being the Sacherer Cracker, a two-pitch alternate to the lower part of The Slack. This 1964 route, done by Sacherer and Mike Sherrick, involved a 120-foot jamcrack that varied in width from 1 to 6 inches. At 5.10a, and difficult to protect (using bong-bongs), this was one of the bolder leads of the mid-1960s. Chouinard, greatly impressed with Sacherer's ability, wrote that he "always climbed on the verge of falling over backwards—using no more energy than was necessary to progress and rarely bothering to stop and place protection. Apparently his belayers have been so completely gripped they were unable to use a camera. I have not been able to find a single photograph of Sacherer on a lead!"

The next major event took place in 1973, when Steve Wunsch and Mark Chapman freed La Escuela. The lower two pitches, once pure, strenuous aid, overnight became a different climb, one involving sustained liebacks at 5.11a. The pair eliminated about 35 aid points!

Another 11a route, Sparkling Give-away, vies for attention. Put up in 1991 by two big-wall tigers, Pete Takeda and Eric Kohl, this short line involves thin moves on the outer face of La Cosita.

All in all, the base of El Cap is a marvelous place, with aesthetic cracks, usually excellent belay ledges, easy rappels, and shaded slabs for picnics and spectators. Oh yes—it's also a favorite haunt of rattlesnakes!

– *Steve Roper*

A. La Escuela   5.11b★★★★

FA: Yvon Chouinard and TM Herbert, 5/62.
FFA: Steve Wunsch and Mark Chapman, 1973.

Polished, sustained, and technical, La Escuela will 'school ya' in classic Yosemite liebacking. The protection is solid but can be difficult to place due to the sustained nature of the climb. Luckily the fall is clean. The crack seeps water early in the season so plan accordingly. A superb route, but the grade keeps traffic down.

B. The Slack, Left   5.10d★★

FA: Chuck Pratt and Royal Robbins, 5/65.
FFA: Pat Ament and Larry Dalke, 1967.

Try this good double-rope toprope after doing Sacherer Cracker. Watch rope stretch as the crux is off the deck. The route has fingers in pin scars with technical stemming to a good 5.8 offwidth to a traversing chimney. Skip the chimney to reduce pendulum potential on toprope.

C. Sacherer Cracker   5.10a★★★★★

FA: Frank Sacherer and Mike Sherrick, 1964.

Sacherer Cracker climbs an excellent, clean, widening crack up a steep wall. Don't underestimate the short 5.7 approach pitch, which is a polished flare that has spit out many a 5.11 climber. The crux is a slowly widening crack that goes from fingers to offwidth and is equally sustained at each size. Fifty feet of beautiful steep hands tests your endurance, and then a rest ledge lets you contemplate the 30 feet of off-hand/fist before the intimidating offwidth. This is the crux for most as it widens so quickly that even big cams don't protect it. A 1.25" cam in a horizontal crack and chockstones at the base of the offwidth are your pro. Stick your right side in and make a few desperate moves (focus on bridging the outside foot). Sacherer Cracker often has a line, so consider La Cosita, Left and toproping Sparkling Give-Away if waiting.

D. The Mark of Art   5.10d★★★★★

FA: Mark Chapman and Art Higbee, 1974.

Outstanding, burly endurance liebacking and off-fingers make this Valley 5.10d testpiece one of the longest and best single pitches in Yosemite. The fact that it starts after the crux fingers to hand crack of Sacherer Cracker (and avoids its offwidth!) only makes this climb more appealing.

E. Short but Thin   5.11b★★★

FA: Tobin Sorenson and John Bachar, 5/74.

Technical and strenuous, Short but Thin makes up for its meager length with fierce moves. Few people lead this, but thin cams and nuts protect it well. Toprope this climb by leading the polished 5.7 flare that begins Sacherer Cracker.

F. La Cosita, Left   5.7★★★★

FA: Bob Kamps, Galen Rowell, Dan Doody, Wally Upton, 6/62.

This is perhaps the steepest 5.7 in the Valley. An intimidating overhanging hand crack protects well (chimney when possible). Jugs appear higher and lead to a final awkward bulge. There is a 5.9 offwidth/squeeze variation behind a flake that takes off left, but it is difficult to toprope safely.

G. Sparkling Give-away   5.11a★★

FA: Pete Takeda and Eric Kohl, 12/91.

This is a wild and challenging toprope. The finger crack traverse rewards the speedy and the crux can be done several ways—from a reachy undercling to a dicey mantel. Higher, staying left on reachy jugs is easier, and staying right is excellent practice for hard, steep slab climbing.

H. La Cosita, Right   5.9★★★★

FA: TM Herbert and Steve Roper, 5/63.

This is the Valley testpiece 5.9 lieback/finger crack. Incredibly slick liebacking off the ground sees many slips and falls, but completely bomber pro makes it safe. The trick is to find the lieback balance—the higher your feet, the more strenuous the climb—yet your feet will cut out at some point. La Cosita will teach you how far you can push it on slick granite. Another lieback section higher is easier since you can get more purchase in the crack with your feet. From the bolted anchor you can toprope La Cosita, Left and Sparkling Give-away.

I. Little John, Left   5.8★★★

FA: Dan Doody, Bob Kamps, Galen Rowell, Wally Upton, 8/62.

This slick, polished fist/tight offwidth crack is an excellent toprope after doing Little John, Right, or a good lead on its own. It is often somewhat obstructed by fixed lines.

J. Hardly Pinnacle   5.10d★★★★

FA: Dale Bard et al, 1972.

Beautiful, clean, steep liebacking is mixed with an intriguing crux of technical stemming. The first 25 feet has two options: either a pumpy lieback or a straight-up finger crack; both are approximately the same difficulty depending on your strengths. This is an outstanding and often overlooked climb. Those willing to trust the normally fixed Heart Ledges lines and capable of safely ascending ropes can jug these lines, then pendulum right to set a toprope.

K. Little John, Right   5.8★★★★

FA: Jack Turner and Royal Robins, 4/62.

Three pitches of 5.8 makes Little John, Right one of the most popular climbs in Yosemite. Many are in for a rude awakening on the first pitch, with its awkward, polished chimney and tricky stemming. Protection is good however, and it's fun to battle with new techniques. The second pitch is excellent, but many miss the traverse to the left and go too high. Study the topo and keep in mind that you are trying to get left when possible. The last pitch has a fun, slick hand crack in a corner. From the bolts at the left end of the last pitch ledge, an 80-foot rappel reaches 3rd class ledges. But before you pack up, toprope Little John, Left—an excellent polished 5.8 offwidth. Do laps on this and you will get great training for the offwidths that you inevitably run into in Yosemite.

L. Moby Dick, Center   5.10a★★★★★

FA: Herb Swedlund and Penny Carr, 5/63.
FFA: Frank Sacherer and Steve Roper, 5/63.

Though it starts with a powerful and technical 5.10a finger crack, most climbers remember Moby Dick for the long battle above with a widening fist crack. For those with small hands, the top of Moby Dick is truly an offwidth, and hand stacking can allow secure rests. Those with large hands will love it, yet the finger crack crux may be correspondingly more difficult. Prepare and plan your pro for the start, as the crux comes right away.

M. Ahab   5.10b★★★

FA: Frank Sacherer and Jim Bridwell, 9/64.

Ahab is a tough offwidth/flare that is a testament to Yosemite climbers of the 1960s. Ninety-nine out of a hundred 5.13 gym climbers will be completely shut down by this climb. Seldom led, it is usually toproped from Moby Dick for practice at that hallmark craft of the hardcore Valley climber—slick and flared offwidth technique.

N. Salathé Wall (Pitch 1 & 2)   5.10c★★★★★

The first pitches of the Salathé Wall are the start for several popular walls as well as Freeblast, a testpiece ten-pitch 5.11. They also have one of the best, most sustained 5.10 finger cracks in the Valley. Fingers, double cracks, and a thin hands crux make for an unforgettable lead. Good footwork helps you make it through the 5.10 technical cruxes. Many do the first 40 feet as a short approach pitch. However, the only good pro for an anchor is also far to the left, making it a problem if you place pro near the start of the finger crack. The best way to safely climb this is to lead the first 40 feet, traverse to the finger crack, get one or two good pieces, and go off belay, then pull your rope all the way through and toss it back down. Then you can lead to the anchors 100 feet above, and either have the follower risk a pendulum, or climb harder terrain directly up to the finger crack, and retrieve the gear on rappel. Before rappelling, consider the excellent and challenging hands/lieback/offwidth next pitch.

O. Pine Line   5.7★★★

FA: Jeff and Greg Schaffer, 7/66.

Pine Line starts from a huge ledge with great views and climbs a fun, short 5.7 finger crack with pin scars. This is an excellent first lead or warm up, it protects with excellent nuts and a few cams, and is a great place for the overly cam-reliant novice climber to train with nuts. Several very good 5.10d-11b slab/thin edge climbs can easily be toproped and are great training. The belay tree is a long way back from the edge and long slings can help extend the anchor past an intermediate bush.

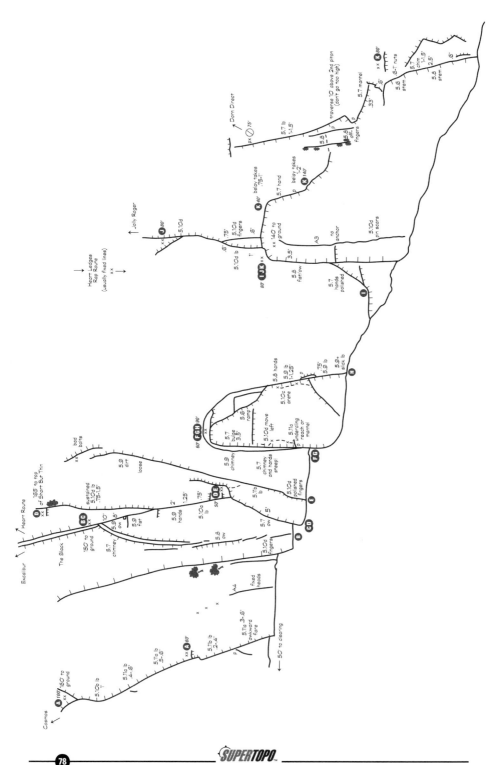

A. La Escuela 5.11b ★★★★ nuts: many extra micro, thin, and sml; cams: many tiny to 2.5", extra .5-.75"

B. The Slack, Left 5.10d ★★ nuts: 1 set, cams: 1 ea 1-3", 2 ea .5-.75", 3.5-6", slings for chockstones

C. Sacherer Cracker 5.10a ★★★★★ nuts: 1 set; cams: 1 ea .5-1", 2 ea 1.25-3.5", optional extra 1.5-2" (One 5" cam can be used for Pitch 1), slings for chockstones; other: big bros for offwidth.

D. The Mark of Art 5.10d ★★★★★ nuts: 1 set; cams: .5-2.5", many extra .75-1.5" (If belaying on ledge, bring three 2.5-3.5" cams for belay)

E. Short but Thin 5.11b ★★★ nuts: 2 sets micro-sml; cams: lots of small/tiny

F. La Cosita, Left 5.7 ★★★★ nuts: 1 set; cams: .6-4", extra 1-2"

G. Sparkling Give-away 5.11a ★★ cams: 1 ea 3.5", optional: .75"; 3 draws

H. La Cosita, Right 5.9 ★★★★ nuts: 1 set; cams: 2 ea .5-2", optional extra .5-2"

I. Little John, Left 5.8 ★★★ nuts: 1 set; cams: 1 set .6-2", 2 ea 2.5-3.5", 1 ea 4"

J. Hardly Pinnacle 5.10d ★★★★ nuts: 1 set; include micro nuts/RPs; cams: 2 ea .5-1.5"

K. Little John, Right 5.8 ★★★★ nuts: 1 set; cams: .5-3", extra 1-2"

L. Moby Dick 5.10a ★★★★★ nuts: 1 set thin-med; cams: 1 ea .5-4.5", extra 2.5-3.5"

M. Ahab 5.10b ★★★ nuts: 1 set; cams: 1 set to 2", 2 ea 2.5-5"

N. Salathé Wall 5.10c ★★★★★ nuts: 2 sets sml to med, 1 set lrg; cams: many .5-1.5", extra 2-4" if doing second pitch, many draws and slings

O. Pine Line 5.7 ★★★ nuts: 2 sets sml-med, 1 set lrg; cams: few .6-1", long slings for tree

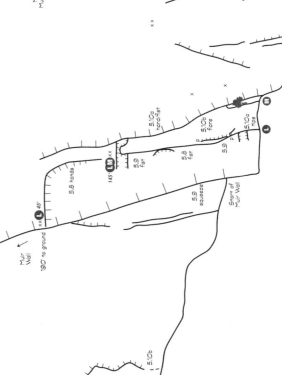

El Capitan Base, Southeast Face

Approach time: **20 minutes**

Sun exposure: **morning to early afternoon**

Height of routes: **80-200'**

The following climbs are located in a spectacular location at the base of El Capitan. They are a good option in mildly bad weather because most routes either dry quickly or may even be sheltered from the rain if there is no wind. Approach all routes by skirting the base of the Southeast Face on a climbers' trail. It's about 10 minutes from the base of The Nose to Gollum.

P. Simulkrime   5.9 R★★★

FA: John Middendorf and Tucker Tech, mid-80s.

Mega runout lead or convenient toprope set up by walking into The Alcove on exposed 3rd class. Lower down a full 200 feet to many fun 5.7-5.9 friction variations. Only the upper 100 feet are dry in the rain.

Q. Gollum, Left   5.10a★★

FA: Peter Haan, Rick Linkert, and David Moss, 3/72.

Wicked adventure in 3-5" cracks. Awkward but possible to toprope that last 100 feet after climbing Gollum, Right.

R. Gollum, Right   5.8★★★

FA: Joe Kelsey, Roman Laba, and John Judson, 9/67.

This stout 5.8 with steep and intimidating cruxes between good ledges is more appropriate for 5.9 leaders. It's like climbing a staircase with all the steps overhanging 10 degrees with a mixture of well-protected hand cracks and wild stemming moves. Use slings on most pieces or face paralyzing rope drag. You can toprope with one 60m rope if belaying up the 3rd class. It's also fun to toprope the face—using some creativity you can find fun 5.10-5.11 face moves. If raining, this route can be dry if there is no wind.

S. The Footstool, Right   5.4★★

FA: Mark Powell Beverly Powell and Bill Feuerer, 1959.

Decent quality climbing leads to a cool platform in a great location (bring your lunch and hang out). After only one pitch, you will feel like you are up on El Cap. Protection is sparse so this is only for 5.6 and better leaders. Rappel to The Bluffer with one 60m rope or bring two ropes to rappel to the ground. After a rainstorm, the route dries quickly. If sunny, this climb is warm on cold winter days.

T. The Bluffer   5.11d★★★

FA: Eric Kohl and Cade Loyd, 1992.

This difficult and quality climb is easily toproped after climbing The Footstool or by scrambling exposed 5.3 to the anchor. Sustained and fun 5.10 and easy 5.11 moves on shallow dishes and thin face lead to a baffling crux that feels harder than 5.11.

Chris McNamara

The Footstool, Right follows the obvious corner.

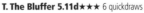

P. Simulkrime 5.9 R★★★ 2 quickdraws

Q. Gollum, Left 5.10a★★ nuts: 1 set; cams: 2 ea .75-4.5", extra 3-4"

R. Gollum, Right 5.8★★★ nuts: 1 set; cams: 2 ea .75-4.5", many slings

S. The Footstool, Right 5.4★★ nuts: 1 set; cams: 1 ea .6-2"

T. The Bluffer 5.11d★★★ 6 quickdraws

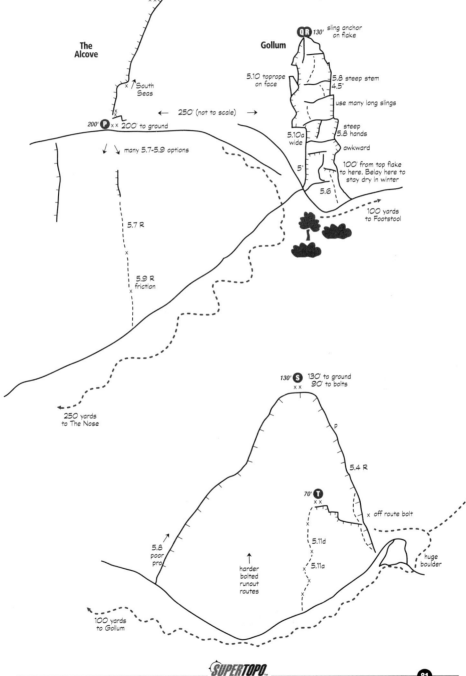

Schultz's Ridge

Most climbers overlook Schultz's Ridge because of its proximity to El Capitan. Those who do brave the 2-minute approach to the base routes find fun and well-protected sport and trad climbs mostly in the 5.9 and 5.10 range. The rock varies from steep and featured dark diorite to classic Yosemite white and slabby granite, often in the course of one pitch.

More adventurous climbers will enjoy the four-pitch The Moratorium, which is located above and to the east of the base routes. It's perfect for those training for Astroman or just wishing to add some technical 5.11 pitches to the start of the East Buttress of El Capitan. The route faces southeast making it great for fall and spring mornings or summer afternoons. It can be wet in winter.

Chris McNamara

Approach

The Moratorium Approach
Park at the first and bigger of two dirt pullouts on the left 1.8 miles west of Camp 4. Walk northeast through the trees for a few minutes to an open talus field. Continue up the talus another 15 minutes directly to the base. Scramble up to a ledge to reach the start of the climb.

Base approaches
Park in the second and smaller of two dirt pullouts on the left 1.8 miles west of Camp 4 (0.2 miles west of Manure Pile Buttress). For Endless Summer Wall, walk 100 feet northwest and hike in the drainage for 10 minutes. For Dan and Jerry's Playground, from the road, walk north 100 yards to the low point/toe of the wall. The climbs start to the left.

Descent

Base descents
Rappel most climbs with one 60m rope.

The Moratorium Descent
Most parties rappel after Pitch 3 (carry two 60m ropes) or continue up the East Buttress of El Capitan. To descend from the top of the climb, walk west along the base of El Capitan for 100 yards until the wall turns to steep gold rock. Turn and descend the talus to the road.

The Moratorium 5.11b★★★★

Time to climb route:	**2-3 hours**
Approach time:	**25 minutes**
Descent time:	**30 minutes-1 hour**
Sun exposure:	**sunrise to early afternoon**
Height of route:	**350'**

This route ascends a beautiful dihedral system and is packed with high quality finger cracks, liebacks, and technical stems. It is great training for the Rostrum or Astroman and has fewer crowds than either. From the last pitch, it's hard to resist continuing up the East Buttress of El Capitan for an incredible 17 pitch link-up. You can pull through the cruxes on gear.

Strategy

The route faces east making it too hot in the summer until the route goes into the shade. Spring and fall are ideal. Winter temps are nice but the crux may be wet.

For both the Pitch 2 and 3 cruxes, unconventional balancy stems are required. For the third pitch crux, clear all gear from your left side, then at the steep thin corner, climb with your left side against the rock using tips, liebacking, and delicate foot placements out right. Don't use the crack too much. Belay at the rap anchor left (if rappelling the route) or continue to a good belay ledge above. A 60m rope will reach the top—use long slings to reduce rope drag.

Retreat

With two 50m ropes, retreat is easy from the first three pitches.

The Moratorium		Pitch 1	2	3	4
Free difficulty	≥5.10	●	●	●	
	5.9				●
	5.8				
	5.7				
	5.6				
	≤5.5				

Rack

micro nuts: 1 set
nuts: 1 set
cams: 2 ea .4-2.5"
    1 ea 3"

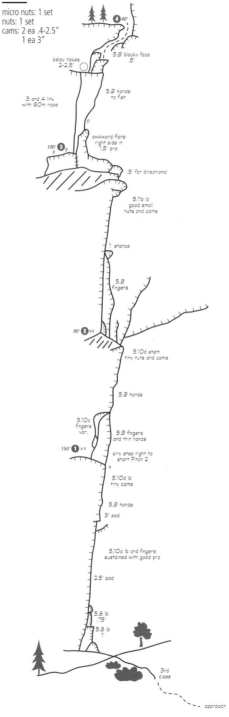

Schultz's Ridge Base, Dan and Jerry's Playground

Approach time: **2-10 minutes**

Sun exposure: **late morning to afternoon**

Height of routes: **35-100'**

Because of the perfect orientation of Dan and Jerry's Playground, it gets mostly sun in fall, winter, and spring but gets morning shade in summer. The rock is steep and dark with half the routes being sport and half being partially bolted and requiring gear. All are well-protected.

A. Dreams of Thailand   5.11d★★★

FA: Dan and Sue McDevitt, Jerry, Sigrid and Lynnea Anderson.

Positive holds on a slightly overhanging face with a surprise crux on what looks like a large jug. Very continuous 5.10 and 5.11 climbing. Use a stick clip to set a toprope. Ratings vary wildly among people who have done this route.

B. Are You Hard Enough?   5.10d★★★

FA: Dan and Sue McDevitt, Jerry, Sigrid and Lynnea Anderson.

After the crux at the second bolt, follow a ramp to a small roof and then to vertical and overhanging moves on positive holds. It looks runout before the anchor, but good hidden holds appear.

C. Just Do Me   5.10d★★★★

FA: Dan and Sue McDevitt, Jerry, Sigrid and Lynnea Anderson.

Start in a fun lieback over a small roof then move right to thin face climbing. Take a good rest before the roof as sustained 5.10 climbing with three separate cruxes continues to the anchor. There are no easy sections on this fun, pumpy route.

D. Second Thoughts   5.10a★★

FA: Dan and Sue McDevitt, Jerry, Sigrid and Lynnea Anderson.

A perfect warm up. There is a single 5.9 move where the flake jogs right and a single 5.10a move at the next to last bolt. A move to the right from the anchor allows setting a toprope on Just Do Me.

E. New Suede Shoes   5.10c★★★

FA: Jerry, Sigrid and Lynnea Anderson.

Super fun 5.10 climbing on tiny but positive holds leads past three bolts to a rest at the 4th bolt. A few crux moves over the roof leads to easier and somewhat lesser quality climbing.

F. Warm Up Crack   5.10a★★

FA: Dan and Sue McDevitt, Jerry, Sigrid, and Lynnea Anderson.

Another good warm up. Don't be fooled by the mellow-looking climbing going right from the last bolt. Make sure you pull down and not out on the first section or the rating could go up in a hurry!

G. Proud Snapper   5.10b★★★★

FA: Dan McDevitt.

Fun bolt-protected face moves lead to a steep and proud stemming corner. The climbing is airy and thought provoking but surprisingly moderate until the last crux move.

H. Hooter Alert   5.10c★★★

FA: Dan and Sue McDevitt, Jerry, Sigrid and Lynnea Anderson.

This climb offers varied and fun climbing starting on a steep featured face. After the first crux the route continues up a slab with positive holds, a little liebacking, and a second crux to clip the anchor.

A. Dreams of Thailand 5.11d ★★★ 5 quickdraws
B. Are You Hard Enough 5.10d ★★★ 9 quickdraws
C. Just Do Me 5.10d ★★★★ 9 quickdraws
D. Second Thoughts 5.10a ★★ cams: 1 ea .6-3.5", 5 quickdraws
E. New Suede Shoes 5.10c ★★★ cams: 1 ea 2.5", 7 quickdraws
F. Warm Up Crack 5.10a ★★ cams: 1 ea .6-3.5", 4 quickdraws
G. Proud Snapper 5.10b ★★★★ cams: 1-2 ea .6-3.5", 3 quickdraws
H. Hooter Alert 5.10c ★★★ 9 quickdraws

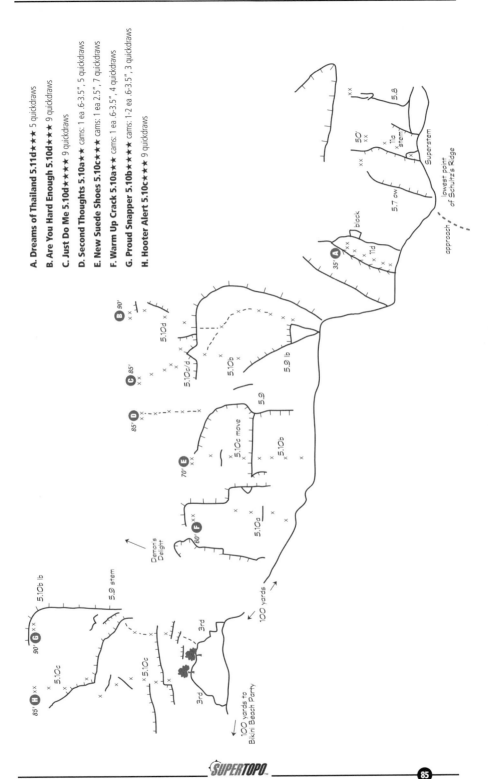

Schultz's Ridge Base, Endless Summer Wall

Approach time: **10 minutes**

Sun exposure: **morning to afternoon**

Height of routes: **90-130'**

Endless Summer Wall gets all day sun making it ideal on cool fall and spring days and in winter. The summer is too hot. All the climbs are bolted face routes and most are well protected. This is a great place to build friction technique. Its prime position under the awesome Southeast Face of El Capitan is reason enough to visit.

I. Bikini Beach Party   5.10a R★★★

FA: Chris Cantwell and Mark Grant, 1980.

This cool face pitch has everything from crystal jugs and incut edges to sporty friction. While the 5.10 crux is well-protected, beware of the 5.7 runout to the top. Easy to toprope after climbing Gidget Goes to Yosemite or Crystalline Passage.

J. Crystalline Passage   5.10b★★★★

FA: Jerry and Sigrid Anderson and Jeff Buhler, 11/02.

This sustained and well-protected pitch is a great first 5.10 friction lead and good training for Crest Jewel. Toprope using a 70m rope. With a 60m rope the belayer must solo 5.4 to the first bolt (tie into both ends of the rope). Descend by rappelling to Bikini Beach Party then to the ground.

K. Gidget Goes to Yosemite   5.9★★★★

FA: Ron White and Bert Levy, 10/88.

A distinct 5.9 friction crux comes between mostly 5.7 friction and crystal jugs. This is a great first 5.9 friction lead. Toprope using a 70m rope. A 60m rope works if the belayer solos up 5.4 to the first bolt. (Tie into both ends of the rope!) From the anchor you can set topropes on the surrounding climbs.

L. Caught at The Lip   5.11a★★★

FA: Chris McNamara, Mark Miller, 12/02.

Moderate moves through featured dark rock lead to a balancy and gripping lip traverse and then sustained thin face moves. You may want a .6" cam before the last bolt and the bewildering finishing mantel.

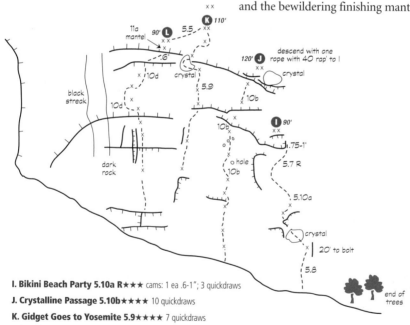

I. Bikini Beach Party 5.10a R★★★ cams: 1 ea .6-1"; 3 quickdraws

J. Crystalline Passage 5.10b★★★★ 10 quickdraws

K. Gidget Goes to Yosemite 5.9★★★★ 7 quickdraws

L. Caught at the Lip 5.11a★★★ cams: 1 ea .6"; 8 quickdraws

Photo by Chris McNamara

Manure Pile Buttress

With its short approach and 600 feet of clean, high-quality rock, the extremely popular Manure Pile Buttress is anything but a heap of shit. While crowds abound, if you are creative and lead 5.8, there is usually something available. This is the site of many climbers' first 5.7 or 5.8 Yosemite multi-pitch route. All routes get sun all day making them usually too hot in the summer. Spring and fall are the ideal times to climb, but winter can be great too.

Approach

From Camp 4, drive west 1.6 miles and park in the paved picnic area lot. From the northeast end of the parking lot, just behind the bathroom, follow a well-traveled trail northeast for a few hundred yards to the base of Manure Pile Buttress. After Six is the 150-foot right-facing corner seen immediately upon reaching the rock face. Nutcracker begins 200 feet to the right (east).

Todd Snyder

Descent

From the top of the climbs, move northwest on a worn trail up a short distance then down and northwest to 200 feet of unobvious 3rd and 4th class which leads to a climbers' trail. Follow this trail as it switchbacks to the base of After Six.

After Six 5.7★★★★

Time to climb route:	**2-4 hours**
Approach time:	**5 minutes**
Descent time:	**25 minutes**
Sun exposure:	**late morning to afternoon**
Height of route:	**600'**

With six pitches of moderate cracks and a short approach, After Six is one of the most popular routes in Yosemite. A step up in difficulty from Munginella, the climbing alternates between cracks and face, exposed terrain, and low-angle 4th class. This is a good way to break into 5.7 multi-pitch climbing. However, some pitches could prove treacherous to the novice leader, especially Pitch 3.

History

It seems likely that we'll never know who discovered Manure Pile Buttress as a climbing objective. Back in the mid-1960s a dirt track led directly to its base from the main Valley road below the Lower Brother, but this side trail seemed to lead only to a gigantic pile of horseshit, for this is where flunkies from the Valley stables deposited it, far from tourists with sensitive noses. Manure Pile Buttress was also known as Ranger Rock, and Camp 4 climbers in the 1960s knew that rangers often practiced their rescue techniques there. What with the stench and the possibility of encountering authority, local Valley hotshots stayed far away. Yet it's likely that weekenders played around on the lower section, a non-threatening beginners' area.

The first complete route, as far as is known, was the brainchild of Yvon Chouinard, who in June 1965 took a beautiful eastern climber, Ruth Schneider, up the most obvious line, named After Six since that's when they started (six in the evening, one might add, not morning). This climb attracted immediate attention for two reasons: it was fun, and it was one of the few Valley climbs where the belayer could sit in the front seat of a car. After Six soon became the most sociable of climbs; beer-guzzling spectators could hurl insults upward without even shouting.

Chouinard returned in 1967 and did a much harder route, just left of After Six. This he accomplished with a handsome Scottish lass, Joy Herron. Chouinard named the route Jump for Joy, a nice pun made even nicer by the rumor—neither confirmed nor denied—that a breathtaking sexual act had occurred on the first big ledge.

– Steve Roper

Strategy

Start early to beat the crowds. The first pitch is the crux and has sustained, awkward jamming with slick footholds and good protection.

Higher on the route, the moves are easier but occasionally not as well-protected. On Pitch 3, the psychological crux, the leader must face climb on the left arête of an exposed wide crack with poor protection. On Pitches 4-6 there are numerous variations and optional belay locations for passing slower parties.

If the climb is crowded and you are comfortable leading 5.8, consider climbing C.S. Concerto or After Seven.

Retreat

Carry two 50m or 60m ropes to retreat. From the first and second belays it is possible to scramble off west on 4th class. There is also an escape at the 4th belay.

After Six		Pitch 1	2	3	4	5	6
Free difficulty	≥5.10						
	5.9						
	5.8						
	5.7	●					
	5.6			●	●	●	●
	≤5.5		●				

A. Hayley's Comet   5.10a★★★

FA: Lance Alred and Jason Torlano.

This fun, featured arête is a sporty lead with just enough bolts to not be runout. Keep a close belay and a spot when clipping the second bolt. Set a toprope by scrambling 4th class around the side then rappelling with one 50m or 60m rope to the anchor.

B. Jump for Joy   5.9 R★★★

FA: Yvon Chouinard and Joy Herron, 1967.

A bold lead or fun toprope after leading Hayley's Comet. The route continues for three seldom climbed pitches.

C. After Seven   5.8★★★★

FA: unknown.

An excellent hand and finger crack to a face climbing crux. The last pro before the crux is just far enough away to grab your attention, but not so far as to make the pitch runout. You can rappel with two ropes after the first pitch, but most climbers join up with After Six. This climb is a great way to pass slow parties starting up After Six.

D. Just Do-do It   5.10a★★★

FA: unknown.

Slick, dicey, and thin face climbing leads to a great thin crack. The crux is before the first bolt so get a good spot. Face climb left of the crack, moving back to place protection.

E. C.S. Concerto   5.8★★★

FA: Yvon Chouinard, Chuck Pratt, and Mort Hempel, 1967.

This three-pitch variation to After Six is as hard and bold as Nutcracker but has fewer crowds. The climbing is consistently good but not spectacular, sparsely protected but only runout on 5.5 or easier ground. The face and finger crack cruxes are well-protected on clean rock. It joins After Six after Pitch 3 where you may need to use the more runout and challenging finishing variations to avoid crowds. There is an escape left at the 4th pitch as well as escapes from Pitches 1 and 2. It is common to climb just the first 80 feet of the first pitch and set a toprope on Fecophilia.

F. Fecophilia   5.9 R★★

FA: Yvon Chouinard, Chuck Pratt, and Mort Hempel, 1967.

Just the first pitch is popular and is most often toproped with one 60m rope by climbing the first 80 feet of C.S. Concerto or scrambling up 3rd class. The fun face and friction climbing to the thin crack is great for practicing footwork. The second pitch is dirty and the upper pitches are runout and seldom climbed.

Chris McNamara on Pitch 3 of C.S. Concerto with El Capitan in the background.

David Safanda

Rack

nuts: 1-2 sets
cams: 2 ea .5-2.5"
          1 ea 3"

A. Hayley's Comet 5.10a★★★
4 quickdraws

B. Jump for Joy 5.9 R★★★
nuts: 1 set; cams: 1 ea .5-.75"

C. After Seven 5.8★★★★
nuts: 1 set; cams, 1 ea .5-2"

D. Just Do-do It 5.10a★★★
nuts: 1 set; cams: 1 ea .5", 1.25-1.5", 2 ea .6-1"

E. C.S. Concerto 5.8★★★
nuts: 1 set; cams: 1-2 ea .5-2.5"

F. Fecophilia 5.9 R★★
nuts: 1 set; cams: 1 ea .5-1.5"

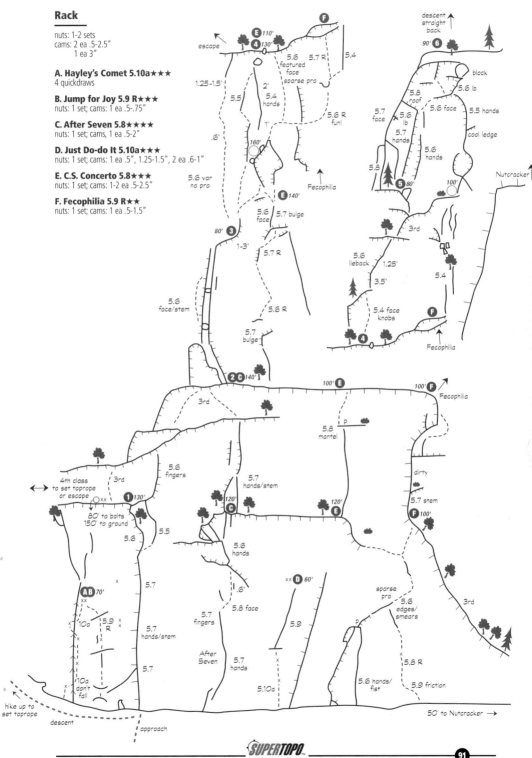

Nutcracker 5.8★★★★★

Time to climb route: **2-4 hours**

Approach time: **5 minutes**

Descent time: **25 minutes**

Sun exposure: **late morning to afternoon**

Height of route: **600'**

Nutcracker is a classic due to its interesting history, easy approach, and five great pitches of perfect Yosemite granite. You will encounter liebacking, hand jamming, finger jamming, delicate smearing, and a bold mantel crux. Nutcracker is a step up from After Six and After Seven. It's hard to pull through the crux mantel on gear so you should be a confident 5.8 leader and practice mantels ahead of time.

History

The first ascent of the most popular Valley climb ever was an historic breakthrough, for it was one of the first routes done solely with nuts. Even though Royal Robbins had climbed twice in England by 1966, he hadn't fully embraced nut use for Yosemite. Royal wrote in June 1966: "I think we can learn a lot from the British, and I see a place in the U. S. for the concept that placing a lot of pitons is not good style and also for the use of nuts at places like Tahquitz, where years of placing and removing pitons have worn the cracks so much as to change the routes." In 1967 Robbins found a magnificent climb at Manure Pile Buttress to test his idea that nuts might be appropriate for Yosemite after all. He named his new route, in his usual punning mode, Nutcracker Sweet. Within months, those ignorant of Tchaikovsky had

shortened the name simply to its first word, which is how it has remained for three decades. An unwritten rule, obeyed by virtually everyone, was that no piton should ever be driven into this route. Many a Valley climber learned how effective nuts could be (this was long before camming devices were available) and left pitons and hammers in camp. Robbins, the king of the big walls, had once again proved that he was the guiding light of 1960s Valley climbing.

Climbers soon swarmed up other routes and variations on Manure Pile Buttress, and the place became a mandatory stop on everyone's itinerary. Even today, you'll see few piton scars, those dreadful excavations still so visible on the popular routes of the early 1960s. Thanks Royal!

– Steve Roper

Strategy

Begin early as this route is extremely popular. There are a number of starting variations but after two pitches there are few ways to pass slower parties. Note that in the winter Pitches 1 and 3 are usually wet. All belays require gear.

The first crux involves friction climbing down low and insecure jamming higher up through the bulge on Pitch 4. The second crux is the exposed 5.8 mantel on the final pitch. Some climbers use small holds above and to the left to avoid the direct mantel move. Take time to find the tricky micro cam and nut placements. Keep a close belay—falls from this move have resulted in broken ankles.

If you arrive at the base and find a long line to start, consider climbing the first pitch of C. S. Concerto (5.6) and toproping Fecophilia (5.9 R). Or if there are way too many people, climb C.S. Concerto in its entirety (see After Six topo).

Retreat

Carry two 50m or 60m ropes to retreat. From the second belay, rappel either the 5.9 variation or the rappel route on the face. Above the second belay, retreat requires leaving gear.

Nutcracker		Pitch 1	2	3	4	5
Free difficulty	≥5.10					
	5.9					
	5.8	●			●	●
	5.7			●		
	5.6					
	≤5.5	●				

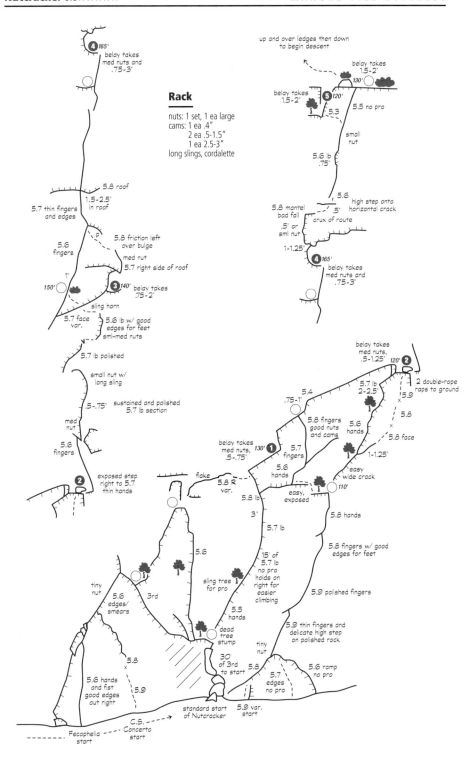

Rack

nuts: 1 set, 1 ea large
cams: 1 ea .4"
     2 ea .5-1.5"
     1 ea 2.5-3"
long slings, cordalette

4 165'
belay takes
med nuts and
.75-3'

up and over ledges then down
to begin descent

belay takes
1.5-2'

5 120'

belay takes
1.5-2'

130'

5.3

5.5 no pro

small
nut

5.6 lb
.75'

5.6

high step onto
horizontal crack

5.8 mantel
bad fall

.5'

.5' or
sml nut

crux of route

1-1.25'

4 165'
belay takes
med nuts and
.75-3'

5.8 roof

1.5-2.5'
in roof

5.7 thin fingers
and edges

5.6
fingers

5.8 friction left
over bulge

med nut

5.7 right side of roof

1'

150'

3 140'
belay takes
.75-2'

sling horn

5.7 face
var.

5.6 lb w/ good
edges for feet
sml-med nuts

5.7 lb polished

small nut w/
long sling

.5-.75'

sustained and polished
5.7 lb section

med
nut

5.6
fingers

2

exposed step
right to 5.7
thin hands

flake

5.8 R
var.

5.8 lb

3'

5.7 lb

15' of
5.7 lb
no pro
holds on
right for
easier
climbing

belay takes
med nuts,
.5-1.25'

120' **2**

2 double-rope
raps to ground

5.7 lb
2-2.5

15.9

x

5.8

x

5.8 face

1-1.25'

5.4

.75-1'

belay takes
med nuts,
.5-.75'

130' **1**

5.7
fingers

5.8 fingers
good nuts
and cams

5.6
hands

5.6
hands

easy,
exposed

easy
wide crack

110'

5.8 hands

5.8 fingers w/ good
edges for feet

5.9 polished fingers

5.9 thin fingers and
delicate high step
on polished rock

tiny
nut

5.6
edges/
smears

3rd

5.6

sling tree
for pro

5.5
hands

dead
tree
stump

tiny
nut

30'
of 3rd
to start

5.8

5.7
edges
no pro

5.6 ramp
no pro

5.8
x

5.6 hands
and fist
good edges
out right

5.9

standard start
of Nutcracker

5.9 var.
start

C.S.
Concerto
start

Fecophelia
start

Camp 4 Wall

Approach time: **15-20 minutes**

Sun exposure: **sunrise to early afternoon**

Height of routes: **100-150'**

Second only to Swan Slab as the closest crag to Camp 4, this area is home to numerous stout 5.9 and 5.10 cracks. This is a great place to improve the hand, offwidth, and chimney techniques demanded on most long Yosemite climbs. The routes face south and are ideal on cool spring and fall days or in the winter. The summer is too hot until the routes become shaded in the early afternoon.

Approach

From the west end of Camp 4, just behind the white Search and Rescue tent cabins, locate a 10-foot-wide drainage that crosses the Valley Loop Trail. Hike up this drainage for a few hundred feet until it widens and becomes a main drainage gully. Follow this gully for about 10 minutes until it comes close to the wall. Just down and left is the Doggie Diversions area. For the Henley Quits area, continue up the drainage for another 100 yards. This area is hard to see at first because it is hidden behind trees.

Descent

Rappel most routes with one 60m rope or two 50m ropes.

A. Doggie Do   5.10a★★

FA: Chris Fredericks.

A short but stout offwidth problem with arm bars in a flaring bulge. Skinny people do better on this one. This climb is usually toproped.

B. Doggie Diversions   5.9★★★

FA: Joe Faint and Yvon Chouinard, 6/67.

The first pitch is a fun squeeze chimney with some small cracks inside for pro. The second pitch is a physical and unrelenting hand, off-hand, and fist crack. There is no real crux—it's sustained the whole way.

C. Doggie Deviations   5.9★★★

FA: Kim Schmitz and Jim Bridwell, 1968.

A challenging 5.9 by either variation. The standard route involves a mixture of finger and hand jams with occasional lieback moves. The crux comes low and the climbing remains sustained above. The right flake variation is easier but poorly protected because most of the placements are behind loose flakes.

D. Cristina   5.11b★★★

FA: Mead Hargis and Dave Davis, 1971.
FFA: John Long et al, 1980.

The first pitch is an awesome 5.10a lieback crack. A bold lead with big cams or a fun toprope after climbing Henley Quits.

E. Henley Quits   5.10b★★★

FA: Mark Klemens and Rick Sylvester, 7/70.

Welcome to Yosemite! This is a classically stout Yosemite 5.10 with offwidth and chimney climbing leading to a steep off-hands crack—tape up! Bring 5-7" cams to protect the first 70 feet unless you are confident soloing 5.8 squeeze chimney. Only one rope is needed to descend by rappelling to the bolted anchor to the west. From here, it is highly recommended you toprope the first pitch of Cristina.

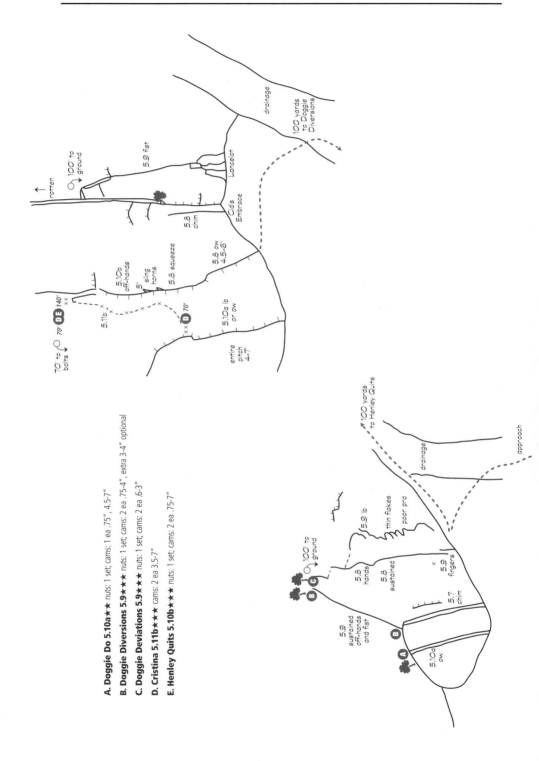

A. **Doggie Do 5.10a**★★ nuts: 1 set, cams: 1 ea .75", 4.5-7"

B. **Doggie Diversions 5.9**★★★ nuts: 1 set; cams: 2 ea .75-4", extra 3-4" optional

C. **Doggie Deviations 5.9**★★★ nuts: 1 set; cams: 2 ea .6-3"

D. **Cristina 5.11b**★★★ cams: 2 ea 3.5-7"

E. **Henley Quits 5.10b**★★★ nuts: 1 set; cams: 2 ea .75-7"

Swan Slab

Approach time: **2 minutes**

Sun exposure: **morning to afternoon**

Height of routes: **30-100'**

Chris McNamara

Within a 5-minute walk of Camp 4, Swan Slab offers the most convenient moderate routes in Yosemite. It's not a single slab as the name implies, but a broad cliff composed of many one- and two-pitch climbs ranging from near-vertical cracks to slabby face climbs. It has everything from 5.1 to 5.11 with emphasis on 5.6-5.8. Most climbs are 30 to 60 feet tall and are great for toproping. Some anchors you can walk to, but in most cases you must lead an easier adjacent climb. Most climbs can be led with the following gear: one set of nuts, one set of cams .5-3", and some long slings. We note when more gear is needed.

This south-facing cliff gets morning to afternoon sun with perfect temperatures in the spring and fall. In summer, the temperatures are okay in the shade, but too hot in the sun. In winter, temperatures are usually good.

Approach

Swan Slab is located about halfway between Camp 4 and the Lower Yosemite Falls parking area. Park in Camp 4 and walk northeast 200 feet to the wide semi-paved trail. Walk east for a few minutes until directly below Swan Slab.

Descent

Rappel most routes with one 50m or 60m rope. On a few climbs you walk off to the west following a faint climbers' trail.

A. Penthouse Cracks   5.8-5.11a★★

These four cracks can be toproped from the same two-bolt anchor. They are perfect for building finger crack, hand crack, and lieback technique. You can walk to the anchor to set a toprope.

B. West Slabs   5.6-5.8★★

This is a great place to toprope and learn 5.6-5.8 slab technique. There are at least five variations from the anchor, which get progressively harder moving right to left. The tree anchor can be walked to and should be backed up with gear.

C. Unnamed gully   5.1★

Great for children and first time climbers.

D. Unnamed flared crack   5.8★★

This steep and powerful route is usually just bouldered because it traverses under a roof and is hard to toprope.

E. Unnamed crack   5.7★★

Work on crack technique without worrying about exposure. Bring gear to set a directional.

F. Unnamed crack   5.9★★

A bouldery start leads to sustained but short lieback moves. Do laps on this climb to refine your liebacking.

G. Swan Slab Squeeze   5.7★★

A good practice squeeze chimney that gets harder the higher you climb. Use foot-bridging technique and face out from the wall. Set a toprope with 1-4" cams by scrambling up 3rd class and some 5.3 past the anchors of D, E, and F to where the gaping crack constricts. The crack is seldom led because it requires 7-10" gear.

H. Swan Slab Chimney   5.5★

This is an unaesthetic climb that does offer

some good chimney practice. If you face into the chimney the climbing is awkward, so face outward with your back to the main wall. This offers the easiest anchor access for Oak Tree Flake or Grant's Crack.

I. Oak Tree Flake   5.6★★★

A 5.6 jam leads to a classic lieback flake. If led, the 3-4.5" cam placements are hard to see. This climb is conducive to doing laps. When setting a toprope, use the bolt anchors and bring slings and cams to set a directional. Continue up Bay Tree Flake for another quality and well-protected 5.6 pitch.

J. Grant's Crack   5.9★★★

This is a great first 5.9 crack lead or toprope. Do a few laps to build finger crack skills. Set the toprope by climbing the 5.5 chimney or Oak Tree Flake.

K. Unnamed thin crack   5.10a★★

This popular toprope develops thin crack and face technique. Set the toprope anchor by climbing the 5.5 chimney or Oak Tree Flake and continuing up a short 5.4 crack.

L. Unnamed seam   5.10c★★

A harder variation to K that requires more face climbing. Set the toprope anchor by climbing the 5.5 chimney or Oak Tree Flake and continuing up a short 5.4 crack.

M. Penelope's Problem   5.7★★

Steep 5.7 hand jams lead to a short traverse. Be sure to set protection before the traverse. To set a toprope, either climb the route or climb Swan Slab Gully. Beware that Swan Slab Gully is so awkward that some climbers may actually find Penelope's Problem easier despite its harder rating.

N. Swan Slab Gully   5.6★★

This is a great first 5.6 multi-pitch lead. The first pitch is awkward and unaesthetic and can be avoided by climbing Hanging Flake or Penelope's Problem. The second and third pitches are mostly low angle and well-protected with 5.6 finger and hand cracks here and there. The route ends on a cool terrace with a nice view.

O. Unnamed face   5.7★★★

Bouldering thin friction moves leads to progressively easier climbing. Set a toprope by climbing Hanging Flake. For the 5.8 variation, start to the left and make a few bouldery face moves before eventually joining the upper part of the main route.

P. Hanging Flake   5.6★★

This is a short and fun introduction to hand jamming. The anchor is fractured and loose so set gear in many locations and equalize.

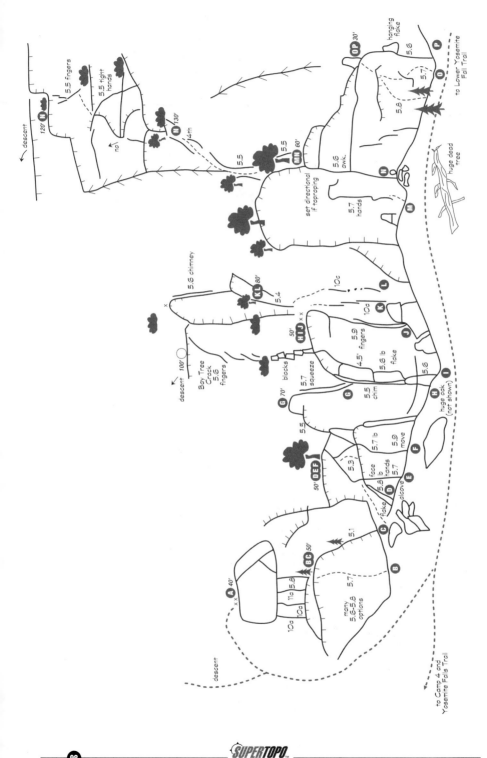

Q. Aid Route   5.10a A0 or 5.11b★★★★

FA: Joe Oliger and Steve Roper, 4/61. FFA: Loyd Price et al, 1967.

This awesome pin-scarred route is perfect training for Serenity Crack. French free 20 feet to the 5.8 crack. Use long slings at the start of Pitch 2. The crux is 5.10a fingers. Two rappels with a 60m rope will get you to the ground.

R. Lena's Lieback   5.9★★★

FA: Kim Schmitz and Jim Madsen.

The first pitch involves sustained and polished liebacking with good protection and is a great toprope (you can also set a toprope by climbing Claude's Delight). The second and third pitches, which are rarely climbed, involve sustained 5.8 underclings and jamming of decent quality. Don't link these pitches as the rope often snags under a roof. Descend from the top by walking down 3rd and 4th class to the east.

S. Goat For It   5.10a★★★

FA: Mark Carpenter, et al late 1980s.

This sporty face climb is usually toproped after climbing Lena's Lieback or Claude's Delight. The route starts after the crux of Lena's Lieback where it traverses right to fun face climbing in a cool position. This climb is for confident 5.10a leaders as there is some big fall potential. If toproping, place gear as a directional 5 feet right of the anchor to prevent a big swing.

T. Claude's Delight   5.7★★★

FA: Claude Fiddler and Peter Olander, 8/72.

This steep, wild, and sustained 5.7 requires good stemming technique. The climbing is unique, fun, and protects well. From the bolt anchors, consider toproping the two climbs to the left. If toproping, place gear as a directional 5 and 10 feet right of the anchor to prevent a big swing.

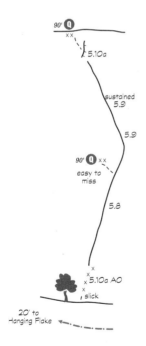

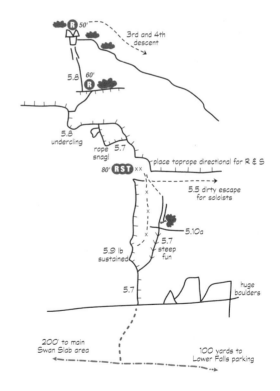

Five Open Books

Approach time: **15-45 minutes**

Sun exposure: **morning to afternoon**

Height of routes: **350'**

Five Open Books has the highest concentration of moderate three- and four-pitch climbs in Yosemite. Most routes are large corners (aka "open books") that face southeast and get sun from sunrise to midday. Temperatures are ideal in the spring and fall. In the winter, climb from morning to mid-afternoon. In summer, climb later when the routes are shaded.

WARNING: Frequent climber-caused rockfall: Always wear a helmet.

A	Munginella	**E**	Try Again Ledge
B	Commitment	**F**	Hanging Teeth
C	The Surprise	**G**	Selaginella
D	The Caverns	**H**	Yosemite Falls Trail

Approach

All routes except Selaginella
Walk toward Lower Yosemite Fall for 100 yards looking left for a climbers' trail marked by a carabiner post. Follow the climbers' trail marked by three more carabiner posts. The fourth post is within 15 feet of the wall and the start of Munginella. For Commitment and all routes to the right, climb the first 20 feet of the Munginella 3rd class and move way right on a ledge. Another option is, from the last carabiner post, to skirt the base of the wall down a few hundred feet then up.

Selaginella
The recommended approach is to climb any lower route at the Five Open Books.

As an alternate approach, follow the approach description above to the base of Munginella. From the fourth and last carabiner post, head west along the cliff to the streambed. Hike the streambed until you can climb slabs (4th class in early season when wet, 3rd class when dry). Move east (right) along the top of the slabs, following the well-traveled climbers' trail

east a few hundred yards to the base of the route. There are many similar-looking right-facing corners, so study the topo carefully. Don't leave anything at the base or you will have to go out of your way on the descent to retrieve it.

Descent

All routes except Selaginella
The descent takes about 15 minutes back to the base (no fun in climbing shoes). Walk west and a little down for a few hundred yards on a climbers' trail until you reach the open slabs area. Continue west across the slabs to a 3rd/4th class descent trail. Consider rappelling this section when wet with one 60m rope (or 50m rope by staying a bit to the left at the bottom). Below the slabs, follow the trail east and downward along the base, then slightly back uphill to the last carabiner post at the start of Munginella. Reverse the approach.

Selaginella
Walk the Yosemite Falls Trail for about one mile to Camp 4.

100
YOSEMITE VALLEY FREE CLIMBS

History

Climbers have always appreciated short approaches, so it's not surprising that the area around Lower Yosemite Fall attracted attention in the 1960s. Only minutes from Camp 4 lay a wealth of possible routes on the various tiers of cliffs. One trouble: these cliffs were not exactly composed of pristine granite. Trees, bushes, munge, loose dark rock—you name it, these cliffs had it. In a valley renowned for its sparkling white granite, this place was an aberration. But let's not forget that approach!

Wally Reed and Jim Posten were the first to explore the area. Five major open books could be seen on the first tier of cliffs, off to the left of the waterfall. But the next tier above looked cleaner, so they proceeded up to it and established a fine 5.7 route, later upticked to 5.8. Reed, fascinated by botany, named the climb Selaginella, after a fern-like plant found on the route.

In June 1966, Jim Bridwell and Phil and Dave Bircheff investigated the lowest tier and climbed the 5.9 Commitment, the second-from-the-left of the Five Open Books. The classic curving lieback on the third pitch was . . . committing!

That same summer Tom Fender and an unknown partner (cleverly called "Vic Tishous" in subsequent guidebooks) did the far-left book, the now-popular Munginella. The name, of course, is a takeoff on

The view from the base.

Selaginella, commemorating the vast amounts of vegetation encountered. Today, all three routes are clear of munge and brush.

– Steve Roper

A. Munginella   5.6★★★★

FA: Tom Fender and Vic Tishous, 1966.

The route name Munginella no longer accurately describes this climb. Every pitch features clean cracks and quality climbing. The route is sustained and challenging for 5.6 and more appropriate for 5.7 leaders. With a 60m rope you can climb the route in two pitches. Expect big crowds.

For some, finding the start is the crux as there is a huge 100-foot-tall right-facing corner to the left of Munginella that suckers in many climbers.

Pitch 2, the crux, requires a few committing face moves with protection below your feet. Use many long slings on this pitch to reduce rope drag. The last pitch is the best but if you need to pass climbers, consider the variation to the right. At the top belay, take extreme care not to send rocks onto climbers below. Retreat with one 60m or two 50m ropes. The first belay has fixed slings for rappelling. Up higher, you will need to leave gear in order to retreat.

B. Commitment   5.9★★★★

FA: Jim Bridwell, Dave Bircheff and Phil Bircheff, 6/66.

This climb warms up with two straightforward pitches before a memorable lieback crux. Although this is the first multi-pitch 5.9 for some climbers, the route's wild crux is, well, committing. It's possible to pull through most crux moves on gear. If too crowded, consider The Caverns or Try Again Ledge.

The first pitch ascends an awesome splitter. The third pitch is the clear crux of the route. It involves 5.9 lieback moves past solid protection. Use long slings around the roof or experience horrible rope drag up higher. Be extraordinarily careful not to drop rocks on the loose topout.

Retreat requires one 60m rope or two 50m ropes.

C. The Surprise   5.10a★★★

FA: Pete Spoecker and Steve Herrero, 4/65.

This is a dirty 5.8, a good 5.10a, or an awesome 5.10c depending on which pitches you start or finish on. We consider the 5.10a variation the standard route because the 5.8 original route is much less classic and more runout. Unlike most Five Open Books routes that ascend big corners, The Surprise mostly climbs splitter cracks on a clean face. This route is usually uncrowded. It's tricky but possible to pull through most of the crux sections on gear.

The 5.8 first two pitches ascend a corner to a sparsely-protected traverse right and then a decomposing ramp/downclimb. This section is difficult to protect and committing for the follower and has a dangerously sharp flake. Pitches 2 and 3 ascend an awesome splitter to a narrow ledge with a bolt. To climb the original route (not recommended), traverse right 10 feet before the narrow ledge on tenuous face to the dirty corner. The better finish is the steep and beautiful 5.10a crack straight above. This crack gets more difficult until you must make a psychological face move to a ledge. Retreat with one or two ropes by leaving gear.

To avoid the not-so-classic 5.8 first two pitches, consider the first pitch of Werner's Ant Trees. This pitch has sustained 5.10a/b moves to a bolt-protected steep 5.10c crux. It sets you up for the stellar upper pitches of The Surprise. Climbed this way the route gets at least four stars.

An obscure and thrilling variation called Old Surprise begins on the 5.8 start and continues up the huge right-facing corner. It involves 5.8 funky chickenwing underclinging with scant protection.

D. The Caverns   5.8★★★★

FA: Jerry Anderson and Jim Pettigrew, 1/70.

This is slightly easier and almost as good as Commitment. Most of the climbing is well-protected fun liebacking with occasional jams or face climbing. The first pitch, the route's crux, has a short but stout 5.8 lieback section. The second pitch is more sustained and features one airy lieback around a wide crack. This section is not possible to pull through on gear. Pitches 3 and 4 climb in or around the wild "Caverns." (See Try Again Ledge text for Pitches 2 and 3.)

Here is a first ascent story from Jerry Anderson: "The route is actually the result of carry-over partying from New Years Eve of 1970. Jim Pettigrew and I were drinking rum and Coke on January 1, 1970 and midday we had the bright idea of doing the first first ascent of the decade. Quite under the influence we got our gear and started off. The only excitement came on the second pitch when I managed to take about a 30-foot fall in an attempt to face climb around the crux 5.8 lieback. Now sobered up, we finished the climb without further mishap."

Brad Goya on the second pitch of The Surprise.

Chris McNamara

E. Try Again Ledge   5.8★★★

FA: Ed Leeper, Dave Trantor, and Steve Herrero, 6/64.

This route features one of the more
memorable moderate chimneys in Yosemite
that doesn't actually need much chimney
technique. The first pitch requires bold 5.8
climbing which keeps the crowds away and
makes the route overall more difficult than
The Caverns, Commitment, or Hanging
Teeth. The first move is the crux—a
committing lieback move with bad fall
potential into a tree. The pitch rarely lets up
and is difficult to protect and pull through
on gear making it only suitable for
confident 5.9 leaders.

The second pitch ascends the wild low-
angle chimney where it appears someone
used a jigsaw with a 2-foot-wide blade on
the rock. The protection is sparse but the
climbing is mostly 5.4 or easier. Anchor off
a questionably strong tree backed up with
cams. Start the last pitch with a well-
protected 5.7 lieback to a wild wide crack
step-across and then glorious hand
traversing. It's also possible to climb directly
in "The Caverns" or on the unprotected
face to the right. Protecting the last 50 feet
requires crack diving.

F. Hanging Teeth   5.8★★

FA: Jim Bridwell and Vic Tishous, 1968.

This memorable climb ascends the most
striking corner at Five Open Books. While
there are no single moves as technical as
Commitment, the route is more sustained
and much harder to protect. The route is
mostly a 5- to 7-inch crack in a huge corner
that is usually liebacked (there is only a
brief section of chimney). Unless you are
comfortable with 10- to 20-foot runouts,
bring a few pieces in the 5-7" range. Even
with big cams, it's not possible to pull
through many of the cruxes on gear. The
second pitch is the endurance crux and
requires sustained 5.7 to 5.8 liebacking. Use
slings to avoid rope drag. The third pitch is
a continuation of the second pitch and
dramatically deteriorates in quality about
40 feet from the top. The Delinquent
Checkup variation avoids this with some
wild hand traversing and awkward wide
moves to fun and slightly runout 5.6 face.

Chris McNamara

Climber on the splitter 5.8 first pitch of Commitment.

G. Selaginella   5.8★★★

FA: Wally Reed and Jim Posten, 9/63.

From lieback cracks and steep faces to
offwidths and chimneys, Selaginella
requires a full arsenal of climbing skills.
Prepare for committing and sustained 5.7
and 5.8 cracks all the way to the route's
great final crux. Because of the sustained
wide cracks and tricky routefinding, this
route is recommended for the more
experienced 5.8-5.9 leader.

There are two starting variations. The
recommended right start has many wide
cracks. An alternate start to the left features
meandering climbing and bad rope drag
and no wide cracks. As with all climbs at
the Five Open Books, the ledge at the top of
this route is loose. Be mindful of dislodging
rocks onto climbers below.

Retreat by rappelling the route with two
50m ropes.

More at SuperTopo.com

View a discussion of the rockfall danger at
Five Open Books so that you can assess the
danger for yourself.

A. Munginella 5.6★★★★
nuts: 1 set; cams, 2 ea .6-3", 1 ea 4", many long slings

B. Commitment 5.9★★★★
nuts: 1 set; cams: 2 ea .4", 2 ea .6-1", 2-3 ea 1.25-3"

C. The Surprise 5.10a★★★ nuts: 1 set; cams: 2 ea .5-1.5", 1 ea. 2-3"

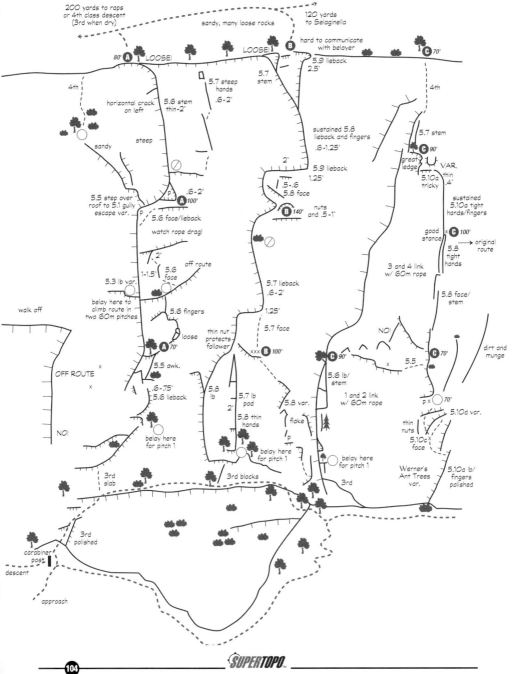

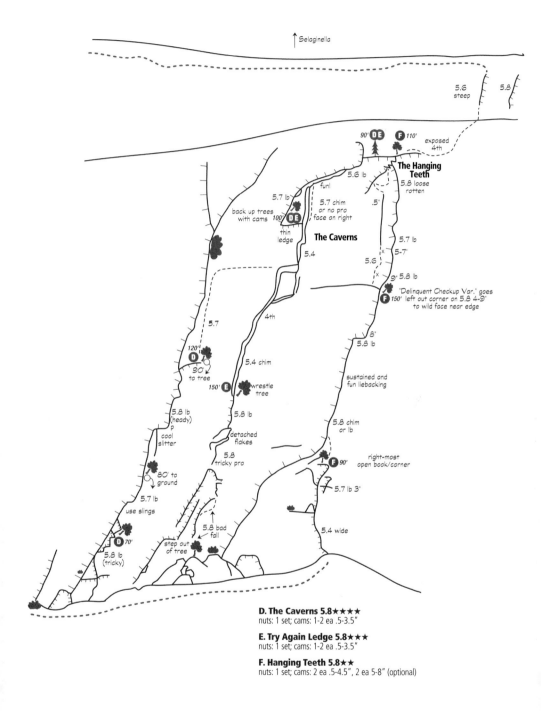

Selaginella

5.6 steep

5.8

90' **D E**   **F** 110'   exposed 4th

The Hanging Teeth

5.6 lb

5.8 loose rotten

fun!

5.7 lb   .5'

5.7 chim or no pro face on right

back up trees with cams   100' **D E**

thin ledge

The Caverns

5.7 lb

5.4   5-7"

5.6   x

x   9' 5.8 lb

"Delinquent Checkup Var." goes
150' left out corner on 5.8 4-9"
to wild face near edge   **F**

5.7

4th

8"
5.8 lb

sustained and fun liebacking

120' **D**
90' to tree

5.4 chim

150' **E**   wrestle tree

5.8 lb
(heady)
p
cool slitter

5.8 lb

detached flakes

5.8 chim or lb

5.8
tricky pro

F 90'   right-most open book/corner

80' to ground

5.7 lb   3"

5.7 lb

use slings

5.8 bad fall

5.4 wide

D 70'

step out of tree

5.8 lb
(tricky)

D. The Caverns 5.8★★★★
nuts: 1 set; cams: 1-2 ea .5-3.5"

E. Try Again Ledge 5.8★★★
nuts: 1 set; cams: 1-2 ea .5-3.5"

F. Hanging Teeth 5.8★★
nuts: 1 set; cams: 2 ea .5-4.5", 2 ea 5-8" (optional)

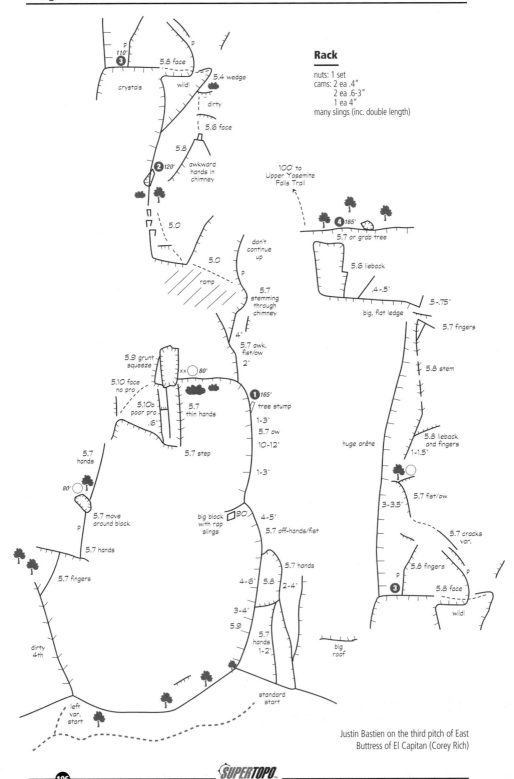

Rack

nuts: 1 set
cams: 2 ea .4"
      2 ea .6-3"
      1 ea 4"
many slings (inc. double length)

p
110'
❸ 5.8 face

crystals   wild!   5.4 wedge

dirty

5.6 face

5.8
❷ 120'   awkward
         hands in
         chimney

5.0

5.0   don't
ramp   continue
            up

4"
5.7 awk.
fist/ow
2"

100' to
Upper Yosemite
Falls Trail

❹ 165'
5.7 or grab tree

5.6 lieback

.4-.5'
.5-.75'
big, flat ledge

5.7 fingers

5.8 stem

5.7 stemming
through
chimney

5.9 grunt
squeeze

5.10 face
no pro

5.10b   .6"
poor pro

xx 80'

5.7
thin hands

5.7
hands

80' ❶

5.7 move
around block
p

5.7 hands

5.7 fingers

5.7 step

❶ 165'
tree stump
1-3"
5.7 ow
10-12"
1-3"

big block
with rap
slings 90
4-5"
5.7 off-hands/fist

5.7 hands

5.8 2-4"
4-6"

3-4"
5.9
5.7
hands
1-2'

standard
start

dirty
4th

left
var.
start

5.8 lieback
and fingers
1-1.5'

huge arête

3-3.5'   5.7 fist/ow

5.7 cracks
var.

5.8 fingers
p   p
❸   5.8 face

wild!

big
roof

Justin Bastien on the third pitch of East
Buttress of El Capitan (Corey Rich)

Sunnyside Bench

Approach time: **10 minutes**

Sun exposure: **morning to afternoon**

Height of routes: **160–400'**

East of the (seasonally) thundering Lower
Yosemite Fall, Sunnyside Bench features a
great introduction to Yosemite cracks in the
5.4 to 5.10 difficulty range. Other than the
Regular Route, most of the climbs are easy
to toprope. All routes face south and receive
sun until the late afternoon, so this can be a
good winter climbing spot. During the
summer, climb early in the morning or
after 5 P.M. when the routes become shaded.
Be aware that the mosquitoes can be
especially nasty in June.

Approach

From the Lower Yosemite Fall parking area,
0.3 miles east of Camp 4, walk north on the
paved trail toward the fall. Cross the bridge
at the base of the fall and continue east
along the trail for 100 yards. Stop where the
trail nears the rock wall. For the Regular
Route, move back left (west) along the base
for 100 feet to the obvious large
gully/corner. For Jamcrack and surrounding
climbs, move up and right (east) following
a climbers' trail that parallels the wall.

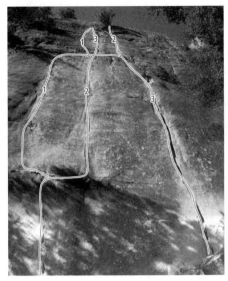

1	Bummer	**3**	Jamcrack
2	Lazy Bum		

Follow the switchbacks for 200 feet.
Jamcrack is the obvious hand crack leading
to a ledge 80 feet up.

Descent

Regular Route Descent
The descent takes about 30 minutes. From
the summit, walk up for 250 feet until you
meet a climbers' trail. Traverse right (east)
on the climbers' trail for about 300 yards
just above the steep slabs. Eventually the
trail starts to peter out and it is possible to
start working your way down to either an
open talus field or a drainage. These lead to
the Lower Yosemite Fall trail, which is
followed back to the start of the route.

Jamcrack and surrounding climbs descent
Descend all routes by rappelling. Two ropes
are required to swing and set a toprope on
Lemon, and to descend from Pitch 2 of
Lazy Bum. Otherwise, a single rope and two
rappels suffice to descend.

History

Where to take girls climbing? This was the
admittedly sexist question for climbers of a
much earlier generation—mine, in fact. Not
that we had anything special in mind, of
course, but it would be fun to find an easy

route, show off a little, and maybe even have a swim at the end. And what better place for this than Sunnyside Bench, with magnificent pools atop it. Even the name was bound to attract the fair sex. Not a "wall," not a "crack," but a bench. And presumably a sunny one at that.

No one knows who discovered the pools atop Lower Yosemite Fall, but it could well have been John Muir, known for prowling around this area (he lived for a few years only 150 yards from the waterfall). In any case, the Bench was well known to climbers of the 1930s. A class 4 route a few hundred yards right of the waterfall was the most direct way up, but one could get onto the Bench via an even easier way, much further east.

The route for which Sunnyside is now renowned for was climbed fairly late. Jamcrack was done with a bit of aid by Kim Schmitz and Loyd Price in 1967. Schmitz returned shortly thereafter to free the route—at 5.9—with Jim Madsen.

– Steve Roper

A. Regular Route   5.4★★★

FA: Unknown.

This is one the best 5.4 multi-pitch routes in Yosemite. While mostly low-angle 3rd and 4th class, the climb has a few exposed and well-protected 5.0-5.4 sections. This is an excellent first Yosemite multi-pitch climb with great views, and a chance to gain significant elevation while getting a feel for the granite. It is also the most direct access to the swimming pools above Lower Yosemite Fall. The climbing is relatively straight-forward but does require some adventurous routefinding and a few chimney moves that may be awkward (but manageable) for beginners. It's relatively easy to retreat with one or two ropes by rappelling the route from the fixed slings. Follow the topo carefully on Pitch 3 so you don't get lost.

B. Lemon   5.9★★

FA: Dave Sessions and Scott Burke, 8/79.

This route is strenuous to protect on lead and is much more appealing as a toprope.

Set a toprope by swinging left on a double-rope rappel from the Pitch 2 anchors on Jamcrack. It is difficult to reach from the Pitch 1 anchors. The route continues half a pitch, but is very dirty with bad bolts and seldom done.

C. Bummer   5.10c★★★

FA: Bruce Morris, Scott Cole, and Peter Thurston, 10/77.

The first pitch features good climbing with a desperate crux. It is usually toproped after climbing Pitch 1 of Jamcrack. Pitch 2 has excellent polished 5.9 face climbing, but is runout and easily toproped from the Pitch 2 anchors of Jamcrack.

D Lazy Bum   5.10d★★★

FA: Eric Beck and Steve Williams, 1971.
FFA: Chris Falkenstein et al, 1972.

Pitch 1 is an excellent finger crack/lieback that is usually toproped after climbing Pitch 1 of Jamcrack. A powerful finger crack start (shared with Bummer) leads to a positive and technical traverse right. Beautiful and sustained steep fingers leads to a thin and delicate 10-foot crux of liebacking (difficult to place pro at crux). Pitch 2 is an excellent technical and endurance challenge. Beware of the munge that is sometimes present if the pitch has not been recently climbed.

E. Jamcrack   5.9★★★

FA: Loyd Price and Kim Schmitz, 1967.
FFA: Kim Schmitz and Jim Madsen.

Because of its solid pro and short crux, Pitch 1 of Jamcrack is the first 5.7 crack lead for many Yosemite newcomers. Consequently, be prepared to wait in line unless you're starting early in the morning. As the name suggests, this is the perfect crack to enhance your hand and finger jamming techniques. You can pull through the cruxes on gear.

A belay can be set in the thin crack 10 feet right of the bolts (start of Pitch 2 of Lazy Bum) if crowds are occupying the bolts. If belaying from the bolts, be sure to set a directional. Linking the two pitches is not recommended due to the 20-foot traverse on the ledge.

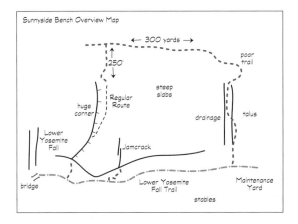

Sunnyside Bench Overview Map

← 300 yards →

250'

poor trail

steep slabs

Regular Route

huge corner

drainage

talus

Lower Yosemite Fall

Jamcrack

bridge

Lower Yosemite Fall Trail

stables

Maintenance Yard

A. Regular Route 5.4★★★
nuts: 1 set; cams: 1 ea .6-2", many slings

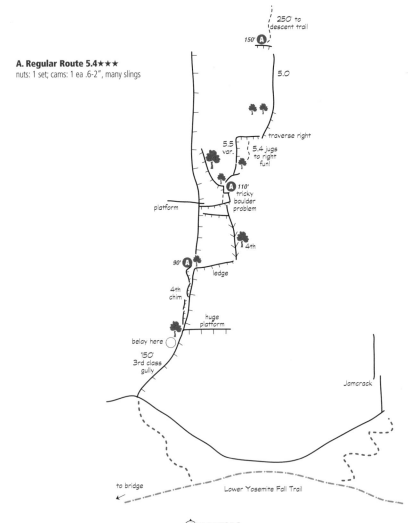

250' to descent trail

150' Ⓐ

5.0

traverse right

5.5 var.

5.4 jugs to right fun!

Ⓐ 110' tricky boulder problem

platform

4th

90' Ⓐ

ledge

4th chim

huge platform

belay here ○

150' 3rd class gully

Jamcrack

to bridge

Lower Yosemite Fall Trail

B. Lemon 5.9★★ nuts: 1 set; cams: 1 ea .4", 2 ea .75-3"

C. Bummer 5.10c★★★ nuts: 1 set; cams: 1 ea .5-2"

D. Lazy Bum 5.10d★★★ nuts:1 set; cams: 2 ea .5-1", 1 ea 1.25-1.5"

E. Jamcrack 5.9★★★ nuts: 1 set; cams: 1 ea .4-.5", 1 ea 2-3", 2 ea .6-1.5"

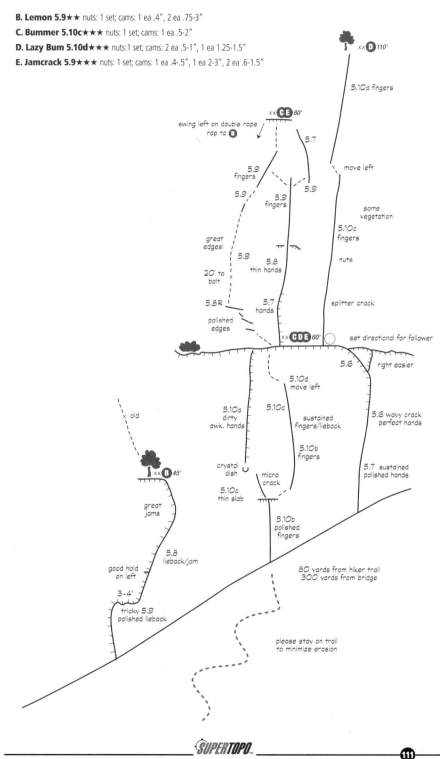

xx **D** 110'

5.10a fingers

xx **C E** 80'

swing left on double rope
rap to **B**

5.7

move left

5.9
fingers

5.9

5.9

some
vegetation

5.9

5.9
fingers

5.10c
fingers

great
edges!

5.9

5.8
thin hands

nuts

20' to
bolt   x

5.8R

5.7
hands

splitter crack

polished
edges

xx **C D E** 60'

set directional for follower

5.6

right easier

5.10d
move left

x old

5.10a
dirty
awk. hands

5.10c

5.6 wavy crack
perfect hands

sustained
fingers/lieback

5.10b
fingers

5.7 sustained
polished hands

xx **B** 45'

crystal
dish

micro
crack

great
jams

5.10c
thin slab

5.10b
polished
fingers

5.8
lieback/jam

good hold
on left

80 yards from hiker trail
300 yards from bridge

3-4"

tricky 5.9
polished lieback

please stay on trail
to minimize erosion

Arrowhead Arête

These are obscure classics with heinous approaches and adventurous climbing. Often mistaken with the cooler-looking Yosemite Point Buttress, both Arrowhead Arête and Arrowhead Spire appear unremarkable until you are climbing on them. The location high above the Valley offers great views of Half Dome and Glacier Point as well as the less aesthetic buildings of the Maintenance Yard.

Chris McNamara

Approach

The approach takes about 2-3 hours, is about 1.5 miles long, and gains 1,500 feet of elevation. It has steep and exposed 3rd and 4th class, and involves tricky routefinding.

From the west corner of the Church Bowl parking area, follow a wide hikers' trail. The trail gradually climbs then begins to descend. After 5-10 minutes, at one of the few clearings and when the trail is dropping, spot the steep and sandy switchbacks on the right. These switchbacks start out poor but quickly improve (it's the old Indian Canyon Trail) then eventually deteriorate again. After 30 minutes of steep uphill and shaded hiking, you'll reach a clearing below 100 feet of dirty 4th class ledges. At the top of the 4th class, angle slightly up and left to the base of a steep wall and then traverse the base of the wall up and left (south). Stay close to the wall, first going up a short ways, then descending a few hundred feet before finally traversing without gaining or losing elevation. Eventually, you turn a corner and reach the steep and wide West Arrowhead Chimney, the crux of the approach. Immediately traverse to the left (west) side of the gully and climb about a hundred feet of sandy 3rd and 4th class that angles back right into the main gully. Continue up the gully to the base of the climbs. Leave your pack here.

Descent

This descent is long, strenuous, and no fun. Allow 1 hour of travel from the last pitch to the base of the route and another 1.5-2 hours from there back to the car. Carry your approach shoes on the climb to use for the descent.

From the last pitch, descend 20 feet west and traverse across a sandy and exposed ledge. Pass through a slot and work up a little (you may see an optional tree rappel left). Keep traversing, going up only when forced to. Eventually scramble down dirty 4th class to the big gully. The gully is mostly scree and talus with three 80-foot rappels over wild chockstones. Be very careful not to knock rocks onto your partner.

From the base of the climbs, reverse the approach. You can avoid the first section of 4th class you encounter with an 80-foot rappel off slings around a tree.

For the seldom-used alternate descent, scramble up 4th class from the last pitch to the rim and descend the Yosemite Falls Trail.

GPS Coordinates

Parking area: 37 44.899, 119 34.862
Leave hikers' trail for steep switchbacks: 37 45.090, 119 35.254
First clearing before 4th class: 37 45.280, 119 35.365
Midway through big traverse to West Arrowhead Chimney: 37 45.447, 119 35.355
End of climbing route: 37 45.411, 119 35.316

Arrowhead Arête 5.9★★★

Time to climb route:	**4-7 hours**
Approach time:	**2-3 hours**
Descent time:	**2-3 hours**
Sun exposure:	**morning to afternoon**
Height of route:	**700'**

This is adventure climbing at its best, especially when linked with Arrowhead Spire. The route is obscure and committing with incredible exposure and a cool knife-edge ridge finish—a Yosemite rarity. With a few exceptions, most pitches are high quality and well-protected, and you'll climb everything from wide cracks to faces. While you can pull through most of the cruxes on gear, this route is only appropriate for confident and fast 5.9 leaders.

Strategy

Climbing this route requires a huge day so start early, as the descent can become epic in the dark. Usually you have the climb to yourself, but occasionally the route is crowded. The climb receives sun all day and despite its high elevation can be too hot in the summer. Spring and fall are the best times to climb. Most belays except for the first are on great ledges. There is not much benefit to bringing a 60m rope.

Start on Arrowhead Spire because you not only avoid the lame approach pitch of Arrowhead Arête, but you also bag an incredible summit. The second pitch starts off a little loose then gets steeper and harder with a tricky move to get from the stemming corner into the wide crack.

The crux third pitch begins with devious routefinding followed by an awkward and wild bulge/stemming corner. From here, the climbing remains sustained and interesting for two pitches until the single unaesthetic pitch before the secure but wickedly exposed knife-edge ridge. Ahh, the knife edge ridge . . . what a finish! In some places the leader may want to belay the follower ahead and break up the ridge into a few pitches. Keep in mind that most routefinding problems on the route are solved by moving right.

Retreat

Retreat Pitches 1-4 by rappelling the climbing route. After Pitch 4, it's probably easier to finish the climb than reverse the pitch. It's possible to retreat with one 60m rope but you will have to leave gear.

A. Arrowhead Spire   5.6★★

This is a great start to Arrowhead Arête but isn't worth the burly approach and descent for the climb itself. This is an old school 5.6 meaning that there is a fair amount of wide awkward climbing that makes it feel much harder. The climbing isn't great but the summit is. From there, you get a superb view of Arrowhead Arête.

Michael Feldman on Pitch 4 of the Arête with the Spire below.

Chris McNamara

Arrowhead Arête	Pitch 1	2	3	4
Free difficulty ≥5.10	●	●	●	
5.9				●
5.8				
5.7				
5.6				
≤5.5				

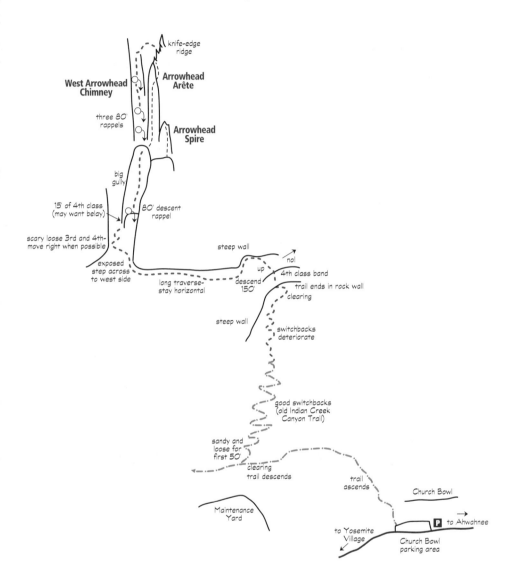

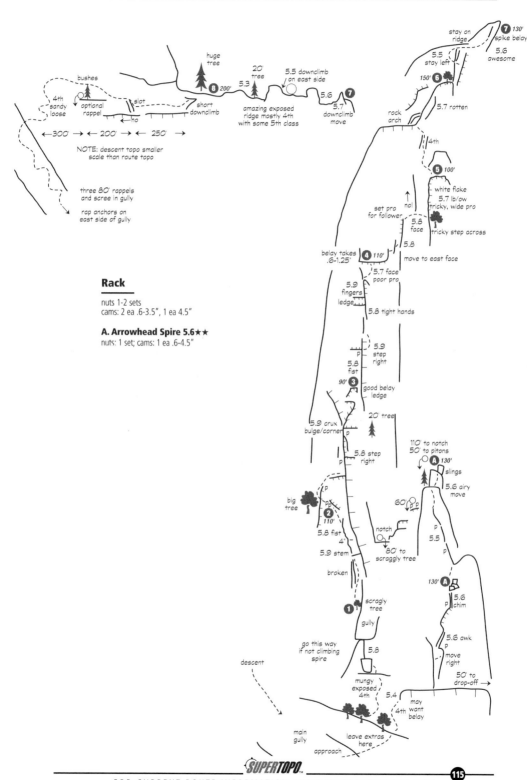

huge tree

🎄 **8** 200'

bushes

4th sandy loose

⭕ optional rappel

slot

no

short downclimb

20' tree

5.3

5.5 downclimb on east side

⭕

5.6

5.7 downclimb move

7

amazing exposed ridge mostly 4th with some 5th class

←300'→ ←200'→ ←250'→

NOTE: descent topo smaller scale than route topo

three 80' rappels and scree in gully

rap anchors on east side of gully

stay on ridge

7 130' spike belay

5.5 stay left

5.6 awesome

150' **6** 🎄

5.7 rotten

rock arch

4th

5 100'

white flake
5.7 lb/ow tricky, wide pro

🎄 tricky step across

5.8 face

5.8

move to east face

set pro for follower

no!

belay takes .6-1.25"

4 110'

5.7 face poor pro

5.9 fingers ledge

5.8 tight hands

Rack

nuts 1-2 sets
cams: 2 ea .6-3.5", 1 ea 4.5"

A. Arrowhead Spire 5.6★★
nuts: 1 set; cams: 1 ea .6-4.5"

5.9 step right

5.8 fist

p

90' **3**

good belay ledge

20' tree

5.9 crux bulge/corner

p

p

5.8 step right

p

110' to notch
50' to pitons

⭕ **A** 130'

slings

5.6 airy move

60' ⭕ p p

big tree
🎄

p

p

2 110'

5.8 fist

4'

5.9 stem

broken

notch

80' to scraggly tree

p

5.5

p

1 🎄 1

scragly tree

gully

go this way if not climbing spire

5.8

🪣

descent

mungy exposed 4th

🎄🎄 leave extras here

🎄

130' **A** 🔧

p 5.6 chim

5.6 awk

p move right

50' to drop-off →

5.4

4th

may want belay

main gully

approach

Church Bowl

Approach time: **1 minute**

Sun exposure: **morning to afternoon**

Height of routes: **175'**

Located between Yosemite Village and the Ahwahnee Hotel, Church Bowl is the Valley's most accessible crag for easy and moderate routes. Church Bowl served as a proving ground in the early development of climbing techniques. The routes remain great training for everything from classic Yosemite chimneys to thin piton scars (for both aid and free climbing practice) to hand jams. The routes have solid protection and easy retreats. There are enough climbs here for a full day of cragging.

Conditions in the spring and fall are perfect. In the summer, climb in the afternoon when the routes go into the shade. For a good link-up of progressively harder finger, hand, and lieback climbs, do Bishop's Terrace followed by Church Bowl Tree and Book of Revelations. Beware of sand on climbs after rainstorms.

Approach

Park 0.3 miles east of Yosemite Village, toward the Ahwahnee Hotel, at the Church Bowl picnic/parking area (a small brown sign can be seen beyond the trash cans). Walk 100 yards to the cliff. If you go to the left through the bushes, you first come to Revival; if you follow the open woods to the right, you come to the cliff between Book of Revelations and Church Bowl Tree.

Descent

Descend all routes by rappel—most require two ropes.

History

Climbers love short approaches, and the Church Bowl area just about wins any timed contest for car-to-cliff. The Church Bowl Chimney, a deep and nasty-looking cleft, was the first route to be done here, probably in the 1950s. Rated only 5.6, this strenuous route today stymies many gym climbers.

Chris McNamara

1	Black is Brown	5	Book of Revelations
2	Uncle Fanny	6	Church Bowl Chimney
3	Church Bowl Lieback	7	Bishop's Terrace
4	Aunt Fanny's Pantry		

Next to fall was Bishop's Terrace. In late December 1959 I spied a beautiful set of jamcracks on the wall above and right of Church Bowl Chimney. Armed with the latest technology—heavy steel inch-and-a-half angle pitons—Dave McFadden, Russ Warne, and I swarmed up the easy lower section. But I didn't know squat about pure jamcracks, and I was scared to boot. To my everlasting shame I used two points of aid on the upper crack. Naturally, the route went free as soon as good climbers got on it, and this happened within months. It was Chuck Pratt who led the first free ascent, so I didn't feel too bad.

Sheridan Anderson came along five years later to put up the pleasant Aunt Fanny's Pantry with Leo LeBon. Sheridan was a true character, a mediocre climber with a love of beer and parties. His satirical climbing cartoons, mostly published in Summit, delighted us for a decade.

Next came the longest route in this area, Book of Revelations, first climbed in 1965 by Gordie Webster and Chuck Ostin. This pair used a fair amount of aid on their five-pitch line, but the route was freed nine years later (with the help of pin scars) at 5.11a by Bob Finn and Chris Falkenstein.

– Steve Roper

A. Black is Brown   5.8★★

FA: Kim Schmitz and Frank Trummel, 1966.

A moderate quality steep crack. Rappel to descend. You can also descend 4th class to the left (west).

B. Deja Thorus   5.10a★

FA: Jim Beyer and Misa Giesey, 1978.

This route involves sustained liebacking with a few face moves. It is not a popular lead, but a fun toprope from the Uncle Fanny belay anchors. Multiple directionals must be set down the flake for toproping, since a nasty fall into the corner could otherwise result.

C. Uncle Fanny   5.7★★

FA: Bruce Price and Michael McLean, 1/70.

A good introduction to chimney climbing. Low angle chimney has excellent 1-2" gear in back. Above, put left side of body into the crack and use heel/toe technique.

D. Church Bowl Lieback   5.8★★★★

This is one of the best climbs at the crag. Use many long slings and take the left finish. This is a good lead reach toprope anchors for other nearby climbs. To belay for a toprope, scramble up to the ledge 10 feet above the ground.

E. Pole Position   5.10a★★

FA: John Harpole et al, late 1980s.

A good introductory friction climb that is unfortunately situated with a nasty fall onto a tree for the leader (or follower) after the second bolt. Excellent climbing on knobs and edges higher. Use directionals on the bolts if toproping.

F. Revival   5.10a★★

Great crack climbing followed by face moves. Use many long slings to avoid rope drag. If toproping, climb straight up from the ground on either side of a large block.

G. Aunt Fanny's Pantry   5.4★

FA: Sheridan Anderson and Leo LeBon, 1965.

This easy and unaesthetic chimney is a good entry-level climb and can be used to access toprope anchors.

H. Book of Revelations   5.11a★★★★

FA: Gordon Webster, Chuck Ostin, 10/65.
FFA: Bob Finn, Chris Falkenstein, 1974.

An extremely awkward crux after 20 feet is followed by hard moves and difficult rests. The crux is often wet during early season and the upper pitches (not shown) are rarely climbed.

I. Church Bowl Tree   5.10b★★★

FA: Mark Jefferson and Dave Collins, 8/70.

Great training for free climbing or hammerless aiding on pin scars. The route involves finger jams in scars and balancy mantels. Getting off the ground can be tricky due to the polish. Most climbers only do the first pitch.

J. Church Bowl Chimney   5.6★★

The next step in chimney training after Uncle Fanny. Great route for doing laps and practicing steep stemming.

K. Energizer   5.11b★★★

FA: Dan and Sue McDevitt, 1990.

Well-protected with bolts, this is a great climb to get comfortable on steep Yosemite face climbing. The crux consists of smears and delicate balancy moves to small edges.

L. Bitches' Terror   5.11a★★★

FA: Walt Shipley and Eric Kohl, 1990.

A quality steep face climb. Approach via the first short pitch of Bishop's Terrace, or better yet, warm up on Bishop's Terrace then rappel 80 feet down and left to the bolt anchor at the start.

M. Bishop's Terrace   5.8★★★★★

FA: Russ Warne, Dave McFadden, and Steve Roper, 12/59.
FFA: Chuck Pratt and Herb Swedlund, 1960.

One of the best 5.8 hand cracks in the Valley. The left start is recommended. Climb in two pitches with 50m ropes or in one pitch with a 60m rope using many slings down low. The climbing consists of glorious hand jams, a brief wide section, and double cracks. If using the alternate right start, it is possible to climb to the upper anchors with one 50m rope. You need a second rope to rappel to the ground.

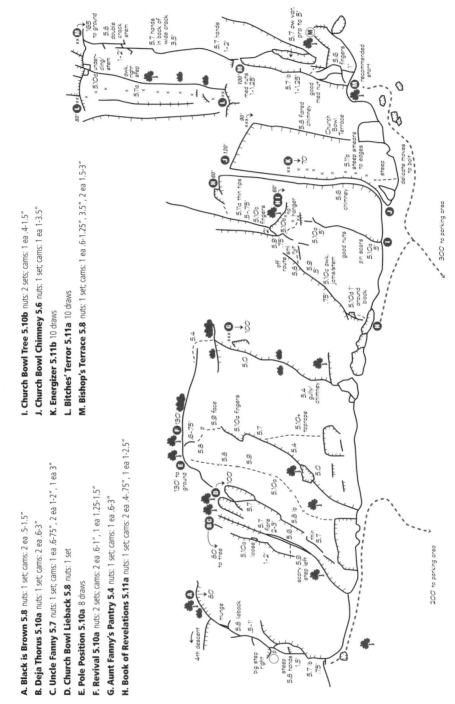

A. **Black is Brown 5.8** nuts: 1 set; cams: 2 ea .5-1.5"

B. **Deja Thorus 5.10a** nuts: 1 set; cams: 2 ea .6-3"

C. **Uncle Fanny 5.7** nuts: 1 set; cams: 1 ea .6-.75", 2 ea 1-2", 1 ea 3"

D. **Church Bowl Lieback 5.8** nuts: 1 set

E. **Pole Position 5.10a** 8 draws

F. **Revival 5.10a** nuts: 2 sets; cams: 2 ea .6-1", 1 ea 1.25-1.5"

G. **Aunt Fanny's Pantry 5.4** nuts: 1 set; cams: 1 ea .6-3"

H. **Book of Revelations 5.11a** nuts: 1 set; cams: 2 ea .4-.75", 1 ea 1-2.5"

I. **Church Bowl Tree 5.10b** nuts: 2 sets; cams: 1 ea .4-1.5"

J. **Church Bowl Chimney 5.6** nuts: 1 set; cams: 1 ea 1-3.5"

K. **Energizer 5.11b** 10 draws

L. **Bitches' Terror 5.11a** 10 draws

M. **Bishop's Terrace 5.8** nuts: 1 set; cams: 1 ea .6-1.25", 3.5", 2 ea 1.5-3"

Timmy O'Neill on Fun Terminal (5.12a). (Corey Rich)

Royal Arches Area

Chris McNamara

Located on the immense wall west of Washington Column, a series of gigantic, water-stained corners and roofs rise 1,400 feet to form Royal Arches. The actual arches are clogged with dirt, water, and vegetation and comprise one of the more notorious and unpleasant climbs in Yosemite: Arches Direct. However, to the left side of Royal Arches lie a number of spectacular climbs including the confusingly-named Royal Arches, Serenity Crack, Sons of Yesterday, and Super Slide.

All climbs face south and receive sun all day. Climbing in summer is uncomfortably hot until you are up a few pitches and get a breeze. Fall and spring are ideal. Winter is great if the routes aren't wet. The longer routes, especially Sons of Yesterday, can be subject to high winds.

1	Super Slide	5	Royal Arches
2	Serenity Crack	6	Arête Butler
3	Sons of Yesterday	7	Y Crack
4	Peruvian Flake	8	Royal Arches Rap Route

Approach

Peruvian Flake, Serenity Crack, Sons of Yesterday, and Super Slide
From the northeast corner of the Ahwahnee parking lot, take the hikers' trail east. After 250 feet, just before a stream crossing (may be dry in summer and fall), locate a climbers' trail on the left. Follow this for 100 feet then move right for Peruvian Flake. For Serenity Crack and Sons of Yesterday, skirt the base up left for another 100 yards to the second major corner system on the right. Scramble up 4th class to a platform. For Super slide, continue skirting the base for another few hundred feet to another obvious 4th class corner on the right.

Royal Arches and Arête Butler
From the northeast corner of the Ahwahnee parking lot, take the hikers' trail east. After 120 yards and 50 feet after a stream crossing (may be dry in summer and fall), locate a climbers' trail on the left. Follow this for 150 feet to a large left-facing corner and the start of the route. For Arête Butler and the alternate Royal Arches starts, skirt the base to the east (right).

Arches Terrace
From the northeast corner of the Ahwahnee parking lot, take the hikers' trail east. When it descends down and almost touches the wall, leave the main trail and skirt the base. Climb faint switchbacks for a few hundred feet and then reach the base of the wall and continue traversing right. Once below the huge open slab right of the enormous corner, continue skirting the base for another few hundred feet down until you can walk out on a ledge, behind a bushy tree, to the start of a distinct left-facing corner.

Royal Arches Area Overview Map

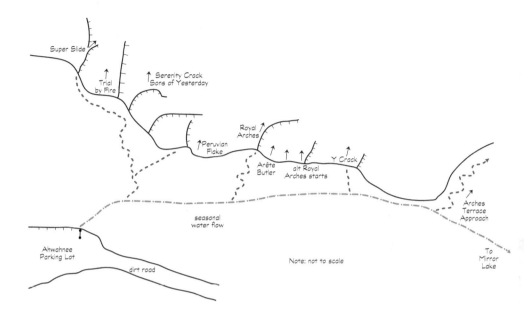

Descent

Super Slide
Rappel the route with two 50m or 60m ropes. At Pitch 3, rappel straight down to a bushy tree and then to the ground.

Serenity Crack and Sons of Yesterday
Rappel the route with two 50m or 60m ropes. From Pitch 2 of Serenity Crack, use the rap anchors to the west of the route (can rap these pitches with one 60m rope).

Royal Arches Descent:

1) Royal Arches Rappel Route
This is the recommended descent (see Royal Arches Rappel Route topo). It requires two 50m ropes or one 60m rope and starts from Pitch 15 of the Royal Arches route. This descent takes 2-3 hours.

2) North Dome Trail to Yosemite Falls Trail
This 8.5 mile descent takes 4-6 hours, requires strenuous cross-country hiking, but has little exposure and no rappels. From the top of Royal Arches, walk north for about 1 mile (no clear trail) and pick up the North Dome trail. Walk west for about 4 miles to the Yosemite Falls Trail. Walk 3.6 miles down to Camp 4.

3) North Dome Gully
If you have North Dome Gully wired, it's the fastest descent from Royal Arches. It takes about 2 hours if you're familiar with the descent, but can take 4 hours if it's your first time and you get off route. See the North Dome Gully Descent description for more information. If not familiar with North Dome Gully, then use the Royal Arches Rappel Route.

Super Slide 5.9★★★

Time to climb route: **3-5 hours**

Approach time: **10 minutes**

Descent time: **1 hour**

Sun exposure: **morning to sunset**

Height of route: **500'**

Super Slide ascends mostly well-protected and sustained 5.7 to 5.8 hand cracks. After a few wandering approach pitches, the bulk of the route follows tasty crack systems in an excellent exposed position. The moves are consistently fun with an exceptional finishing crack. This is a good introduction to 5.9 multi-pitch climbs. You can pull through all cruxes on gear except on the second pitch.

FA: Gene Drake and Rex Spaith, 1971.

Chris McNamara

Strategy

Most climbers rope up for the standard 5.2 start. For more climbing, start on Trial By Fire (5.8) followed by two pitches of wandering and mungy 4th and moderate 5th class with bolted belays.

The only poorly protected part of the climb comes on the second pitch. At the top of this pitch, manage the rope carefully or you may drop rocks on your belayer.

Now the climb gets good. The next three pitches become gradually harder as you alternate between liebacking, stemming, and straight-in jams. All the belay stations were recently rebolted by the American Safe Climbing Association. The final 40 feet of the last pitch are gorgeous.

On the last rappel of the descent, consider setting a toprope on Rupto Pac (5.11c) for some delicate slab practice.

Retreat

Retreat by rappelling with two 50m or 60m ropes.

A. Trial by Fire   5.8★★★

FA: Chris Falkenstein and Don Reid, 3/74.

A clean and sustained wide crack that varies from a groove to a chimney with a distinct awkward crux halfway. Climb two more wandering pitches to join Super Slide. Two ropes are needed to toprope.

B. Demimonde   5.11c★★★

FA: Eric Mayo, Andy Roberts, Dave Caunt, and Rick Harlin, 1991.

This sustained and demanding steep face climb is relatively well-protected. Two ropes are needed to toprope. It is also possible to rappel left of Trial by Fire and set a toprope from a tree on Peter's Out, a cool 5.12 thin crack on the slab.

Super Slide		Pitch 1	2	3	4	5
Free difficulty	≥5.10					
	5.9					●
	5.8				●	
	5.7		●	●		
	5.6					
	≤5.5	●				

Rack

nuts: 1 set
cams: 1-2 ea .6-3.5"

A. Trial by Fire 5.8★★★
nuts: 1 set; cams: 2 ea .75-4.5"

B. Demimonde 5.11c★★★
10 quickdraws

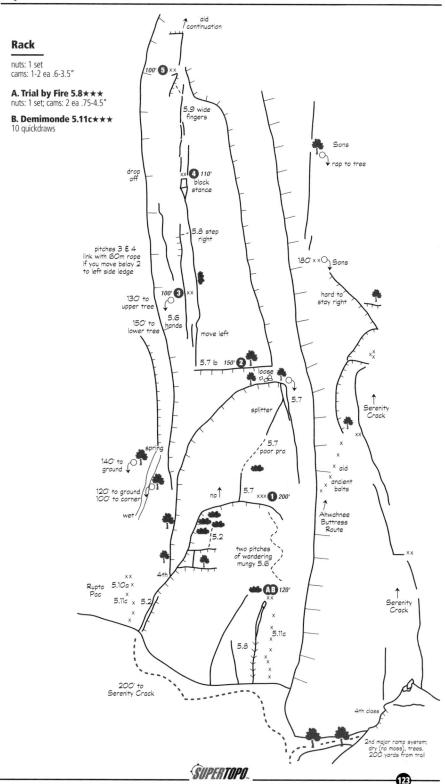

Serenity Crack 5.10d★★★★★

Time to climb route: **3 hours**

Approach time: **5 minutes**

Descent time: **30 minutes**

Sun exposure: **morning to sunset**

Height of route: **400'**

This route climbs a continuous 400-foot pin-scarred crack right above the Ahwahnee Hotel. The scars are ugly but fun to climb and sometimes involve unusual pinches and jams. As you climb higher the scars diminish and the difficulties increase. The short, powerful 5.10d finger crack crux on the last pitch has decent protection, a clean fall, and is an excellent place to push your free climbing limits to a higher level. You can pull through all the cruxes on gear except for the first pitch.

History

Anyone who doubts that pitons can damage granite should check out this climb. The dozens of atrocious pin scars on the lower route allow the line to go free at a moderate rating—a mixed blessing. Glen Denny and Les Wilson established this classic in 1961, using huge amounts of aid up a long, bottomed seam that could hardly be called a crack. The team battered chrome-moly pitons into this seam an inch or so and then tied them off. Since it was a perfect place to learn the art of moderate aid climbing, the route was done hundreds of times in the early 1960s. The scars appeared early on for the simplest reason: steel is harder than granite. The back-and-forth pounding done during piton removal scraped out a hole in the seam, and this is where the next party would place its own pin. When an excavation became wider than it was

Serenity Crack		Pitch 1	2	3
Free difficulty	≥5.10	●	●	●
	5.9			
	5.8			
	5.7			
	5.6			
	≤5.5			

A stellar day on the Royal Arches. (Corey Rich)

deep—meaning the pin placement could get dicey—the process would begin once again in an untouched part of the seam. It's amazing that any portion of the original seam is visible!

By 1967 so many holes existed that many people were doing the lower two pitches free: this segment had become a 10a jamcrack! A much harder section at the top of the route—a steep and strenuous finger crack—resisted free attempts for a time, but Tom Higgins and Chris Jones managed the feat in 1967. For several years this short section, rated 5.11, stood as one of the toughest free climbs in the Valley. Around 1976 it was downgraded to 5.10d.

– Steve Roper

Strategy

Serenity Crack is extremely popular. If the route is too crowded, consider climbing Super Slide. In early season, the first 50 feet are wet, making this infamous, hard-to-protect section even more intimidating. A few poor cam placements lead to a bolt 35 feet up, the first solid protection.

Pitch 2 has two options: climb 30 feet and traverse to the right crack (less intimidating) or climb up all the way to where the crack ends and make delicate face moves and a big reach (very intimidating). Use many slings to avoid rope drag.

The third pitch crux has few footholds and gear is strenuous to place. Some hang out and place gear while more confident climbers run out the bulk of the crux. The variation to Pitch 3 is easier, but much less classic. The rock is slightly decomposing in sections and the gear can be tricky.

While some climb only Serenity Crack and then rappel, it is a crime to quit before doing Sons of Yesterday. The combination of the two climbs is probably the best and most sustained 5.10 crack route in Yosemite.

Retreat

Retreat by rappelling with two 50m or one 60m rope using bolt anchors west of the route.

Sons of Yesterday 5.10a★★★★★

Time to climb route:	**3-3.5 hours**
Approach time:	**2-3 hours**
Descent time:	**1 hour**
Sun exposure:	**morning to sunset**
Height of route:	**500'**

Sons of Yesterday is a beautiful, consistent line soaring up the buttress beyond Serenity Crack. To approach the route, you must climb Serenity Crack, or one of several hard free or aid routes leading to Sunset Ledge. Pitch 4 of Sons is perhaps the single best hand crack splitting a clean face of granite in Yosemite. Up higher, the route offers four more pitches of exposed and strenuous cracks, mostly in the thin hands and hands size. The link-up of Serenity Crack to Sons of Yesterday offers the best and most consistent 5.10 crack climbing in Yosemite. You can pull through most cruxes on gear.

Strategy

A fair number of parties rappel after Serenity Crack, tending to reduce the traffic on Sons. However, unless you are one of the first groups up, the parties rapping down on you can be annoying and time consuming. It's easy and common to be hit by pulled ropes and more than a few climbers have come away with rope burns from descending parties. Serenity requires many smaller cams; Sons requires many medium to hand-sized protection.

The 5.10a second pitch can be more of a challenge than even the crux pitch of Serenity if you are not strong on off-fingers, slightly flared jamming. The perfect hand crack on this takes only 1-1.25" protection for about 60-70 feet. While the bomber

hands allow most to comfortably run the pitch out, only two 2" cams will prevent a huge fall.

The key to the first 5.10a pitch is to stay calm, concentrate on your feet and trust the often tenuous off-finger jams. The bulk of this pitch requires endurance with its steep thin hands and hands. To negotiate the crux, the offwidth bypass, move left on slippery 5.10a face with no crack to plug pro. At the belay, while standing on the tree manage the rope carefully. It is easy to snag the rope on the tree's hidden branch stubs, which can cause problems for the leader on the next pitch.

On Pitch 5, a cool, traversing, offset off-finger crack heads left. If you traverse with your hands in the crack, it is possible to place pro, but it's hard. Alternatively, if you place a piece and then carefully "walk the plank" on the one-inch offset ledge, there will be no hand holds and no chance to place pro. This option is much easier, but scary! The wide crack at the end of this pitch is easy even if you have no offwidth experience. Simple liebacks to the left, with careful footjams, gain the top quickly. A 4 inch cam protects this well, but most people just run this section out rather than carry the extra weight of the piece.

The 6th pitch, a short slab to a tree, is rarely done.

All anchors were replaced by the ASCA in 1998.

Retreat

Rap the route with two 50m or 60m ropes then rappel Serenity Crack.

E. Peruvian Flake   5.10a★★★

FA: Bruce Morris, Kevin Leary, and Bill Taylor.

This climb's start is difficult, but quickly eases making it an ideal first 5.10 lead. The protection is solid, especially at the distinct 5.10a finger crack crux. You can barely toprope the climb with a 60m rope. (Bring a few extra big cams and long slings to extend the anchor.) Descend by scrambling back to the wall and then down 3rd class (wet in spring).

		Pitch					
Sons of Yesterday		**1**	**2**	**3**	**4**	**5**	**6**
Free difficulty	≥5.10	●			●		
	5.9		●	●			
	5.8					●	
	5.7						
	5.6	●					
	≤5.5						

SUPERTOPO

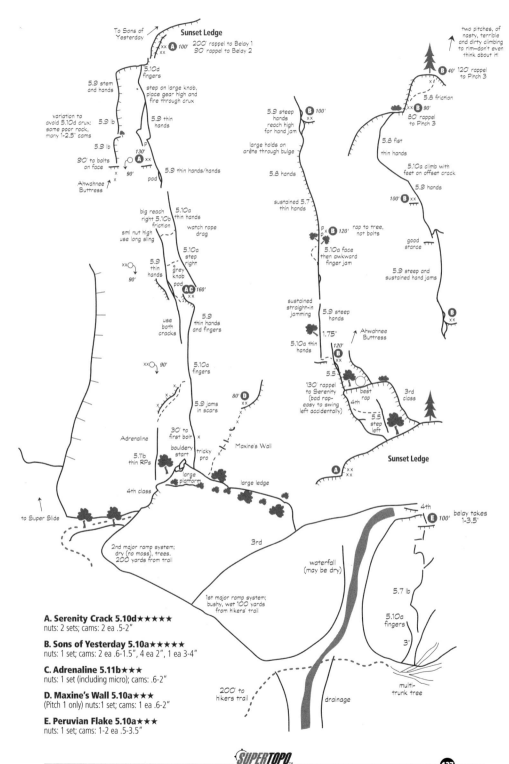

To Sons of Yesterday

Sunset Ledge

A xx xx 100' 200' rappel to Belay 1
90' rappel to Belay 2

5.10d fingers

step on large knob, place gear high and fire through crux

5.9 stem and hands

variation to avoid 5.10d crux: some poor rock, many 1-2.5" cams

5.9 lb

5.9 thin hands

5.9 lb

A xx 130'
90' to bolts on face
x 90'
x

Ahwahnee Buttress

5.9 thin hands/hands

pod

big reach right 5.10b friction

5.10a thin hands

watch rope drag

sml nut high use long sling

5.10a step right

grey knob pod

5.9 thin hands

AC xx 160'

use both cracks

5.9 thin hands and fingers

xx 90'

5.10a fingers

5.9 jams in scars

80' **D** xx

30' to first bolt x

Adrenaline

5.11b thin RPs

bouldery start

tricky pro

Maxine's Wall

4th class

large platform

large ledge

to Super Slide

2nd major ramp system; dry (no moss), trees. 200 yards from trail

3rd

1st major ramp system; bushy, wet 100 yards from hikers' trail

5.9 steep hands reach high for hand jam

B xx 100'

large holds on arête through bulge

5.8 hands

sustained 5.7 thin hands

p x **B** 120' rap to tree, nat bolts

5.10a face then awkward finger jam

sustained straight-in jamming

5.9 steep hands

1.75"

5.10a thin hands

5.10a thin hands **B** xx 120'

5.5

130' rappel to Serenity (bad rap- easy to swing left accidentally)

best rap

4th

5.5 step left

Ahwahnee Buttress

B xx

3rd class

Sunset Ledge

A xx xx

two pitches, of nasty, terrible and dirty climbing to rim—don't even think about it!

B 40' 120' rappel to Pitch 3

5.8 friction

B xx 90' 80' rappel to Pitch 3

5.8 fist
thin hands

5.10a climb with feet on offset crack

5.9 hands

100' **B** xx

good stance

5.9 steep and sustained hand jams

B xx

4th **E** 100' belay takes 1-3.5"

waterfall (may be dry)

5.7 lb

5.10a fingers

3'

multi-trunk tree

200' to hikers trail

drainage

A. Serenity Crack 5.10d★★★★★
nuts: 2 sets; cams: 2 ea .5-2"

B. Sons of Yesterday 5.10a★★★★★
nuts: 1 set; cams: 2 ea .6-1.5", 4 ea 2", 1 ea 3-4"

C. Adrenaline 5.11b★★★
nuts: 1 set (including micro); cams: .6-2"

D. Maxine's Wall 5.10a★★★
(Pitch 1 only) nuts: 1 set; cams: 1 ea .6-2"

E. Peruvian Flake 5.10a★★★
nuts: 1 set; cams: 1-2 ea .5-3.5"

Royal Arches

5.10b or 5.7 A0★★★★★

Time to climb route:	**7-10 hours**
Approach time:	**10 minutes**
Descent time:	**2-3 hours**
Sun exposure:	**morning to sunset**
Height of route:	**1400'**

With more than 1,600 feet of climbing, Royal Arches is the easiest long route in Yosemite Valley. Short 5.7 moves are mixed in with long stretches of 3rd and 4th class circuitous climbing. The only hard section, a 5.10b traverse, is easily bypassed with a fixed pendulum. That said, Royal Arches is committing and has benighted more than a few climbers. The climbing varies from 3rd class walking on large ledges and 5.4 friction to 5.7 finger and hand cracks. The climb is well-protected except for a few moderate but intimidating friction-climbing sections.

History

In 1936, with both Cathedral Spires climbed and the virgin Lost Arrow defining the impossible, the Valley pioneers reconsidered the walls. Pinnacles had real summits, places where no one had ever trod, yet there weren't too many more lurking about. Some walls were out of the question, like El Cap and Sentinel. Others proved unattractive or had no obvious crack systems. An exception was the shining wall above the Ahwahnee Hotel, just left of the Royal Arches. If a few key features could be linked, a thrilling route might lead to the rim.

The enormous, layered arches left of Washington Column spring directly out of the forest and curve upward until they fade out horizontally close to the rim. So prominent are these onionskin-like features that the Indians had several names for the formation. "Scho-ko-ni" referred to the arched shade of an infant's cradle; and "hunto" meant an eye. Morgan Harris, a zoology junior at UC Berkeley, was obsessed by this area and lounged for hours near the recently-built hotel, studying the face with binoculars. He knew the main Royal Arches couldn't be climbed—clearly, that was for a future generation. But just to the left lay lower-angled terrain, studded with trees, devoid of overhangs and blessed with cracks.

One attempt in torrid weather failed, and Harris spent a week in a hospital recovering from sunstroke. After yet another attempt, Harris, Ken Adam, and Kenneth Davis succeeded on October 9, 1936. The climbing on the route was not especially tough, but the routefinding and rope techniques proved daunting. One new procedure, called by Harris a "swinging rope traverse," overcame a blank section. (Later this technique became known as a "pendulum.") Harris, wishing to cross a smooth slab in order to reach a narrow ledge some 20 feet to his left, climbed straight upward about 25 feet, placed a piton and had his belayer lower him from it. Then, held tight by the rope from above, Harris began running back and forth across the wall, straining to reach the narrow ledge and finally succeeding.

Later, after yet another pendulum, the trio reached what they described as "an old tree-trunk," a feature soon to become

Royal Arches	Pitch	1	2	3	4	5	6	7	8	9	10	11	12	13	14	15	16
Free difficulty	≥5.10									●							
	5.9																
	5.8																
	5.7				●	●	●					●					
	5.6	●	●						●				●				
	≤5.5			●				●		●				●	●	●	●

famous as the Rotten Log. This 25-foot-long, foot-thick dead log bridged a deep chasm, affording a unique method of reaching the other side. Harris had spotted this golden trunk from the Valley floor and hoped it would be strong enough to hold his weight. It was, although it vibrated crazily as he led across it. The three men reached the rim a few hours later, having completed the Valley's longest route.

The climb, often the first serious one that beginners mastered, became immensely popular during the 1950s and 1960s. Hundreds of climbers endured their first bivouac at the top of the route or on the descent, for the climb was a long one—16 pitches with short ropes. Those who started late, or who hadn't yet dealt with multi-pitch routes, had campfire stories to tell forever.

The Rotten Log was the chief attraction of the route, and many thousands shuffled with trepidation across this tilted, shaky pole. It finally parted company with the rock in the spring of 1984. Pieces of the "True Log," soon scooped up from far below by Dr. Gus Benner, ended up on various Berkeley shelves as relics. A moderate but undistinguished alternate to the Log surfaced immediately, but never again would the route have the same cachet.

– *Steve Roper*

Strategy

Expect crowds on the climb and start early. Water pours down much of the route in winter and early spring (Tip: when Pitch 10 is wet, it's easier to climb barefoot). If climbing during this period, be prepared to improvise a route around wet sections. Some parties spend an entire day or more on this climb. Others have done the route in less than an hour, car to car. Be prepared to pass parties or to be passed at the intermediate belay stations, or by using the variations noted in the topo. If you arrive and find a massive queue on the first pitch, consider the other two starting variations. It is easy to pass parties until Pitch 5; above this there are few opportunities to pass.

The last pitch, a friction traverse above a 1400-foot drop-off, is the psychological crux of the route. Regardless of how you do this pitch, the follower is looking at the same long pendulum fall as the leader. The lower option is easier, and a bolt protects the scary traverse across a blank slab. Keep all your weight on your feet, stand up straight (don't lean forward), and make small steps. Another option: if you're scared or in bad weather, clip the old bolt and simply lower off into the dirt/pine needles below. The follower can leave a biner on the bolt and lower off to the dirt, then hike up, clip into a tree, and untie fully. Then the leader can pull the rope through the leaver biner and toss it back down to the follower. If night falls as you finish the last pitch, it is possible to bivy in the trees or above on the rim.

Retreat

Rappel the route with two 50m or 60m ropes. Retreating from below Pitch 15 requires leaving gear at some stations.

A. Arête Butler   5.10a★★★
FA: Norman Boles, George Watson, and Brian Bennett, 1986.

A bouldery start leads to a small ledge and a fun, continuous, well-protected slab. Above, an easier right-facing flake leads to the finishing vertical crack. Bring a full length sling to thread through a hole to protect the moves into the final crack. Rappel with two ropes.

B. Y Crack   5.10a★★★
FA: Gene Drake, et al 1975.

This sustained finger and lieback crack is mostly 5.9 with a distinct 5.10a crux at the top. Tricky gear placements 20 feet up make this route only suitable for confident 5.10a leaders. The unrelenting last 40 feet put your endurance to the test. There are a few ways to climb the crux, none of which are obvious. Descend by rappelling with two ropes. The route can barely be toproped with one 70m rope. Otherwise, use two ropes to toprope.

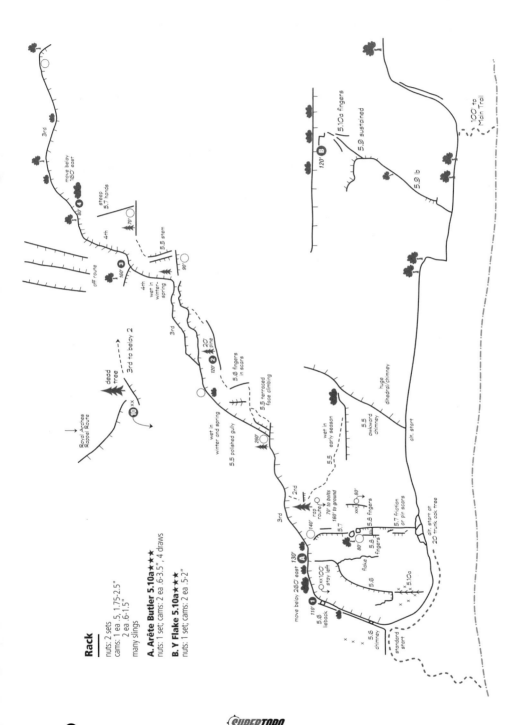

Rack

nuts: 2 sets
cams: 1 ea .5, 1.75-2.5"
        2 ea .6-1.5"
many slings

A. Aréte Butler 5.10a★★★
nuts: 1 set; cams: 2 ea .6-3.5", 4 draws

B. Y Flake 5.10a★★★
nuts: 1 set; cams: 2 ea .5-2"

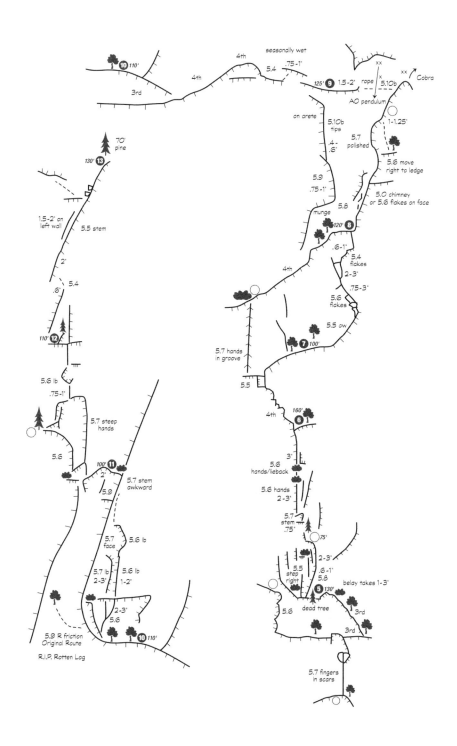

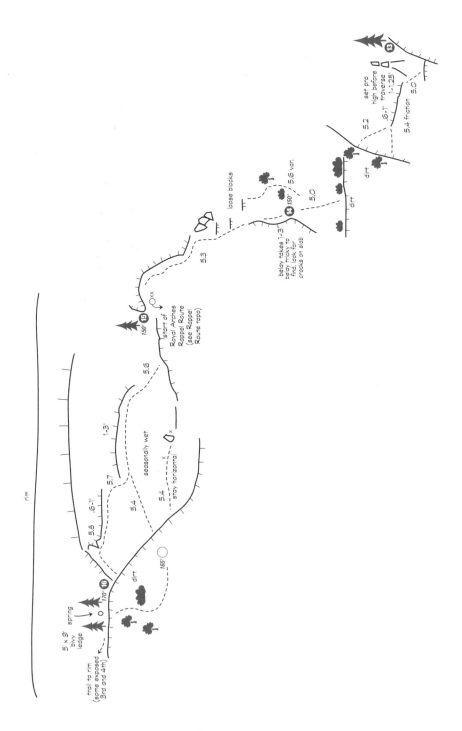

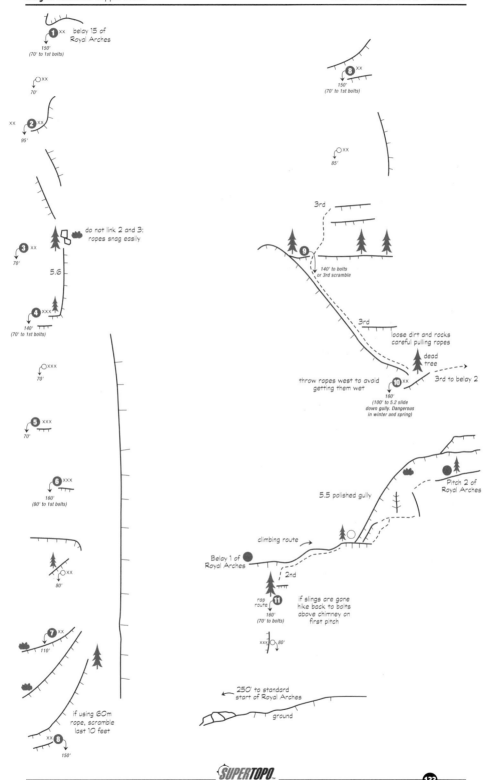

1 xx belay 15 of
Royal Arches
150'
(70' to 1st bolts)

xx
70'

xx 2 xx
95'

do not link 2 and 3:
ropes snag easily

3 xx
70'

5.6

4 xxx
140'
(70' to 1st bolts)

xxx
70'

5 xxx
70'

6 xxx
160'
(80' to 1st bolts)

xx
80'

7 xx
110'

if using 60m
rope, scramble
last 10 feet

xx 8
150'

8 xx
150'
(70' to 1st bolts)

xx
85'

3rd

9
140' to bolts
or 3rd scramble

3rd

loose dirt and rocks
careful pulling ropes

dead
tree

throw ropes west to avoid
getting them wet

10 xx
160'
(100' to 5.2 slide
down gully. Dangerous
in winter and spring)

3rd to belay 2

Pitch 2 of
Royal Arches

5.5 polished gully

climbing route

Belay 1 of
Royal Arches

2nd

rap
route 11
160'
(70' to bolts)

if slings are gone
hike back to bolts
above chimney on
first pitch

xxx 80'

250' to standard
start of Royal Arches

ground

Arches Terrace 5.8 R★★★

Time to climb route: **2-4 hours**

Approach time: **15 minutes**

Descent time: **30 minutes**

Sun exposure: **sunrise to afternoon**

Height of route: **400'**

This adventurous old school classic is half two-star crack climbing and half four-star slab climbing. This is a semi-serious route. While you're not usually looking at a dangerous fall, there is some big sliding potential and some of the cracks are flared and difficult to protect. Both the leader and follower should be confident 5.8 friction climbers. 60-meter ropes are mandatory.

Strategy

This route receives sun most of the day making it too hot to climb during the summer. Cool fall days are ideal and early winter is good as long as no big storms have activated the water seepage down the route. Only in exceptionally dry winters and springs is the route climbable between December and May.

The first pitch has a short almost runout 5.7 section before the anchor. The second pitch traverses horizontally on sustained 5.7 and 5.8 friction for 150 feet. This is a classic pitch and while sporty, is rarely runout for the leader. The follower on the other hand looks at a nasty swing after unclipping from the 4th bolt. The third pitch starts with a 5.7 runout but you can place gear right before it gets too scary. Aliens help a lot in the flared and pin-scarred crack.

Many climbers rappel from the tree. Another two pitches of mostly bushy 4th class climbing lead to Arches Terrace and is probably worth visiting once. There is a 100-foot-tall 5.10c incipient fingertip crack right of one of the 4th class pitches. It protects with small nuts and is named Anorexia Crack because as first ascensionists James Selvidge and Bernie Rivadeneyra put it, "it's just a little too thin to be healthy!"

Retreat

Descend or retreat by rappelling with two 60m ropes. Rap the route to the second belay. From here, rappel down and a little east for 190 feet to 4th class ledges. Downclimb 4th class for another 60 feet to the ground.

Rack

nuts: 1 set
cams: 2 ea .5-2"

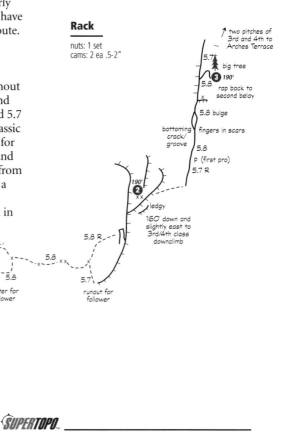

North Dome

North Dome is a Tuolumne-like dome with Yosemite Valley quality rock. One of Yosemite's larger domes, most ignore it due to a long approach and little publicity. Those willing to hike will find great climbing with stunning views of Yosemite Valley and the high country.

Approach

Access North Dome from Porcupine Creek Trailhead, by climbing Royal Arches, or by reversing the North Dome Gully (see North Dome Gully page). Porcupine Creek Trailhead is the fastest and most popular approach. However, if you climb fast, the Royal Arches option makes for a combined total of 24 classic pitches. Both approaches are long and make for a demanding day.

Approach from Porcupine Creek Trailhead
This approach is about 5 miles long and is flat until it descends to the base of the dome. Park at the Porcupine Creek Trailhead (1 mile east of Porcupine Flat or 4.5 miles west of Olmstead Point). Hike the trail for 4 miles to just before North Dome. Leave the trail and hike cross-country down the drainage on the west side of the dome. Traverse across when steep slabs are encountered. When you hit the large ramp system, hike up. You may encounter bad bushwhacking. Contour around when possible to a ramp leading to the base of the South Face route, which is marked by the huge obvious dihedral. Note: This approach is only viable when Highway 120 (Tioga Road) is open, usually between June and November, depending on the snow year.

Approach from Royal Arches
After climbing Royal Arches, head east on a climbers' trail toward Washington Column. At the slabs, walk up and slightly right over the slabs aiming for the lower of the two obvious terraces with trees at the base of North Dome. Skirt a large rock ridge along its left side and gain the base of the dome at the eastern end of the terrace. The route is the obvious left-facing dihedral. From the

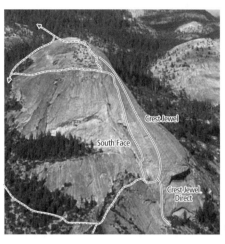

Chris McNamara

top of Royal Arches, the approach is 0.8 miles long and gains 500 feet of elevation.

Crest Jewel Direct Approach
Where the North Dome Gully trail emerges onto the North Dome/Washington Column saddle, there is a large boulder with a carin on it marking the North Dome Gully trail. If coming from Royal Arches, this is the boulder that you pass just as you leave the top of Washington Column and drop down slightly to traverse across to the gully. Go behind this boulder on a good trail that heads through manzanita and oak for about 50 feet. Head straight up the rocky/sandy slope until it ends at a medium-sized sloping boulder. The fairly well-marked and visible trail goes left and wanders across another small boulder field heading toward a large Jeffrey pine up higher. Past the pine, you climb a ramp along a slab up and right. Go to the highest point of the large slab.

Descent

From the last pitch, head up and left to the summit. Once on the summit, either pick up the hikers' trail back to Porcupine Creek Trailhead or descend the north side to the trees. A climbers' trail through the trees leads down and west along the base of the dome. Follow the trail until reaching the same slabs used for the approach and continue across (east) and then down the North Dome Gully.

South Face 5.8★★★★

Time to climb route: **5.5-6 hours**

Approach time: **1-6 hours**

Descent time: **2-3 hours**

Sun exposure: **morning to afternoon**

Height of route: **1000'**

Distinguished by its remoteness, ultra-clean rock, and stunning view of the face of Half Dome, the South Face is a true gem. There's only one problem: the approach. If the route were down near the Valley floor it would be climbed as often as Nutcracker. As it is, it's a neglected beauty. Every pitch is fun, but it is the wild low traverse and incredible liebacking up high that make this climb memorable. The route requires every technique, especially liebacking. You can't pull through most cruxes on gear.

History

Wally Reed and Mark Powell were the two best Valley free climbers during the late 1950s. In the spring and summer of 1957 they got together and established five exceptional routes. Among these is one of the classics of today, the South Face of North Dome.

Reed described the climb later in his matter-of-fact style. "After three pitches of easy friction and lieback climbing we were at the base of a 15-foot overhanging wall which diagonals to the left across the lower third of the face. Three sixth-class pitons overcame that problem, which was followed by two moderate friction pitches." Soon the pair arrived at the crux, a right-facing open book that stretched upward out of sight. Reed again: "Arranging a belay stance from a lieback position 100 feet up was difficult, as was the single crack which continued to

a small ledge above and which was partly filled with dirt and grass. Thirty feet beyond the ledge all cracks terminated. By placing a piton at his feet, Mark was able to make a difficult pull-up and a delicate friction step to easy scrambling and the summit. It took us about six hours."

Reed and Powell had accomplished the route in superb style, using only three aid placements. Other climbers of the time would have used many more.

Because of the gruesome approach, no one repeated this route for more than three years. One cool October morning in 1960, I was restless, eager to do something different from the usual routine. I talked Mort Hempel and Irene Ortenburger into trying the route, and soon we were staggering up the North Dome Gully, complaining just as much as Reed and Powell must have. But, unlike them, we still had the climb ahead of us on the same day, and didn't rope up until early afternoon. We somehow avoided the aid on the "15-foot overhanging wall" (it seemed not that overhung and only wild 5.7, so perhaps we discovered a variation), and then raced the sun to the summit. The liebacks at the top proved thrilling indeed, but the descent was not.

– Steve Roper

Strategy

An alpine start is mandatory. A 60m rope allows linking some pitches and is needed to avoid simul-climbing on Pitch 4, which is 180 feet.

There are three distinct cruxes. Pitch 3 is the routefinding crux (most climbers are lured by off route slings and go too high). After this the routefinding is pretty easy. Pitch 4 is the psychological crux as you must travel a long ways on 5.6 runout slab. Pitch 7 is the endurance and technical crux with a section of insecure 5.8 liebacking. Overall, the route is sustained with almost every pitch involving at least 5.7.

Retreat

Carry two ropes to retreat. From Pitches 1 and 2 there are slings on trees but after that you will have to leave gear.

South Face		Pitch 1	2	3	4	5	6	7	8
Free difficulty	≥5.10								
	5.9								
	5.8							•	
	5.7			•	•	•			
	5.6	•	•				•		•
	≤5.5								

Rack

nuts: 1 set
cams: 1 ea .4-1"
     2 ea 1.5-2"
     1 ea 3"
other: several long slings, cordalette

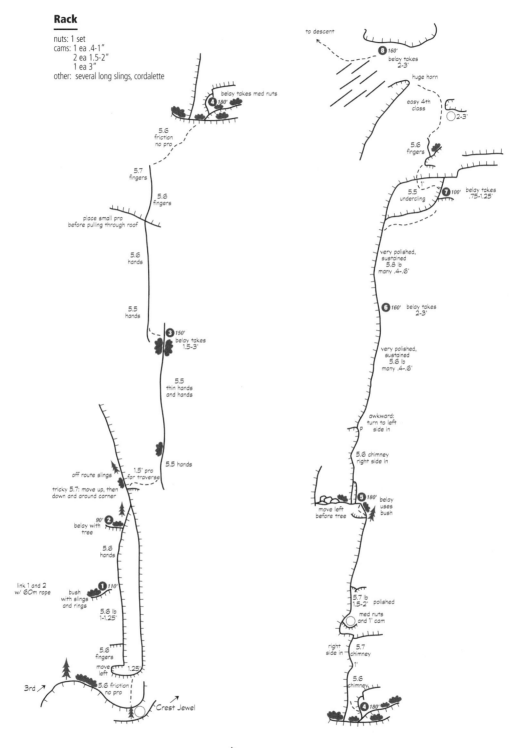

to descent

8 160' belay takes 2-3'

huge horn

easy 4th class

○ 2-3'

5.6 fingers

4 180' belay takes med nuts

5.6 friction no pro

5.7 fingers

5.6 fingers

place small pro before pulling through roof

5.6 hands

5.5 hands

3 150' belay takes 1.5-3'

5.5 thin hands and hands

5.5 hands

5.5 undercling

7 100' belay takes .75-1.25'

1'

very polished, sustained 5.8 lb many .4-.6'

6 160' belay takes 2-3'

very polished, sustained 5.6 lb many .4-.6'

awkward: turn to left side in

P

5.6 chimney right side in

off route slings

1.5' pro for traverse

tricky 5.7: move up, then down and around corner

2 90' belay with tree

5.6 hands

link 1 and 2 w/ 60m rope

1 110' bush with slings and rings

5.6 lb 1-1.25'

5.6 fingers

move left

1.25'

3rd

5.6 friction no pro

Crest Jewel

5 180' belay uses bush

move left before tree

5.7 lb 1.5-2' polished

med nuts and 1' cam

right side in

5.7 chimney

1'

5.6 chimney

4 180'

Crest Jewel 5.10a★★★★★

Time to climb route: **3-5 hours**

Approach time: **2-3 hours**

Descent time: **3-4 hours**

Sun exposure: **all day**

Height of route: **1000'**

Crest Jewel is likely the best climb of its type and grade on the planet. The immaculate featured slab hangs thousands of feet above the Valley floor and the huge north face of Half Dome sits directly across. Combined with the popular approach of climbing Royal Arches, this route covers an immense amount of 5th class terrain. Most cruxes are well-protected but there are some runouts on 5.8 and easier terrain.

FA: Dan Dingle and Michael Lucero, 9/81.

Strategy

Many parties epic in the dark coming off Crest Jewel. Start early, go fast on Royal Arches, and don't dawdle on the climb, which like many low-angle climbs looks much shorter than it is. Alternate approaches include hiking up North Dome Gully (not a bad idea if you're planning on descending that way and have not been there previously), and hiking down and back from Highway 120. The latter has a long bushwacking descent that is difficult to find, but a relatively mild hike from the top back to your car. Crest Jewel Direct adds five more pitches (with a short and tightly-bolted crux pitch) to the mix.

All lead and protection bolts were replaced by Larry Scritchfield and Greg Barnes with support from the ASCA in 2002.

Retreat

Rappel is possible from any pitch with two ropes; care must be taken on the severely traversing pitches at top and bottom. Because of this, rappelling in the dark is a dangerous proposition.

A. Crest Jewel Direct   5.10d★★★★

FA: Dan Dingle and Steve Swann, 6/02.

By adding five pitches to Crest Jewel, the Direct makes one of the longest and highest quality 5.10 face routes anywhere even better. Not only do you get an extra 400 feet of fun thin face and friction moves, it avoids the longer standard approach. The climbing is similar to Crest Jewel but slightly steeper and harder. It's possible to pull on bolts through some of the cruxes but you still should be a confident 5.10 slab climber.

The Crest Jewel first ascent team originally intended to start from the base of North Dome. However, upon arriving at the base, they were deterred by the steep face climbing and improbable-looking roofs. It didn't help that one of the climbers, Dan Dingle, had tennis shoes instead of the then state-of-the-art EBs (just consider that EBs were far less sticky than modern shoes!) They opted instead to start Crest Jewel by traversing in from the side.

Twenty years later and with better footwear, Dingle returned with Steve Swann and started from the base. The overhangs and face moves, while challenging, proved on par with the difficulty of the original route. The result is a more natural and aesthetic start to an already incredible Crest Jewel.

It should be noted that the first ascent team graciously used some extra sweat and time to place good 3/8" protection and anchor bolts.

Crest Jewel		1	2	3	4	5	6	7	8	9	10
Free difficulty	≥5.10		●					●			
	5.9	●				●					
	5.8			●	●		●		●		
	5.7										●
	5.6										
	≤5.5							●			

Rack

nuts: none
cams: optional one .5 or .6"
many slings and draws
buffed calves

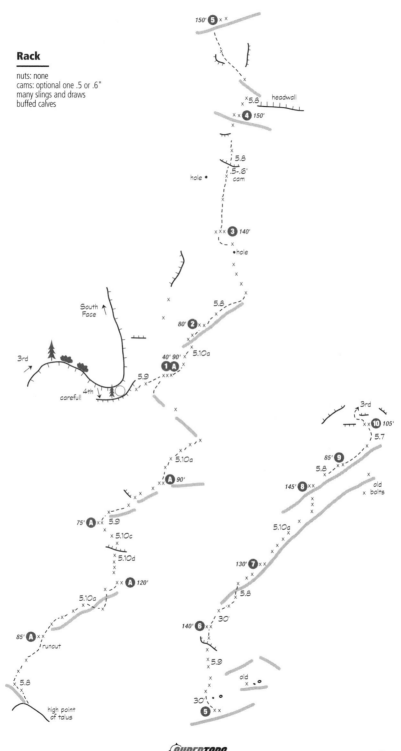

Washington Column

To the east end of the Valley juts an impressive prow of overhanging rock. Washington Column bears its name from a supposed resemblance to our first president. Its 1,100 feet of golden granite is divided into two distinct faces. The East Face sports long, clean, continuous cracks on a steep and intimidating wall. The lower-angle South Face features are more varied and vegetated with a surprising number of trees. Making convenient anchors, these trees inspired one of the first serious roped climbs in 1933. Though unsuccessful, the attempt opened minds to the possibilities of Yosemite's walls.

Approach

This approach is about a mile long, takes 40 minutes, and gains 1,000 feet in elevation. From the Ahwahnee Hotel parking area, hike east along a dirt road (through the valet parking area) until reaching the bike path. Continue east (left) for about 0.5 mile to a point where the bike path and horse trail (on the left) nearly meet. At the point where the bike path turns right, head left, cross the horse path, and continue into the trees. (Don't worry if you miss this trail— just walk up the hill, meet the wall, and walk right.) A climbers' trail winds up to the base of a wall and then continues up and right to the base of the East Face of Washington Column.

Descent

From the top of Washington Column there are three descent options:

North Dome Gully

Though by no means enjoyable, this is the best and fastest descent option. Allow 1-2 hours if experienced with the descent and 2-4 hours if it is your first time. Do not attempt it at night unless you're familiar with the descent.

For this descent, refer to the North Dome Gully Descent description.

Chris McNamara

Royal Arches Rappels

This option depends on your ability to find the top of the Royal Arches route. This is a difficult task unless you have already climbed the Royal Arches. This option takes 2-4 hours.

North Dome Trail

This is the longest and most grueling descent but may be the best option if you are descending in a storm and are unfamiliar with the North Dome Gully. For this descent, walk northwest until you pick up the North Dome Trail. Follow this for about 8 miles until you reach Camp 4.

Astroman 5.11c★★★★★

Time to climb route:	**10 hours**
Approach time:	**40 minutes**
Descent time:	**1.5 hours**
Sun exposure:	**sunrise to early afternoon**
Height of route:	**1100'**

Astroman is one of the best long free routes in the United States. When first established, it was the domain of only the most honed climbers in the world. Today, still considered a Valley testpiece, Astroman has lost little of its stature or mystique. It's the gold standard of long and hard free climbing and most tall climbing areas have some route which is measured against it. Climbers who have the skill and nerve to attempt Astroman will find tremendous exposure, flawless rock quality, and mostly solid protection. The climbing involves every technique imaginable, from balancy face moves and boulder problems to sustained hand jamming and a squeeze chimney.

History

I was not too happy with the route name Astroman when I first heard it. Sure, the word itself had a fabulous ring to it, but the newly named route already had a name. This was what disturbed me. Never mind that the old name was pedestrian: the East Face of the Washington Column. This was back in 1975, and the arrogant notion of re-naming a route once it had been freed was fairly new. (I'm still not thrilled by this dying trend—and pleased that Lynn Hill didn't re-name The Nose!) And yet the climb christened Astroman, so radically different from the East Face route of 1959, perhaps demanded a new name.

When John Bachar, Ron Kauk, and John Long topped out on that afternoon a quarter-century ago, they knew they had done something remarkable—the most continuously difficult free climb in the world. Of the 12 pitches, two were easy, five were 5.10, and five were 5.11!

The original ascent, made by Warren Harding and Chuck Pratt, had been a fixed rope effort from bottom to top—a year-long adventure. In addition, the trio had used aid on virtually every pitch—probably 225 aid placements altogether. The route overhung for much of its 1100-foot height and it leaned annoyingly to the right on many pitches, making even the aid strenuous. Pratt and I, along with Eric Beck, made the fifth ascent in 1967 and used about 150 aid placements. The idea that the route would ever go free was ludicrous. Even that great crack specialist Pratt never harbored such a thought, though he did some scary and innovative 5.10 climbing on this route.

Kauk and Bachar, both 18 years old, went up on the route early in 1975 to see if a long, steep corner low on the route could be freed. Incredibly continuous, the corner (soon named the Enduro corner) did indeed go free at 11c. Kauk later called this severe pitch the "key to the door." The remainder of the route didn't look much worse, and when John Long heard this news he persuaded the pair to head back up with him.

Bachar led a short but fierce 11c "boulder problem" near the bottom for the first time. Kauk led both the Enduro corner and the 11a section just below the fabled Harding Slot in great style, but aid climbers above slowed the party by mid-afternoon. The trio descended to a bivy ledge, leaving a few ropes fixed. The next morning saw

		Pitch											
Astroman		**1**	**2**	**3**	**4**	**5**	**6**	**7**	**8**	**9**	**10**	**11**	**12**
Free difficulty	≥5.10	●	●	●		●	●	●	●	●			●
	5.9				●								
	5.8												
	5.7	●										●	
	5.6												
	≤5.5												

Long tackling the horrendous difficulties above the Harding Slot, including a harrowing mantelshelf of 11a, and higher, a short section of 11b. A few hundred feet of "moderate" crack climbing followed, then Long led the summit pitch, a loose and unprotected 10d face.

Climbing historian Jim Vermeulen sums up the achievement: "In two short days, the trio had changed the rules of wall climbing." From this point onward, the lure of a first free ascent was just as powerful as the idea of a first ascent, and the Valley's hard men and women soon turned to even more intimidating walls, knowing that anything was now possible.

Kauk and Bachar both returned to Astroman within a year, and the climb quickly became a testpiece for climbers who wished to test their crack skills and/or gain notoriety. Werner Braun, who has lived and climbed in the Valley for 30 years, has done the route some 50 times. At least two climbers have soloed the wall unroped: Peter Croft (in 1987—and he did it several times) and Dean Potter (in 2000). Croft's ascent stunned the climbing world as the boldest ascent in Valley history. Generations of roped climbers will find the route strenuous, historic and more than enough exercise for a day's outing.

– Steve Roper

Strategy

There are many crux sections but the main difficulty is maintaining mental and physical stamina through the consecutive 5.10 and 5.11 pitches. Despite its fame, the hard climbing keeps the crowds away. While you can pull through crux hard moves on gear if necessary, only solid 5.11 climbers should try this route.

Pitch 3, the Boulder Problem, is the technical crux and requires powerful lieback moves with thin protection. The Enduro Corner is steep and sustained and sets the pace for the demanding pitches above. The Harding Slot, Astroman's most notorious pitch, has reduced many talented climbers to curses and whimpers. (Tip: retie your knot so that it hangs well below your waist and out of the way.) This pitch is wet in the winter and early spring. The dangerous and runout last pitch is protected largely by fixed pitons and copperheads and is wet in spring. Find out the condition of this pitch before heading up on the route.

Sun hits the route first thing in the morning and leaves the face at 1 P.M. Spring and fall are the best times to climb. During the summer, only exceptionally fast teams are able to climb the route while completely in the shade and even then heat may be a problem.

Retreat

Two 50m ropes are needed to retreat. The route can be rappelled easily from Pitch 1-6. Beyond Pitch 6, retreat is difficult due to the steep and traversing nature of the route. Above Pitch 8 you will need to leave gear in order to retreat.

More at SuperTopo.com

Download a free color version of the Astroman topo at www.supertopo.com.

Rack

micro nuts: 1 set
nuts: 2 ea sml, med
cams: 1 ea .4"
      2 ea .5-.75"
      3 ea 1-2.5"
      2 ea 3-3.5"
      1 ea 4"
60m ropes useful

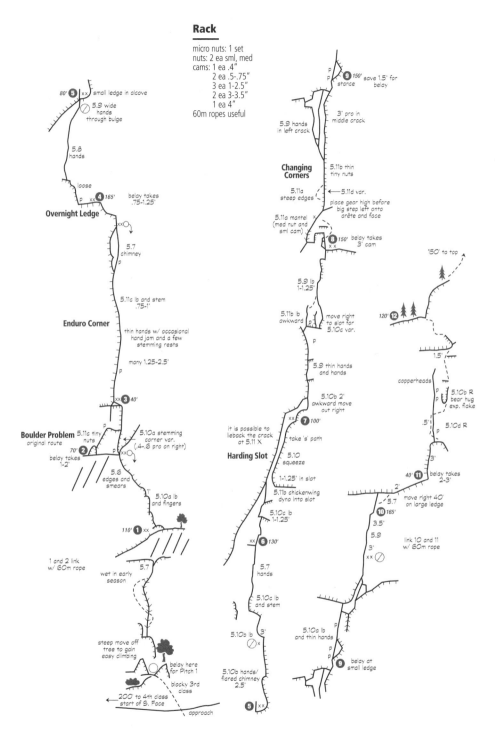

80' **5** xx small ledge in alcove
5.9 wide hands through bulge

5.8 hands

loose

4 165' belay takes .75-1.25'

Overnight Ledge

5.7 chimney

5.11c lb and stem .75-1'

Enduro Corner

thin hands w/ occasional hand jam and a few stemming rests

many 1.25-2.5'

3 40'

Boulder Problem 5.11c tiny nuts
original route
70' **2** belay takes 1-2'

5.10a stemming corner var. (.4-.6 pro on right)

5.6 edges and smears

5.10a lb and fingers

110' **1** xx

1 and 2 link w/ 60m rope

5.7 wet in early season

steep move off tree to gain easy climbing

belay here for Pitch 1

blocky 3rd class

200' to 4th class start of S. Face

approach

---

9 150' save 1.5' for stance belay

3' pro in middle crack

5.9 hands in left crack

Changing Corners 5.11b thin tiny nuts

5.11a steep edges 5.11d var.

place gear high before big step left onto arête and face

5.11a mantel (med nut and sml cam)

8 150' belay takes 3' cam

5.9 lb 1-1.25'

5.11b lb awkward

move right to slot for 5.10c var.

5.9 thin hands and hands

5.10b 2' awkward move out right

7 100'

it is possible to lieback the crack at 5.11 X

take 's' path

Harding Slot 5.10 squeeze

1-1.25' in slot

5.11b chickenwing dyno into slot

5.10c lb 1-1.25'

6 130'

5.7 hands

5.10c lb and stem

5.10b lb 3'

5.10b hands/ flared chimney 2.5'

5 xx

150' to top

120' **12**

1.5'

copperheads

5.10b R bear hug exp. flake

.5'

5.10d R

40' **11** belay takes 2-3'

5.7 move right 40' on large ledge

10 165'

3.5'

5.9

link 10 and 11 w/ 60m rope

3'

5.10a lb and thin hands

9 belay at small ledge

North Dome Gully

The North Dome Gully requires tricky routefinding on exposed terrain. It is strongly advised that you travel with someone who is familiar with the descent. If it is your first time and you must descend at night or in a storm, consider hiking to the North Dome Trail and walking about 8 miles to Camp 4.

Mark Kroese

From Royal Arches Last Pitch

If you have the North Dome Gully memorized, it is the fastest way to descend from Royal Arches and takes 1-2 hours. If it is not familiar, the North Dome Gully can be a nightmare and take 4 hours due to the ease of getting off route. We strongly recommended the Royal Arches Rappel Route (a topo is located with the SuperTopo for the Royal Arches route).

From the last pitch of Royal Arches, follow a climbers' trail west (some 3rd and 4th class required) to the **rim (1)**. Continue on the climbers' trail as it turns east. For the next 5-10 minutes the trail will stay roughly 100-300 feet north of the edge. The trail eventually moves north (farther from the edge) and enters bushy terrain, then **trees (2)**. The climbers' trail leaves the trees and continues through manzanita as it climbs up to a **ridge (3)**. Next, follow the instructions in the section titled, "From Washington Column Ridge."

From Washington Column Summit

This is the best descent option for Washington Column and takes 1-3 hours.

From the top of Washington Column, walk north toward North Dome on a climbers' trail through manzanita staying just west and below the ridge. After 5-10 minutes gain the **ridge (3)**. Next, follow the instructions in the section titled, "From Washington Column Ridge."

From Washington Column Ridge

From the ridge, walk north, and look for a sandy, mildly exposed **climbers' trail (4)** that drops down the east side of the ridge and then continues traversing exposed terrain. This trail is difficult to locate but once you find it, the climbers' trail is well-defined. The next 100 yards are the crux. In general, traverse horizontally without ever gaining or losing more than 100 feet of elevation. If you ever contemplate a steep rap, you are off route.

A few hundred feet after leaving the ridge, work briefly up an **eroding hillside (5)** then move down and make a short but exposed **4th class traverse (6)**. Move back up a short section and then continue traversing above an **exposed cliff (7)** until it is mandatory to downclimb 40 feet of **4th class and tree branches (8)**. From here, move east, cross a 50-foot-wide rocky **drainage (9)**, and continue traversing east into the trees until a steep, slippery, and dusty trail leads down through the **trees (10)**. This trail leads out into the open to a long section of loose but well-worn **switchbacks (11)**. These switchbacks lead to a few short but exposed sections of **4th class downclimbing (12)** that some parties may want to rappel (there are bolts but sometimes no slings). From the base of the North Dome Gully, either skirt the base back to the East Face of Washington Column or continue straight down on a well-worn **climbers' trail (13)** that eventually leads to the horse trail and then the **bike path (14)** near the Indian Caves. Follow the bike path or horse trail back to the **Ahwahnee Hotel (15)**.

Photo by Chris McNamara

Half Dome,
Southwest Face

In his book *The Yosemite*, John Muir called Half Dome, "the most beautiful and sublime of all the wonderful Yosemite rocks." With a summit that towers nearly 5,000 feet above the Yosemite Valley floor and a sheer face of 2,000 vertical feet, Half Dome offers breathtaking views of Yosemite Valley and the High Sierra.

In the 1860s, the California Geological Survey deemed Half Dome unclimbable, "a perfectly inaccessible [peak] which never has been, and never will be, trodden by human foot." But in 1875, George Anderson, a Scottish trail-builder and carpenter made it to the summit. He painstakingly drilled 6-inch-deep holes into the 300-foot 45-degree eastern slab. After hammering iron pegs into these holes, Anderson attached ropes and ascended the dome. Just days later, Sandy Dutcher, wearing a long dress, became the first woman to climb Half Dome.

Approach

The 6-mile approach gains about 2500 feet of elevation and is extremely strenuous. Start early and plan for at least 3 hours of hiking. Park at Curry Village and either walk or take the shuttle bus to Happy Isles. Follow the John Muir Trail for one mile to the Mist Trail. Follow the Mist Trail for 2.1 miles to the top of Nevada Fall and again pick up the Muir Trail. After about 0.75 miles, the rock on the left that forms the shoulder of Liberty Cap will gradually recede to nothing. At this point, pick up a climbers' trail on the left and walk northwest for about one mile, passing Lost Lake, to the open slabs. Here the trail ends and you must walk directly toward the South Face of Half Dome on talus and slabs with some bushwhacking. Cairns are abundant and may or may not guide you on the right path. Skirt the base of the South Face on sometimes exposed ledges and 3rd and 4th class to the sandy switchbacks that lead to the base of the Southwest Face and the start of the route.

Snake Dike

Chris McNamara

Approach between Mt. Broderick and Liberty Cap: This more scenic variation is slightly faster but devious. Few people find the quickest way on their first attempt. On the Mist Trail, before the final steep granite switchbacks leading to the top of Nevada Fall, pick up a climbers' trail to the left where Liberty Cap touches the trail. Skirt the base of the South Face of Liberty Cap. Follow cairns and switchbacks up and right through the trees to an open talus slope that leads to the base of a steep cliff. Contour left along the cliff, following it as it trends right above a steep drop-off and drops down slightly left into the chasm between Mt. Broderick and Liberty Cap. Continue through the chasm (stay right) and scramble up 3rd class rocks as the brush becomes thicker. Near the top of the chasm, move left into a flat area and follow a streambed. Trend back right and into trees until Half Dome becomes visible on your left—at this point look for cairns leading left. Follow the trail north and then east, and merge with the standard approach at Lost Lake.

Descent

Allow 3-4 hours for the 9-mile descent. From the summit, descend the cables. The cables are in place year-round. During the winter and spring the uprights are removed, but the cables are still easy to descend. Continue on the Half Dome Trail until it joins the Muir Trail, which leads back to Happy Isles.

SUPERTOPO

YOSEMITE VALLEY FREE CLIMBS

Snake Dike 5.7 R ★★★★★

Time to climb route: **3-4 hours**

Approach time: **3-4 hours**

Descent time: **3-4 hours**

Sun exposure: **late morning to sunset**

Height of route: **800'**

A dramatic setting with clean and exposed climbing qualifies Snake Dike as one of the most glorious moderate climbs on the planet. The long and aesthetic approach will take you past two beautiful waterfalls, through the backcountry and past an isolated lake to the southwest toe of Half Dome. The route climbs an 800-foot salmon-colored dike that wanders up the dramatic southwest face of Half Dome. The combination of a 6-mile hike to the base, eight pitches of climbing, and a 9-mile descent back to the Valley makes for a full adventure and may require more than one day.

History

Climbers who made the long trek up to the base of the massive Southwest Face of Half Dome before 1965 went there for one reason only: to do the classic Salathé-Nelson route. This demanding aid line wandered up unconnected crack systems, but it was the only way to the top since everyone knew that the rest of the wide face was crackless, and obviously impossible. When Camp 4 inhabitants heard in July 1965 that a second route had been put up nearby, the sense of disbelief was audible. When the first ascensionists—Eric Beck, Jim Bridwell, and Chris Fredericks—bragged that their route was trivial, disbelief turned to disdain. When they claimed that they had placed only two pitons and about

Snake Dike	Pitch	1	2	3	4	5	6	7	8
Free difficulty	≥5.10								
	5.9								
	5.8								
	5.7	●	●	●					
	5.6					●			
	≤5.5				●		●	●	●

six hurried bolts, disdain evolved to thoughts that the three men should be committed. A far easier route than Salathé's? But it was true. Beck had been the instigator of the route soon named Snake Dike; he had spotted a potential route on a reconnaissance and had talked the two others into making the horrendous approach. To their great surprise they put up the new route in a day from Camp 4 back to Camp 4.

Years later, Beck reminisced about their climb. "We were expecting a much harder route and only had twelve bolts, so we did our best to conserve them where the climbing was easy. What I really imagined happening was that we would get up a few pitches, fix the ropes, and return with more bolts. Also, our original choice of line was to follow a dike leading up and right on Pitch 3. This was Bridwell's lead and he climbed up about 20 feet, got in a bolt, but didn't like it. This caused more uncertainty about routefinding and wasting our bolts. I then gained the lead and had a look to the left. This proved to be the best way."

Two years later I grabbed a stranger named John Gibbons and we set off at dawn from a campsite in Little Yosemite, armed with a hefty bolt kit. Ordinarily, taking a bolt kit for an easy second ascent would have made me a laughingstock. But Beck, Bridwell, and Fredericks, feeling that they had created a potential death route for beginners, had given me permission to replace their bad bolts and stick in new ones where I deemed necessary. This was the first time in Valley history that first ascensionists had given someone permission to add bolts to their route.

At the end of two pitches Gibbons and I realized that the Dike was truly a splendid route, and I made sure my bolts were bombproof and properly spaced. That is, I did this for a while. My fingers and arms soon began to throb from all the hand drilling. Morning turned to afternoon. I inspected my dulled drill bits. I listened as Gibbons called up anxiously, "You finished?" Soon I simply ran out the pitches and relied on the sporadic and wretched first ascent bolts. We rappelled the route and staggered down through the brush to our camp below, arriving just as the owls began to hoot.

Snake Dike hadn't been totally retrofitted, but it had been a good day and a good start. We spread the word and within a few years many more bolts had been added, and Snake Dike became the most popular climbers' route to the top of the most spectacular hunk of granite in North America.

– Steve Roper

Strategy

Start early, as the day will be long. Snake Dike is extremely popular even during a weekday. Prepare for crowds, unexpected weather changes, and a late finish. A 60m rope allows more options for linking pitches, but is not required. Many of the belays are at uncomfortable stances, so roomy climbing shoes are recommended.

On the first pitch crux it's possible to climb high up and right to set pro, then back down before moving left to 5.7 friction. The third pitch crux is both the technical and psychological crux of the climb: an exposed 5.7 friction traverse. At the end of the traverse is an alternate belay/rap station with two bolts. To better protect your follower on the traverse, clip these bolts with an extra long sling, or skip the bolts and climb up the dike to the next bolt, which offers a better rope angle for the follower on the friction traverse. From here on up, easier climbing wanders up the salmon-colored dike for four pitches with very runout 5.4 R and 5.3 R sections. On the worst runouts, you will climb as much as 75 feet of 5.4 R without any protection, clip a bolt, and then climb another 75 feet of 5.4 R to the anchor. Climb carefully on these amazing, secure, and dangerously runout sections.

The sun hits the climb by mid-morning and temperatures range from very hot to

Endless 5.4 jugs (and a big runout) on Pitch 4.

Mark Kroese

windy and cold. During the summer, afternoon thunderstorms are common and lightning strikes on Half Dome's summit have killed. Be respectful of approaching thunderclouds and do not hesitate to retreat if the risk of lightning arises.

Many climbers give themselves more time by camping at either Lost Lake or Little Yosemite Valley the night before starting the route. Consult the Wilderness Center for permits and information or visit www.nps.gov/yose/wilderness/permits.htm.

Wild-at-heart climbers are sometimes found climbing this route by full moon.

Retreat

The route can be rappelled easily from any point using two 50m or 60m ropes.

More at SuperTopo.com

View a photo gallery of Snake Dike at www.supertopo.com.

Rack

nuts: 1 ea med, lrg
cams: 1 ea .4-1"
6 quickdraws
slings

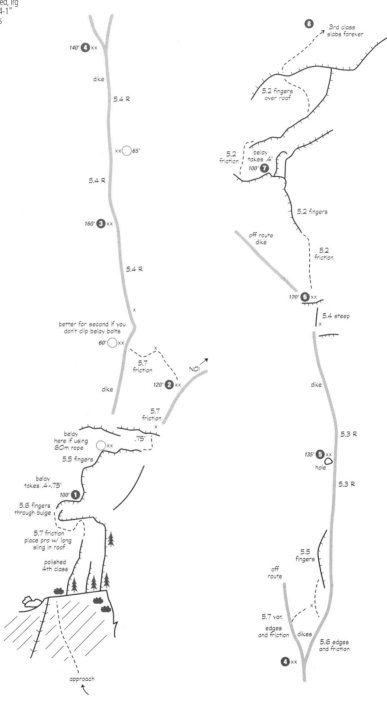

140' **4** xx

dike

5.4 R

xx◯65'

5.4 R

160' **3** xx

5.4 R

x

better for second if you
don't clip belay bolts

60'◯xx   x

5.7
friction   NO!

dike   120' **2** xx

5.7
friction
x

belay
here if using
60m rope   ◯xx   .75'

5.5 fingers

belay
takes .4-.75'

100' **1**

5.6 fingers
through bulge

5.7 friction
place pro w/ long
sling in roof

polished
4th class

approach

8   3rd class
                    slabs forever

5.2 fingers
over roof

5.2   belay
friction   takes .4'
            100' **7**

5.2 fingers

off route
dike   5.2
                     friction

120' **6** xx

5.4 steep
x

dike

5.3 R

135' **5** xx
        hole

5.3 R

5.5
fingers

off
route

5.7 var.
edges
and friction   dikes   5.6 edges
                            and friction

4 xx

Glacier Point Apron

Approach time: **5-15 minutes**

Sun exposure: **morning**

Height of routes: **30-500'**

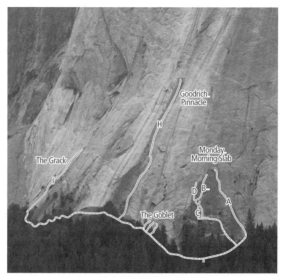

Glacier Point Apron is a one-thousand-foot-high and quarter-mile-wide slab of smooth granite with a reputation for scary runouts and rockfall. While this reputation is true for some routes, relatively safe and well-protected climbing does exist. Most of the face climbs are runout, but the apparently featureless wall holds a few high-quality cracks, many in the 5.5-5.8 range. Most of these routes are two pitches or longer. There are only a few topropes, which are mostly at The Goblet.

The two massive and deadly rockfalls (and many smaller rockfalls) in the last ten years occurred east of The Cow and west of Monday Morning Slab. These rockfall zones are still active and dangerous. However, if you climb in between them on the routes included in this book, you're probably in no more danger than anywhere else in Yosemite. Visit www.supertopo.com for rockfall updates and user discussions on the topic.

The Apron faces north and northeast, which means some of the areas like Monday Morning Slab are usually shaded, but climbs near The Grack receive morning sunlight. It's one of the cooler Yosemite crags in the summer (but can still be too hot), is perfect in the spring and fall, and too cold in the winter.

Approach

From Curry Village, drive 0.2 mile east toward Half Dome. At the 3-way stop, turn right and drive a few hundred yards to the road barriers and turn into a huge dirt parking lot under Glacier Point Apron.

From the parking lot, it's about a 5-minute hike to Monday Morning Slab and 15 minutes to The Grack and The Cow.

From the northeast corner of the parking lot, walk 100 feet on a hikers' trail and turn right (south) onto a climbers' trail. Hike uphill for a few minutes to the base of Monday Morning Slab. For Harry Daley and Right Side, go up and right 100 feet. For The Grack and all other routes, go left and uphill. After 100 yards, you reach The Goblet and then the trail flattens out at the base of Goodrich Pinnacle. Continue along the base for 100 yards, then down dirt switchbacks for a few hundred feet to a drainage crossing. Skirt the base for another few hundred yards to the point where the tree cover opens up again and you can see the massive rockfall to the southeast. Look above and locate The Grack, Center that is the beautiful splitter crack on the smooth and slabby face. The Cow is 150 feet left.

Descent

Descend all routes by rappelling. You generally need two 50m or 60m ropes.

A. Monday Morning Slab, Right   5.4★

FA: Don Goodrich and Mac Fraser, 1958.

One of the few multi-pitch 5.4s in Yosemite. Mostly 3rd and 4th class climbing leads to a few tricky 5.4 sections on the last pitch. While the climbing is never great, you gain some elevation and reach the top of a cool formation with a cozy ledge and a nice view. Be careful of the occasional rotten rock. Descend by rappelling with two 50m or 60m ropes.

Chris McNamara

B. Harry Daley   5.8★★★★★

FA: Ken Weeks and Harry Daley, 1960.

This is one of Yosemite's best two-pitch 5.8 climbs. The first pitch climbs tricky and sustained 5.8 fingers in pin scars. The difficulties ease as you move left and walk the crack. Keep the follower in mind when placing pro for this section. Belay at the tree under the roof, especially if climbers above need the bolted rap station to descend.

The second pitch is incredible. Strenuous but solid jams over a roof lead to a zig-zagging splitter hand and finger crack with a distinct 5.8 fingers crux midway. Descend by rappelling with two ropes and consider toproping Variation on a Theme.

C. Variation on a Theme   5.10b R★★★

FA: Paul Cowan et al, 1974.

This combination of friction and knob face climbing is a great toprope after climbing Harry Daley (or a bold lead). Toprope it from the chain anchors with one 60m rope.

Marshall Minobe

The deadly 1998 rockfall that released a few hundred yards west of Monday Morning Slab.

D. Chouinard Crack   5.8★★★

FA: Yvon Chouinard, et al.

This climb starts beautifully, but finishes too quickly. It's a good option if the second pitch of Harry Daley is crowded.

E, F, G. The Goblet, Right, Center, and Left
5.5-5.6★★

These short topropes are ideal for friction practice. The Goblet, Right is the only well-protected way to reach the central two-bolt anchor. Use this two-bolt anchor when toproping all routes—don't set up a toprope off one bolt! There are two variations to the Left route and many variations to the Center route. Try to find the hardest slab moves you can (there are many 5.6-5.9 variations).

H. Goodrich Pinnacle, Right 5.9 R★★★★★

FA: Royal Robbins, Liz Robbins, and TM Herbert, 5/64.

This is one of the better climbs of its length not only on the Apron but also in the entire Valley. Every pitch is clean and offers interesting and varied climbing from slab to polished cracks to face and even an easy chimney. There are some moderate and long runouts on 5.6 and 5.7, but anything 5.8 or harder is fairly well-protected. Two ropes are needed to rappel (60m recommended). Do not rappel from the fourth belay all the way to the second belay or your ropes will get stuck.

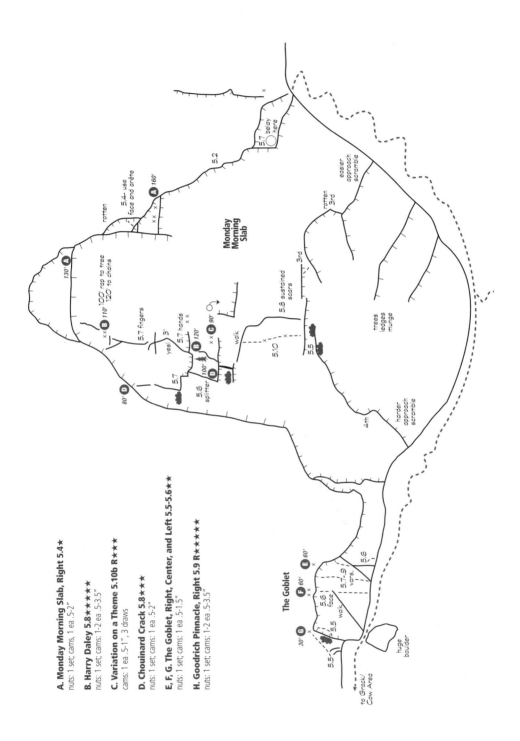

A. Monday Morning Slab, Right 5.4 ★
nuts: 1 set; cams, 1 ea .5-2"

B. Harry Daley 5.8 ★★★★
nuts: 1 set; cams: 1-2 ea .5-3.5"

C. Variation on a Theme 5.10b R ★★★
cams: 1 ea .5-1", 3 draws

D. Chouinard Crack 5.8 ★★★
nuts: 1 set; cams: 1 ea .5-2"

E, F, G. The Goblet, Right, Center, and Left 5.5-5.6 ★★
nuts: 1 set; cams: 1 ea .5-1.5"

H. Goodrich Pinnacle, Right 5.9 R ★★★★★
nuts: 1 set; cams: 1-2 ea .5-3.5"

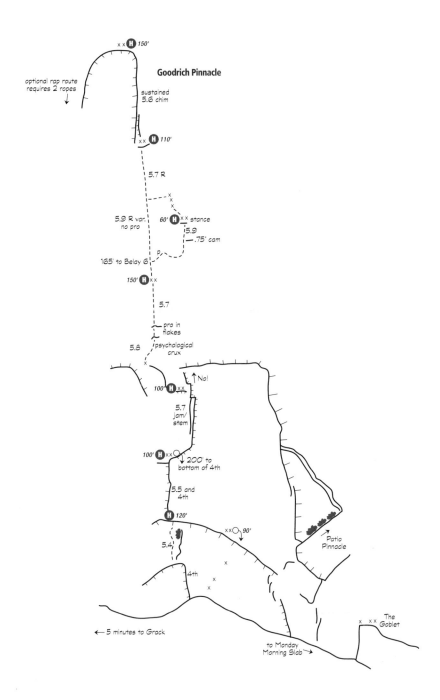

x x **H** *150'*

Goodrich Pinnacle

optional rap route
requires 2 ropes
↓

sustained
5.6 chim

x x **H** *110'*

5.7 R

x
x

5.9 R var.   *60'* **H** x x stance
no pro   5.9
                    .75' cam

165' to Belay 6   P

150' **H** x x

5.7

pro in
flakes

5.8   psychological
crux
x

↑ No!

100' **H** x x

5.7
jam/
stem

100' **H** x x   ↓ 200' to
                    bottom of 4th

5.5 and
4th

H *120'*

x x   90'

5.4

Patio
Pinnacle

x

4th

x
x

The
Goblet
x   x x

← 5 minutes to Grack

to Monday
Morning Slab →

I. Marginal   5.9 R ★★★★★

FA: Ken Boche, Mary Bomba, and Joe McKeown, 5/70.

This is the best pure 5.9 friction climb in Yosemite. It's low-angle and has few features, holds, or protection points. The climb is runout but you're rarely looking at longer than a 20- to 30-foot-slide. You usually get protection right before it gets too scary. All three pitches are sustained at 5.7 and 5.8 with a few 5.9 moves.

J. The Grack, Center   5.6 ★★★★★

FA: Bill Sorenson and Jack Delk, 1967.

This is the best 5.6 in Yosemite. Such incredible moderate crack climbing is rare, which makes the route extremely popular. This climb is well-protected until 15 feet of unprotected 5.6 friction at the top that spooks out those unaccustomed to low-angle holdless climbing. The route faces east and is very hot on summer mornings but bearable by the afternoon. Temperatures in the spring and fall are ideal. If too crowded, climb The Grack, Left Side, or The Cow. Descend with three rappels using two 60m ropes or four rappels using two 50m ropes on the Marginal anchors.

K. The Grack, Left   5.7 ★★★

FA: Bob Kamps and Andy Lichtman. 8/63.

This is a good consolation prize if The Grack, Center is too crowded. The climbing is a mixture of straight-in jamming, stemming, and liebacking and is well-protected. Rappel the route with two ropes to descend.

L. The Cow, Right   5.7 ★★★

FA: Ken Boche, 5/70.

The first pitch is varied with some awkward sections and some straightforward splitter cracks. The protection can be tricky at times. The second pitch is technical and wild but rarely climbed and may be munge-filled.

M. The Cow, Right (var.)   5.6 R ★★

This pitch involves mostly face climbing and "walking" up the crack with very little protection. After 50 feet, if you want better protection, step right onto The Cow, Right.

N. The Cow, Center   5.5 R ★★★

FA: Jeff and Greg Schaffer, 7/66.

If not for the tricky and loose anchor, the first pitch would be a great first lead. It involves mostly face climbing with a crack for protection and the occasional jam. The second pitch has a huge runout on 5.5 friction before turning to a well-protected, short, and fun lieback. Beware that if you rappel after the first pitch, the only fixed anchor is a sketchy slung chockstone (be careful!). Descend from the second pitch by rappelling with two ropes to the bolt anchor of The Cow, Left.

O. The Cow, Left   5.8 R ★★★

FA: Ken Boche and Mary Bomba, 3/70.

The first pitch offers great but very runout friction climbing. The second pitch is more moderately runout before turning to a well-protected and fun 5.8 lieback. Few climbers lead the first pitch. Instead they access the second pitch via The Cow, Center and then rappel to the first pitch anchors to toprope it with one 60m rope (great friction practice).

More at SuperTopo.com

View a discussion of the rockfall danger at the Glacier Point Apron so that you can assess the danger for yourself.

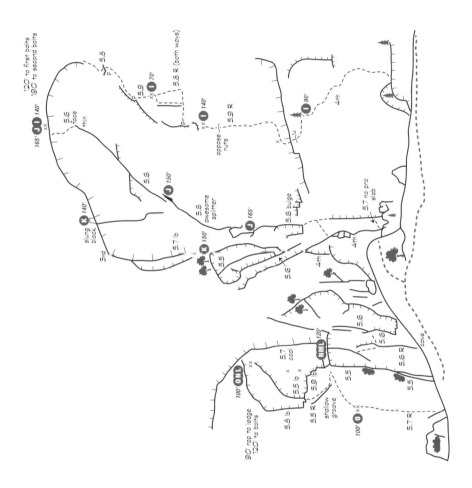

I. Marginal 5.9 R ★★★★★
nuts: 1 ea sml; cams, 1 ea .5-1", 4 draws

J. The Grack, Center 5.6 ★★★★★
nuts: 1 set; cams: 2 ea .5-2"

K. The Grack, Left 5.7 ★★★
nuts: 1 set; cams: 1-2 ea .5-2.5"

L. The Cow, Right 5.7 ★★★
nuts: 1 set; cams: 1-2 ea .5-3"

M. The Cow, Right (var.) 5.6 R ★★
nuts: 1 set; cams: 1 ea .5-1.5"

N. The Cow, Center 5.5 R ★★★
nuts: 1 set; cams: 1 ea .5-2"

O. The Cow, Left 5.8 R ★★★
nuts: 1 set; cams: 1 ea .5-1.5"

Sentinel Rock

The sentinel . . . is perhaps the least variable in expression of all the notable cliffs of the valley, standing resolutely muffled until the sun begins to sink to its eclipse behind the high promontory of El Capitan. Then his face glitters with fine Plutonian lines, hard and grim as steel on iron.

– J. Smeaton Chase, 1911

Approach

This 1.5-mile-long approach gains about 1,500 feet in elevation. Park at the paved pullouts for the Four Mile Trail (1.8 miles from El Cap Meadow) and hike up the trail about 0.5 mile to a creek crossing (dry in late season). Just before the creek crossing, leave the trail and hike up the talus slope. Cairns mark the trail as it switchbacks up the talus. At a point near the base of the rock, the trail splits; hike up and right toward the large ramp. Continue up this ramp and slightly right until you reach a trail contouring west (right). This trail traverses a ledge and passes trees to another ramp leading up and right. Continue several hundred feet up the talus to a somewhat loose and blocky corner on the left that leads to a ledge with trees. The route begins in the corner on the right side of this ledge.

Stecke Salathé

Randy Spurrier

Descent

From the top of Sentinel Rock, hike north and east following a trail through the bushes and over boulders into the gully. Continue down and eastward through the gully, being careful of loose rock. Once down the gully, cross a creek and continue over slabs down and right. Scramble down the slabs past bushes and trees. Once at the base of the slabs, hike along the right side of the trees and down a bit (with more slabs on the right). Cut left through the trees and contour over to the point where the approach trail splits. Follow the trail back down the talus to the Four Mile Trail and return to the trailhead.

Steck Salathé 5.10b★★★★

Time to climb route: **6-8 hours**

Approach time: **1-1.5 hours**

Descent time: **1.5-2 hours**

Sun exposure: **morning to afternoon**

Height of route: **1600'**

This Yosemite wide-climbing testpiece ascends a striking line up Sentinel Rock's imposing North Face. While many fear the route, those with good offwidth and chimney technique will have a blast. Steck Salathé has all the ingredients necessary for a big adventure: stout wide cracks, some tricky routefinding, big exposure, many pitches, and an awesome summit. The climb is one of the *Fifty Classic Climbs of North America*. You can't pull through many of the cruxes on gear.

History

Even in the infancy of Valley climbing, Sentinel Rock beckoned. Its northern escarpment, especially at sunset, glistened with cracks and dihedrals, some perhaps climbable. Pioneers of the 1930s ventured up the lower, tree-covered part of the formation, returning humbled by the nightmare above: a 1,500-foot wall of tremendous steepness and disconnected crack systems.

Yet after the Lost Arrow Chimney climb of 1947, the upper north wall of Sentinel became the "next great problem," and the route was never in question: head for the top of a prominent buttress (soon named the Flying Buttress) and enter the Great Chimney, which led to the top.

In 1948 Robin Hansen, Fritz Lippmann, and Jack Arnold made the first attempt—and quit after 100 feet. Jim Wilson and Phil

Bettler were next, a year later: they got one pitch higher. Wilson and Bettler soon returned with two of the most competent climbers of the day, Allen Steck and Bill Long, but this team turned back after two days and 450 feet. Long and Bettler came back in May 1950, reaching the halfway point, the top of the Flying Buttress. They retreated.

Four attempts, four retreats. Steck had watched the last bid with great interest, and was not unhappy with the outcome. "I lay awake many a night in Berkeley," he later wrote, "wondering what this north wall was like above the buttress; it was almost an obsession with me." Steck was no stranger to difficult climbing. In 1949 he had become the first American to climb one of the fabled "Six Great North Faces" of the Alps when he did the Cima Grande in the Dolomites.

In late June 1950, Steck asked the renowned John Salathé to try the wall with him and the 51-year-old Swiss instantly agreed. The pair reached the top of the Flying Buttress late on Day Two. Ahead lay new ground: the Headwall. Salathé labored for more than ten hours on this pitch, placing six bolts and many marginal pitons. Finally, the two men were able to work across a slab and enter the Great Chimney, the gateway to the summit.

Meanwhile, the pair had to deal with an even more malevolent enemy: the heat. The wall became a furnace. Steck acutely remembers their thirst: "Standing there in slings, with his hammer poised over the star drill, John would turn his head and say, 'Al, if I only could have just a little orange juice!'"

On the morning of Day Four, Salathé took the lead toward the now-notorious Narrows. A perfect back-and-foot chimney led upward from a small chockstone ledge.

Steck Salathé	Pitch	1	2	3	4	5	6	7	8	9	10	11	12	13	14	15	16
Free difficulty	≥5.10				●					●							
	5.9					●			●		●	●				●	
	5.8	●	●				●										
	5.7			●									●	●			
	5.6							●									●
	≤5.5						●										

Ten feet higher, the chimney narrowed abruptly at a ceiling. A hole, dark as a house chimney—and nearly as tight—shot upward out of sight. Salathé, an aid specialist, wanted nothing to do with this claustro-horror, so he worked his way sideways to look at the prospects outside of the main chimney. Using aid and placing a few bolts, he managed to bypass The Narrows, a feat few have repeated.

At dawn on Day Five, thirsty Steck tried not to watch as Salathé placed his false teeth into a cup, using the last of the water to moisten them enough to insert. And Steck was not especially pleased to hear Salathé soon say, "Allen, you should do the Arrow Chimney—now dot's a real climb!" At noon on July 4, 1950 the pair reached the top and staggered down the complex descent gullies toward the stream below. Steck hurled himself, fully clothed, into a shallow pool.

Chris McNamara

"The reason, the incentive, the motive for all this?" Steck asked in his splendid 1951 article about the climb. "It is an intangible, provocative concept that I shall leave to the reader to explain." Steck was neither the first nor the last climber to avoid trying to illuminate the rationale for the peculiar sport of rockclimbing. His article contained one remark he now wishes he'd never written: ". . . the second ascent should do better, if there should ever be one." Ironically, Steck was to do the route five more times, the last one on the fiftieth anniversary of his first ascent!

That bold and haughty youth Royal Robbins led the next two ascents, the first in 1953 (at age 18) and then again in 1956. Unlike Salathé, Robbins was able to thread his way through The Narrows, the claustrophobic route virtually everyone has followed since. The Steck Salathé was done only nine times during the 1950s, and only 37 times during the 1960s. But by the early 1970s it was a trade route, appreciated as a classic crack climb, not terribly hard but long, strenuous, and historic.

– *Steve Roper*

Strategy

Get a dawn start (or earlier), as the

combination of the approach, climb, and descent is demanding." Bring plenty of food and water as well as a headlamp and jacket. The route receives a limited amount of sun in the afternoon keeping the temperatures cool even during mid-summer. A 60m rope is not mandatory but allows doing the route in as few as 10 pitches.

The first crux is the Wilson Overhang, which seems to keep getting harder due to rockfall. The second and most feared crux is The Narrows. Here you must climb a spooky squeeze chimney inside the rock or climb even harder terrain outside. Make sure your squeeze chimney technique is dialed before attempting this pitch.

Retreat

Retreat from this route can be accomplished with two 50m ropes. There are usually fixed rappel anchors to use for the entire route except on Pitch 10. With only one rope (50m or 60m), you will be required to leave gear to retreat. The route follows a major watercourse and will become potentially dangerous during rain. If you are forced to bivy, there are a number of good ledges on which to be relatively comfortable.

Rack

nuts: 2 sets
cams: 2 ea .5-3.5"
        1 ea 4.5"
        1 ea 5-7" (optional)
For aid variation on Pitch 9
bring hooks and micronuts.

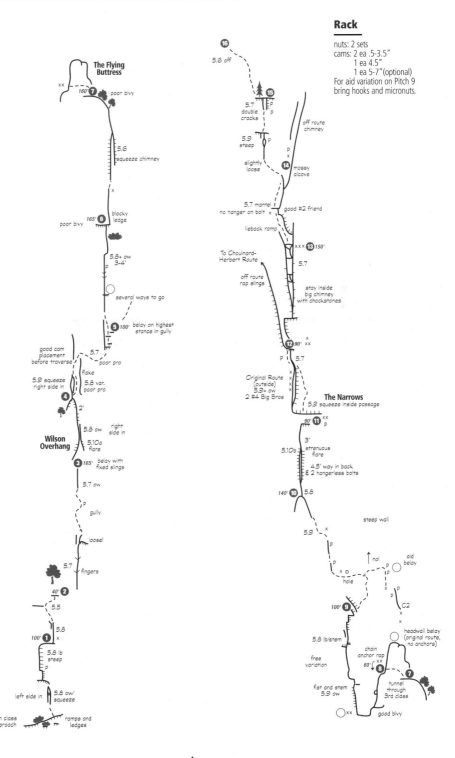

The Flying Buttress

xx

160' **7** poor bivy

5.6 off

5.7 double cracks

5.9 steep

slightly loose

off route chimney

5.6 squeeze chimney

x

165' **6** blocky ledge
poor bivy

5.8+ ow 3-4'
p

several ways to go

100' **5** belay on highest stance in gully

good cam placement before traverse
5.7
poor pro

flake
5.8 var.
poor pro

5.9 squeeze right side in

4

2'

right side in

5.8 ow

5.10a flare

Wilson Overhang

3 165' belay with fixed slings

5.7 ow

p

gully

loose!

5.7 fingers

40' **2**

5.5

100' **1**

x

5.8

5.8 lb steep
p

left side in   5.8 ow/ squeeze

4th class approach   ramps and ledges

5.7 mantel
no hanger on bolt   x

good #2 friend

lieback ramp

To Chouinard-Herbert Route

off route rap slings

14 mossy alcove

xxx **13** 150'

5.7

stay inside big chimney with chockstones

x
xx

12 90'

p   5.7

Original Route (outside)
5.9+ ow
2 #4 Big Bros

x
x
x
x

The Narrows

5.9 squeeze inside passage

90' **11** xx
p

3'
5.10b   strenuous flare

4.5' way in back
& 2 hangerless bolts

140' **10** 5.8

steep wall

5.9

x
p
p

no!

x o
hole

100' **9**

aid belay

C2

x

5.8 lb/stem

free variation

fist and stem
5.9 ow

chain anchor rap
60' **8** xx

headwall belay (original route, no anchors)

7

tunnel through 3rd class

xx

good bivy

16
15
p
p
p
x

Lower Cathedral Spire

By and large, the two Cathedral Spires climbs of 1934 set a marvelous standard for future climbers. An ethic had unconsciously evolved—one that seems to me to speak volumes about the character of the three climbers involved. Train hard for a climb and know what you are getting into. Be bold—but practice proper safety measures. Don't be afraid to turn back. Most of all, don't subdue the rock with technology: use sophisticated gear—but use it wisely.

– Steve Roper, Camp 4

Approach

If driving from Camp 4: take Northside Drive to El Capitan Meadow. Turn left at the triangle and drive east to just before you meet Southside Drive (the one-way road). Park on the side of the road and walk 300 feet west on Southside drive to the pullout on the left (south). If driving into Yosemite Valley: on Southside Drive, park 300 feet before the turnoff to El Capitan Meadow at the paved pullout on the right.

This 0.8 mile approach gains about 1,500

feet of elevation. From the middle of the pullout, locate a trail and walk 300 feet, passing a climbers' information sign, to the Valley Loop Trail. Turn left (east) and walk 300 feet until an unmarked climbers' trail is visible on the right. Follow this for a few hundred yards until the trail wraps around two large trees side by side, right before an uphill grade. Left of the trees leave the main climbers' trail and pick up a faint climbers' trail on the left that passes The Cathedral Boulders and then starts up the hill. From here the trail is hard to follow—use your intuition.

Follow the faint trail with cairns into the broad boulder field/gully. Hike up this for 40-60 minutes, passing a small formation on the right, until you are even with the obvious bulk of Lower Cathedral Spire.

Head through dense forest toward the south face of the Spire stopping about 200 feet short of the notch and looking for a dead log wedged into a crack.

Descent

Rappel with two 50m ropes or one 60m rope with some 4th class downclimbing. From the base, reverse the approach.

Lower Cathedral Spire as seen from Higher Cathedral Spire. (opposite) Cathedral Spires. Photo by David Safanda

South by Southwest

5.11a★★★★

Time to climb route: **3-5 hours**	
Approach time: **1-2 hours**	
Descent time: **1-2 hours**	
Sun exposure: **morning to noon**	
Height of route: **450'**	

From the instant Walt Shipley and Keith Reynolds climbed South by Southwest in 1993, it has been recognized as a classic. The route is beautiful, extremely exposed, perfectly protected, and has one of the most amazing summits in the country. The absence of awkward or poorly-protected climbing makes it an excellent climb for those wanting to break into the grade.

The summit is simply astounding. It is nestled among Higher Cathedral Spire (only a few hundred feet away), the awesome northwest face of Higher Cathedral Rock, and Middle Cathedral Rock. From here you'll get perfect views of El Capitan, Sentinel Rock, and Taft Point.

Strategy

South by Southwest is becoming increasingly popular, however the long approach hike and the grade make crowds unlikely. The first two pitches are shared with the Regular Route and thus may require a wait. Note that many parties rappel South by Southwest regardless of their ascent route, yet potential problems would only arise at the Pitch 5 belay or on the 6th pitch.

The route is south facing yet fairly near the Valley rim. As a result, mid-summer can be hot, but breezes are common. In early season, damp conditions may be present on the approach pitches.

South by Southwest		Pitch 1	2	3	4	5	6
Free difficulty	≥5.10					●	●
	5.9						
	5.8						
	5.7			●			
	5.6	●					●
	≤5.5		●				

Be aware of loose rock, primarily a danger on the first two pitches and mostly a problem if there are parties in front.

If you finish early, consider rappelling to the main ledge, walking out right, and climbing the Regular Route. Then, rappel back down South by Southwest to the main ledge and continue to the ground.

Retreat

Rappel from any belay except the top of the 4th pitch where you would need to leave a cam or two to back up the manky fixed sling held in place with a knot jam. Better to leave a cam than to trust the old webbing. There are no major watercourses on the route, but you will get wet if caught unprepared.

A. Regular Route　　　　5.9 or 5.7 A0★★

This is a must-do for any historic climb trophy collector. Only months after climbing Higher Spire, the same team of Eichorn, Leonard, and Robinson returned to Lower Spire and started up the Southeast Face. The route turned out to be less sustained than the Higher Spire but more risky due to one large feature on the third pitch: a menacing, thin flake detached 10 inches from the wall. The mindset necessary to climb the flake bordered on insanity. First, they lassoed a projection on the flake and then climbed hand-over-hand until they could mantel the flake. If liebacked, the fragile flake would break, so the leader used a hammer to chip footholds. Moving upward, the leader delicately balanced his weight to keep from pulling the feature—and himself—from the wall.

Today, the detached flake still looks suicidal and all climbers avoid the original direct line with a variation to the right. This variation starts with a 5.9 boulder problem or an A0 move off a bolt. Next, the climbing follows steep, loose, and poorly protected 5.7 flakes that will scare even the solid 5.9 leader. The rest of the route has no good pitches. However, the summit and overall experience make this a worthy outing.

To descend, rappel South by Southwest.

Rack

nuts: 1 set
cams: 2 ea .5-1.25"
     3 ea 1.5-2.5"
     2 ea 3"

A. Regular Route 5.9 or 5.7A0 ★★

nuts: 1 set; cams: 2 ea .6-3", 1 ea 4.5"(optional)

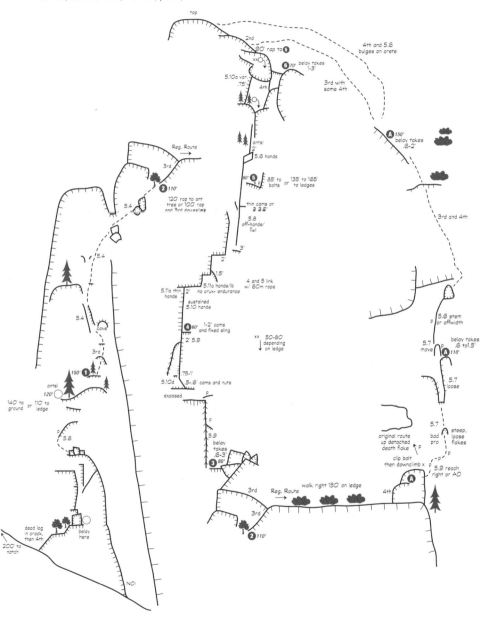

Higher Cathedral Spire

Higher Cathedral Spire was the testpiece Valley climb at the time of the first ascent in 1934 by climbing legends Jules Eichorn, Bestor Robinson, and Dick Leonard. During the 1930s, the techniques for roped climbing were still new and the modern climber can only imagine the terror of climbing this classic route with heavy boots, almost no pro for the leader, and ropes that were unlikely to survive a lead fall.

Regular Route

Greg Barnes

Approach

If driving from Camp 4: take Northside Drive to El Capitan Meadow. Turn left at the triangle and drive east to just before you meet Southside Drive (the one-way road). Park on the side of the road and walk 300 feet west on Southside drive to the pullout on the left (south). If driving into Yosemite Valley: on Southside Drive, park 300 feet before the turnoff to El Capitan Meadow at the paved pullout on the right.

This 0.8 mile approach gains about 1,500 feet of elevation. From the middle of the pullout, locate a trail and walk 300 feet, passing a climbers' information sign, to the Valley Loop Trail. Turn left (east) and walk 300 feet until a climbers' trail is visible on the right. This trail is not marked by a carabiner post. Follow this trail up switchbacks to the talus slope. Cairns mark the easiest path up the talus. Trend left whenever there is any question. Continue past the Lower Cathedral Spire and follow

the contour of the west face of Higher Cathedral Spire up and around the south side. The trail is well-traveled and switchbacks up loose dirt and talus, then cuts left to a cleft at the start of the route. A cross is etched into the rock at the base of the route.

Descent

Rappel the route and reverse the approach. You can rappel the route with one 50m rope, but it is much easier with a 60m rope.

Regular Route 5.9★★★★

Time to climb route: **3-5 hours**

Approach time: **1.5-2 hours**

Descent time: **2.5 hours**

Sun exposure: **noon to afternoon**

Height of route: **300'**

Nearly 70 years after its first ascent, Higher Cathedral Spire remains a great adventure and challenge. It is classic in every way possible: a beautiful formation, a compelling line, an intriguing first ascent history, and an awesome summit. Unlike most rock in Yosemite, the Higher Spire contains numerous face holds and fractured, loose rock. The standard route avoids straight-in crack climbing when possible in favor of wild and circuitous face moves. Some of the cruxes are hard to pull through on gear.

History

It's hardly surprising that the pioneer climbers of the early 1930s chose the Higher Cathedral Spire for their first serious outing. These adventurers had started as mountaineers, where reaching an actual summit (rather than a nondescript rim or a ledge partway up a cliff) was a demonstrable sign of success. And what better place to head for than the Higher Spire, North America's largest freestanding pinnacle? This phallus of granite rises some 400 feet above the ground at its upper edge and more than 1,000 feet on its downhill side. Naturally, it was to the upper side of the tower that the pioneers approached, for they wanted success, not an epic.

On the historic Sierra Club trip of Labor Day 1933—the first-ever climbers' visit to the Valley—Jules Eichorn, Dick Leonard,

Regular Route		Pitch 1	2	3	4	5
Free difficulty	≥5.10					
	5.9	●	●	●	●	
	5.8					
	5.7					
	5.6					
	≤5.5	●				

and Bestor Robinson had hiked up to the southern base of the spire. Leonard's first impression: "After four hours of ineffectual climbing on the southwest face, and three hours more upon the southeast and east faces, we were turned away by the sheer difficulty of the climbing." It's no wonder they failed—their "pitons" on this reconnaissance were 10-inch-long nails!

On November 5, armed with pitons and carabiners obtained by mail from Sporthaus Schuster, a large sporting-goods store in Münich, the trio returned to the southern face and managed to climb two pitches before darkness forced a retreat. "By means of pitons as a direct aid," Leonard wrote, "we were able to overcome two holdless, vertical, 10-foot pitches."

This attempt is historic, for it signified the first use of artificial aid in Yosemite—and one of the first times in the country. The technique of driving pitons into the rock in order to grab them, or to stand on them, or to attach slings to them—in other words, to use them to gain elevation—was common in the Alps. Robert Underhill, the trio's mentor, had trained in Europe and might have been expected to embrace this technique, but he was unyielding on the use of artificial aid: "Every pitch," he once wrote, "must be surmounted by one's own unaided abilities. . ." The pioneer Yosemite climbers respected Underhill, of course, but confronting firsthand the smoothness and sheerness of the Valley's cliffs, they realized they would not get far unless they used, occasionally at least, some form of "artificial" techniques. The trick, as they saw it, was to use as little direct aid as possible: the game was climbing, not engineering. This adventurous attitude was to be emulated by most of the better climbers in the years to come.

After ordering more pitons from Sporthaus Schuster (they now possessed 55), the trio was set to go as soon as spring arrived. The Valley's first climbing spectators accompanied Eichorn, Leonard, and Robinson to the base of the Higher Spire on April 15, 1934, and present were two high-powered ones: Francis Farquhar, the president of the Sierra Club, and Bert Harwell, the park's chief naturalist, on hand to witness history. In a few hours the trio had reached its previous high point, a ledge at the base of a steep orange trough later known as the Rotten Chimney. Here, Eichorn and Leonard alternated pounding in the crude spikes, hanging on to them to inch upward. Where the crack ended, Leonard made a clever traverse to reach easier ground. Finally, as the Valley turned golden, the men nailed a final pitch to the spacious summit and planted an American flag—surely the only time this silly patriotic practice ever took place in Yosemite.

With the route known, the climb became popular almost immediately, though there were so few good climbers in the 1930s that only 12 ascents had been made by Pearl Harbor. Raffi Bedayn, that kind-hearted soul who helped preserve Camp 4 in the 1970s, obviously loved the route: he did it four times between 1937 and 1941! Bill Hewlett, later to become famous as the co-founder of the Hewlett-Packard organization, did the route in 1937—the eighth ascent. Though the first ascensionists had used lots of aid, this was naturally whittled down until by 1940 only 10 feet of aid remained. This section, on the Bathtubs

Pitch, was finally climbed free by Chuck Wilts and Spencer Austin in 1944.

– Steve Roper

Strategy

The best time to climb this route is between May and October. Most of the route is in the shade until about 1 P.M. so start early in the hot summer months. Most pitches are protected by a combination of gear and pervasive fixed pitons. Loose rock and tremendous exposure make this a climb best suited for confident and experienced 5.9 leaders. A single 60m rope is optimal and will allow you to rappel the route at convenient spots. The route can also be descended with a single 50m rope but this is not recommended.

The variations on the second pitch and last pitches offer steep and strenuous 5.9 crack climbing. Use these variations to add more crack climbing to the route or to pass slower parties.

Retreat

Retreat by rappelling the route with one 60m rope. The fourth belay is difficult to retreat from. If rappelling, be conscious of parties that may be climbing below.

Randy Spurrier on the summit of Higher Cathedral Spire.

Rack

nuts: 1 ea med, lrg
cams: 1 ea .5-1"
        2 ea 1.5-2"
        1 ea 3"
many slings

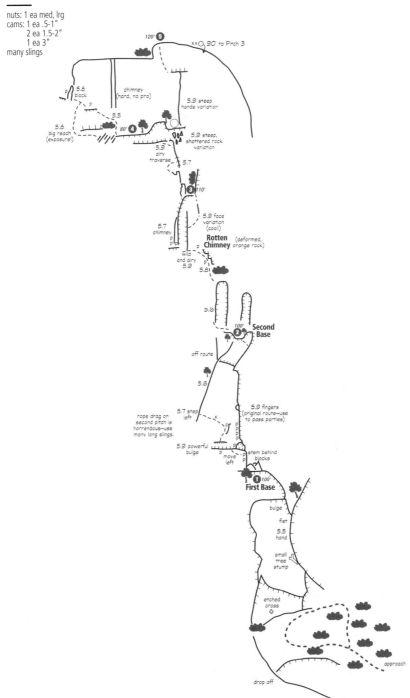

Higher Cathedral Rock

Higher Cathedral Rock is one of the most ignored formations of the Valley, thanks to its modest position between its massive sibling, Middle Cathedral, and the soaring Cathedral Spires. If HCR is hardly an earthshaking sight from the valley floor, the opposite is true once you stand beneath it. This is one steep and beautiful crag!

– Steve Roper

Approach

If driving from Camp 4: take Northside Drive to El Capitan Meadow. Turn left at the triangle and drive east to just before you meet Southside Drive (the one way road). Park on the side of the road and walk 300 feet west on Southside drive to the pullout on the left (south). If driving into Yosemite Valley: on Southside Drive, park 300 feet before the turnoff to El Capitan Meadow at the paved pullout on the right.

From the middle of the pullout, walk 300 feet, passing a climbers' information sign, to the Valley Loop Trail. Turn left (east) and walk 300 feet until a climbers'

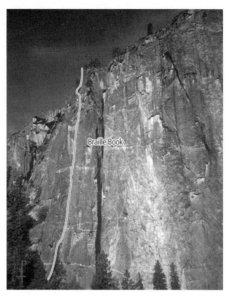

Braille Book

Chris McNamara

trail is visible on the right. Follow this trail for 1-1.5 hours, at times scrambling over boulders, until a few hundred feet before the northeast face of Higher Cathedral Rock. Braille Book starts about 150 feet left of an enormous, ominous-looking corner. The Northeast Buttress Route starts under a huge roof on the right side of the face.

Descent

Braille Book
From the top of Braille Book, hike up and south for 150 feet, then cut left on a climbers' trail through brush. Follow the ridgetop down to the main notch between Higher Cathedral Rock and the valley wall. Follow the well-traveled climbers' trail as it switchbacks down through trees and brush onto talus. Hike down the talus until you meet the approach trail.

Northeast Buttress
From the last pitch, hike south and west toward the summit. From near the high summit, walk south and down the ridgetop through brush and sandy ledges to the main notch between Higher Cathedral Rock and the valley wall. Follow the well-traveled climbers' trail as it switchbacks down through trees and brush onto talus. Hike down the talus until you meet the approach trail.

NE Buttress

Braille Book 5.8★★★★

Time to climb route:	**3-5 hours**
Approach time:	**1-2 hours**
Descent time:	**45 minutes-1.5 hours**
Sun exposure:	**morning to afternoon**
Height of route:	**700'**

Amazing surroundings and atypically juggy face holds make the Braille Book a must-do. However, the cruxes all involve stemming on slick holds and/or flared chimneys and there is not always good protection. This is an old school 5.8 and will feel much harder if you lack solid chimney skills. High points are the Cathedral Spires looming behind you, a surprise view of a giant chasm high on the route, and the unforgettable final pitch of huge 5.4 jugs on a steep spectacular wall.

While the approach is daunting for some, the trail is generally good, and with limited boulder-hopping it goes quickly. The descent is neither treacherous nor long, and thus far fewer people than you might expect are forced to bivy. You can't pull through many of the cruxes on gear.

History

Some routes aren't worth a long approach (the West Face of North Dome springs to mind). Some routes definitely are. The approach to the Braille Book is not much fun: one must thrash up a steep, unpleasant forest and then ugly talus—1,800 vertical feet in all. But once this is out of the way, a delightful route awaits. When Jim Bridwell, Chris Fredericks, Brian Berry, and Joe Faint established this climb in June 1966, they knew they had a winner. Within weeks the quality line was repeated and word soon

spread. The origin of the name will be obvious to anyone who climbs the route: knobs abound and even a blind person could probably do the route. This is not to say the route is easy, as Bridwell protégé Jim Stanton realized one day. He fell high on the route, popped a few pitons, and plunged 160 feet. Incredibly, considering the rough rock, he escaped with only a knee injury.

- Steve Roper

Strategy

Unfortunately, the approach hike and hot summer temperatures don't keep the crowds down and many parties end up turning around due to the line—start early. A great backup option is the Regular Route of Higher Cathedral Spire—only a few hundred yards east of the start of Braille Book. A 50m rope is sufficient for Braille Book, since extending pitches with a 60m does not gain better belay points or allow linking pitches.

While jugs are everywhere on the first half of the route, the crux sections involve surprisingly burly moves, usually stemming off of slick holds, with some fist and offwidth moves. For the less experienced, the best possible practice for Braille Book is to work on flared stemming and flared chimneys. Some sections of chimneying are protected only with micronuts.

Although high above the Valley floor, Braille Book is baked by summer sun until afternoon, and on hot days this is a route to avoid. Early season sees snow at the base and some wet sections. There are loose holds and blocks on the route, and as with any multi-pitch climb parties above always present some danger.

Retreat

Retreat by rappelling from trees, your own gear, and/or bolts if you are high enough to gain the bolts on the new routes to the right. Two ropes are required unless you leave more gear.

Braille Book	Pitch	1	2	3	4	5	6
Free difficulty	≥5.10						
	5.9						
	5.8	●	●	●			
	5.7					●	
	5.6						
	≤5.5						●

Rack

micro nuts: 1 set
nuts: 1 set
cams: 1 ea .6-2"
      2 ea 2.5-4"
      optional 4.5-7"

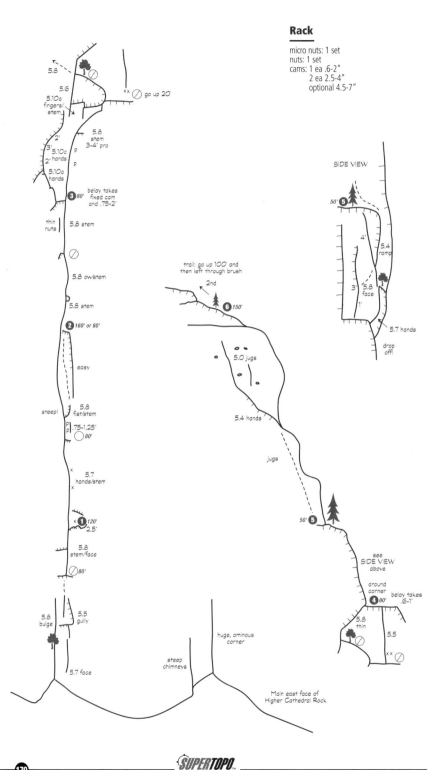

5.8

5.6
5.10a
fingers/
stem

xx ⊘ go up 20'

5.8
stem
3-4' pro

2'

3' 5.10c
2" hands

5.10a
hands

P
P

❸ 80' belay takes
fixed cam
and .75-2"

thin
nuts

5.8 stem

5.8 ow/stem

5.8 stem

❷ 160' or 80'

easy

steep!

5.8
fist/stem

P
P .75-1.25"
◯ 80'

x
x

5.7
hands/stem

x ❶ 120'
2.5'

5.8
stem/face

⊘ 80'

5.8
bulge

5.5
gully

5.7 face

huge, ominous
corner

steep
chimneys

Main east face of
Higher Cathedral Rock

SIDE VIEW

50' ❺

4'

5.4
ramp

3'

5.8
face

1'

5.7 hands

drop
off!

trail: go up 100' and
then left through brush

2nd

❻ 150'

5.0 jugs

5.4 hands

jugs

50' ❺

see
SIDE VIEW
above

around
corner

❹ 80' belay takes
.6-1"

5.8
thin

5.5

xx ⊘

Northeast Buttress

5.9★★★★★

Time to climb route:	**7-9 hours**
Approach time:	**1 hour**
Descent time:	**1.5 hours**
Sun exposure:	**morning to afternoon**
Height of route:	**900'**

With pitch after pitch of amazing climbing in a spectacular location, this is possibly the best long 5.9 in the Valley. Though not as technically difficult as routes such as Serenity Crack or Sons of Yesterday, this climb is much more committing and requires routefinding and wide crack skills. From sustained and steep jams to mandatory offwidths and chimneys, this route requires experience on 5.8 and 5.9 cracks.

History

Most of the significant Valley first ascents up until the early 1960s were made by a select few. Six men—Dave Brower, John Salathé, Allen Steck, Mark Powell, Warren Harding, and Royal Robbins—account for the vast majority of the best routes. The Northeast Buttress of HCR is a remarkable exception: three climbers, hardly possessing household names, did the first ascent, and in impeccable style.

One day in early 1959 while climbing the Higher Cathedral Spire, 24-year-old Dick Long looked west across the talus and scanned the Higher Rock's gray-and-gold buttress. Hundreds of climbers had seen this exact same view, but Long was the first to spy a possible route. Long had a small side-business making pitons and by 1959 was a rival of Chouinard's. A superb

climber—daring, talented, and inventive—Long once said, with no hint of bragging, that he could have been as good as Robbins if only he'd climbed full time.

One weekend in June, Long grabbed two climbers even more unknown than himself, Ray D'Arcy and Terry Tarver. D'Arcy, an Ivy League physicist who talked so fast that spittle spewed constantly from his lips, was known for his far north adventures (in 1955 he had been on the first expedition to the Cirque of the Unclimbables), but he was mainly a snow-and-ice specialist. Tarver had been climbing in the Bay Area for a few years but had never done even a Grade IV. It was an unlikely team for such an imposing buttress.

Yet two days later the trio topped out, having used no bolts and having done much of the route free. Long, a modest fellow, wrote up the climb for the Sierra Club Bulletin, summarizing the route in a single sentence: "This climb can be well-protected and offers a variety of difficult climbing." No kidding! What Long neglected to say was that they had encountered wild flared chimneys, complex routefinding and strenuous jamcracks. It was a job well done.

For this ascent Long had brought along some of his prototype giant angle pitons, nearly 3 inches wide, the largest ever made. Various climbers on the Higher Spire during those same two days had heard these pitons being driven and returned to Camp 4 mystified about the "bonging" sound emanating from the cliff. The term "bong-bong" soon became the name for any piton wider than 2 inches. To make these steel monstrosities lighter, Long had drilled holes all over them, another first. Yvon Chouinard, seeing these angles after the climb, was mightily impressed: his biggest

	Pitch										
Northeast Buttress	1	2	3	4	5	6	7	8	9	10	11
Free difficulty ≥5.10											
5.9						●	●				●
5.8	●	●					●		●		
5.7				●							
5.6	●				●						
≤5.5							●				

angle was only an inch-and-a-half wide.
Long later accomplished what I consider to
be one of the most impressive
performances of the 1960s. This was back
in the days when one was either a rock
specialist or a mountaineer, but rarely both.
Long and Allen Steck were exceptions.
During a ten-month period in 1965 and
1966 the pair made the first ascent of Mt.
Logan's Hummingbird Ridge and the third
ascent of the Salathé Wall. Talk about well-
rounded climbers!

- Steve Roper

Strategy

Start early. The first few pitches have short
cruxes and large belay ledges. It is much
easier to pass parties down low than up
high.

   Prepare for an intense day of hiking and
climbing. Though there are a few notable
crux sections, the hardest part of this climb
is staying fresh on pitch after pitch of
sustained, steep, and physical terrain. The
climb also has a few routefinding
difficulties. Look for obvious lines of
weakness in the upper pitches to avoid
getting off-route.

   The route receives early light then goes
into the shade in the afternoon.
Temperatures can be scorching or windy
and cold on any given day. Be prepared for
both extremes with plenty of water and a
wind jacket. Most parties should also bring
a headlamp in case the climb takes longer
than expected.

Retreat

Two 50m ropes are required for retreat.
From Pitch 5 or below the climb can be
rappelled without much difficulty. From
above Pitch 5, retreat becomes more
difficult due to the traversing nature of the
route.

More at SuperTopo.com

Check out beta from other climbers at
www.supertopo.com.

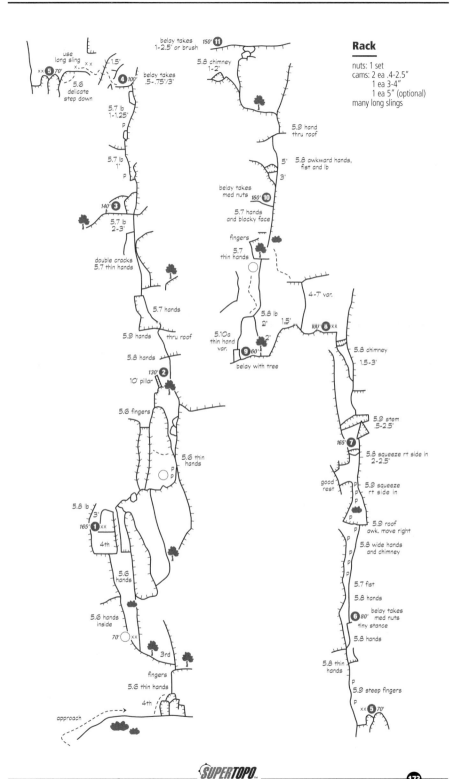

Rack

nuts: 1 set
cams: 2 ea .4-2.5"
      1 ea 3-4"
      1 ea 5" (optional)
many long slings

use long sling

1.5°

5 70' xx x—x xx

belay takes .5-.75'/3'

4 100'

5.6 delicate step down

5.7 lb 1-1.25'

P

5.7 lb 1'

P

140' 3

5.7 lb 2-3'

double cracks 5.7 thin hands

5.7 hands

5.9 hands thru roof

5.8 hands

130' 2
10' pillar

5.6 fingers

5.6 thin hands

P P

5.8 lb 3'
165' 1 xx
4th

5.6 hands

5.6 hands inside

70' xx

3rd

fingers

5.6 thin hands

4th

approach

belay takes 1-2.5' or brush

150' 11

5.8 chimney 1-2'

5.9 hand thru roof

5' 5.8 awkward hands, fist and lb
3'

belay takes med nuts
160' 10

5.7 hands and blocky face

fingers

5.7 thin hands

5.8 lb 2'
1.5'

5.10a thin hand var.
2'

9 60'

belay with tree

4-7' var.

100' 8 xx

5.8 chimney
1.5-3'

5.9 stem .5-2.5'

165' 7

5.8 squeeze rt side in 2-2.5'

good rest

5.9 squeeze rt side in
P
P
P

5.9 roof awk. move right
P
P
5.8 wide hands and chimney
P

5.7 fist

5.8 hands

6 80' belay takes med nuts
tiny stance

5.8 hands

5.8 thin hands

P

5.9 steep fingers

xx 5 70'

Middle Cathedral Rock

If Half Dome is forbidding, and El Cap smooth, then one must regard this rock as interesting, both to look at and to climb on. In certain lighting one can see thousands of the tiny ramps and flakes which makes climbing largely free and incredibly enjoyable. Much of the climbing consists of face climbing rather than cracks—this should come as a pleasant surprise to those who think the Valley is all nailing, 5.10 cracks, and ghastly friction. Approaches to the routes are obvious—it is the descents which force people into occasional bivouacs.

– *Steve Roper,* Climber's Guide To Yosemite, *1971*

Approach

If driving from Camp 4: take Northside Drive to El Capitan Meadow. Turn left at the triangle and drive east until just before you meet Southside Drive (the one way road.) Park on the side of the road and walk 300 feet west on Southside drive to the pullout on the left (south). If driving into Yosemite Valley: on Southside Drive, park 300 feet before the turnoff to El Capitan Meadow on the paved pullout on the right.

From the middle of the east most pullout, locate a trail and walk 300 feet, passing a climbers' information sign, to the Valley Loop Trail. (Don't start from the pullout to the west or all the following distances will be wrong.)

From here, follow different trails depending on which route you are climbing:

East Buttress

On the Valley Loop Trail, walk 300 feet right (west) until a climbers' trail is visible on the left marked by the first carabiner post after the climbers' information sign. After 5 minutes the trail leads into a boulder-strewn gully. Follow the gully to a carabiner sign in the middle of the boulders and another carabiner sign to the right marking a trail. After 150 feet you will reach a large platform with a great view of El Cap. The route starts here.

Central Pillar of Frenzy / Kor-Beck

On the Valley Loop Trail, turn right (west) and walk 350 yards until you see the second carabiner post after the climbers' information sign marking a climbers' trail. Walk up the hill to another carabiner post at the base of the wall. Walk 50 feet right to the start of the route.

To reach the start of Kor-Beck, from the Central Pillar carabiner post, skirt the base east for 100 yards until you must scramble up and left on 3rd class switchbacks. Move back right to the large recess in the face. To the right of the recess, climb 3rd class to an exposed pedestal.

Direct North Buttress

Turn right (west) and walk 500 yards until you see the third carabiner post after the climbers' information sign marking a climbers' trail. Head uphill to the toe of the buttress and then up right to a left-facing dihedral with a wide flared crack.

Descent

WARNING: There has recently been major rockfall in the descent gully for the East Buttress and DNB. Check conditions at www.supertopo.com before climbing these routes.

East Buttress

From the last belay, head right and up for 50 feet and then up and left on 3rd class. A trail becomes more distinct and contours left. After 250 feet look for a campfire ring/large cairns at a small clearing right before the first section of dense trees. Do not take the trail heading up and right. Instead, head down left through trees on a trail, which is not obvious at first. Follow the trail for 300 yards of easy but exposed 3rd class until it ends at the awesome chasm between Higher and Middle Cathedral Rocks. Scramble down this, with three single-rope rappels. Continue all the way down the gully, looking for the East Buttress approach trail (marked by carabiner posts) on the left at the point

Chris McNamara

where trees close in almost at the bottom. Reverse the approach trail to the road.

Kor-Beck
Rappel the route with two 50m or 60m ropes.

Central Pillar
Rappel on bolted anchors to the east of the climbing route (see topo).

Direct North Buttress
From the Kat Walk, follow a ledge trending slightly downward for 200–300 feet. When you reach a pillar (tree below it, ledges at base), work up the pillar to its top, then drop steeply down the other side through brush and small trees (careful!). About 100 feet after the pillar is the most dangerous section, a sloping ledge with no good holds (careful!). Another 200 feet around on the

ledge, you will spot the trees, dirt and brush of the East Buttress walk-off about 150 feet below you. Continue contouring, then drop down 3rd class dirt until you gain the obvious East Buttress descent trail just before the campfire ring/large cairns (see descent below).

Thank You Climb for Yosemite

The carabiner posts at Middle Cathedral Rock, Five Open Books, Reed's Pinnacle, and Fairview Dome were provided by the sweat and money of Climb for Yosemite, an annual fundraising climb-a-thon in the Bay Area. Thanks to the organizers, participants, and National Park Service for purchasing and installing these posts that eliminate the confusion and erosion caused by unnecessary extra climbers' trails.

East Buttress

5.10c or 5.9 A0★★★★★

Time to climb route: **8-9 hours**

Approach time: **30-40 minutes**

Descent time: **1.5 hours**

Sun exposure: **morning to afternoon**

Height of route: **1100'**

Included in *Fifty Classic Climbs of North America*, the East Buttress clearly stands out as a Yosemite gem. Pitch after pitch of moderate Yosemite cracks are occasionally interrupted with short, well-protected crux sections. The view of El Capitan is astounding and only surpassed by the dreamy climbing moves. Solid protection and very few awkward wide sections make the East Buttress a great entry climb to long Yosemite 5.9s and 5.10s. You can pull through most cruxes on gear.

History

Middle Cathedral Rock rivals El Cap in an odd sort of way. It isn't as high or as monolithic or as majestic, but it certainly has more "character" than its cross-Valley neighbor. If El Cap is gray and forbidding, much of Middle Cathedral is colorful and inviting. If El Cap defines Big Wall Climbing, then Middle Cathedral stands for Medium Wall Climbing. What can be more intriguing than Yosemite's neglected orphan?

Warren Harding craved Middle long before he became fixated on the Big Stone. In May 1954 he had pioneered, with three others, the 2,000-foot north buttress of Middle, by far the longest roped climb yet done in North America. Three months later he shifted his eyes left to the shorter but much more compact east buttress. A few hundred feet above the ground, Harding, Bob Swift, and John Whitmer twisted their way through an ant-infested tree (one of the little-known hazards of Valley climbing) and later arrived on a narrow platform below a crackless wall 40 feet high. This 65-degree slab was featureless, the biggest holds a mere quarter-inch wide. Any first ascensionist who wanted the east buttress would have to deal with this smooth wall, and no climber of the time (and very few today) could have done this unknown section free with zero protection. Artificial aid was needed and so out came the bolt kit. But down went the sun.

Bob Swift remembers the next events: "It was pitch dark when we heard voices below, in the forest. Some friends of ours were worried about us and had hiked up to check. They yelled up, 'How's the bivouac?' 'Bivouac? Hell, we're still climbing', was Warren's reply. The monotonous tink-tink of the hammer on the drill began again as work was started on the next bolt hole. Beside me on the belay ledge John rasped away furiously at sharpening a spare drill." Harding, later famous for his all-night drilling session on the first ascent of The Nose in 1958, had learned this nocturnal trick in 1954!

With the bolt ladder almost completed, they bivouacked and resumed climbing at dawn. The 50-foot section above the bolt ladder proved spectacular and thrilling. A long, serrated flake shot up the 70-degree wall, and the orange-colored granite was dotted liberally with knobs. It wasn't hard, yet it wasn't trifling either. One could rest on certain knobs and the protection was excellent. The exposure was sensational. But several pitches higher the trio ran out of steam and rappelled rather than face another bivouac.

East Buttress	Pitch	1	2	3	4	5	6	7	8	9	10	11
Free difficulty	≥5.10					●						
	5.9											
	5.8		●	●		●		●		●		
	5.7				●			●		●		●
	5.6	●										
	≤5.5											

The buttress now sported the longest continuous bolt ladder in the country—about nine. Bolts were not controversial back in 1954 and this ladder occasioned little comment at the time. In retrospect, however, this attempt can be seen as a radical Valley event. The old-timers had first sought out climbs with "inaccessible" summits like the Higher Spire and later routes that had natural lines, like the Column and Lower Brother. Harding was one of the first to see that hundreds of routes would open up if one simply placed a few bolt ladders to connect crack systems. (Much later, however, Harding's "excessive" use of bolts would cause a great rift in the climbing community.)

Little competition for routes existed in 1954 and Harding waited nine months before returning, knowing the route would remain virginal. Bob Swift and newcomer Jack Davis joined him on Memorial Day Weekend 1955, and thanks to the nine bolts, quickly reached the previous high point. After a bivouac near the top of the route, the trio finished the climb with alacrity and descended via the Kat Walk, the first ever to do so (William Kat, back in the 1920s, had wandered up this complex but easy route to the top of Middle). The Kat Walk later became the routine descent for many thousands of climbers.

Incredibly, this classic route was done only twice more during the 1950s. This obscurity was short-lived, however. A major variation—the one followed by most today—was put up in 1961 by Yvon Chouinard and Mort Hempel. Leaving the original route not far above the bolt ladder, this duo traversed up and right to a series of superb cracks that shot upward, meeting the original line three or four pitches higher. Hundreds of adventurers did the improved route in the early 1960s, but all used aid on the bolt ladder. Then in 1965, the legendary Frank Sacherer climbed the bolt ladder free, a startling achievement for its time.

– *Steve Roper*

Strategy

Start early and bring a headlamp and warm jacket. Many people underestimate the length of the route and end up spending a night on the rock. Also, this is an exceptionally popular climb and you may get stuck behind slower climbers. Bring plenty of water.

The 5.10c crux on Pitch 5 is easy to avoid by pulling on the closely spaced bolts (no aiders needed). The climbing on the 50 Crowded Variation is excellent. This variation is easier than the bolt ladder and a great opportunity to pass bottlenecked parties.

After the crux pitch, there are two finishes to the climb. To the left, the original route heads up wide, strenuous, and uncrowded terrain. To the right, Pitch 6 of the recommended route opens up with a spicy section of runout 5.6 and continues up stellar finger and hand cracks. A fall for the leader or follower will result in a pendulum.

Retreat

Two 50m or 60m ropes are required to retreat. The route can be rappelled from any pitch but requires leaving gear at many belay points. Retreat after Pitch 5 is difficult because the climb traverses to the right and left.

More at SuperTopo.com

In early 2002, rockfall swept through the descent gully. Check www.supertopo.com to read current climber beta on the conditions of the gully so that you can assess the risks for yourself.

A. Stand and Deliver   5.8★★

Good intro to fingers, hands and lieback cracks. Well-protected with many rests.

B. The Pedestal   5.8★★★

A consolation prize if the East Buttress is too crowded. An awkward wide crack start leads to an awesome corner that can be jammed, liebacked, or climbed using the crack and arête.

Rack

nuts: 1 set
cams: 2 ea .5-3.5"
other: slings/cordalette
60m ropes useful

A. Stand and Deliver 5.8★★
nuts: 1 set; cams, 2 ea .6-2.5"

B. The Pedestal 5.8★★★
nuts: 1 set; cams, 2 ea .6-2"

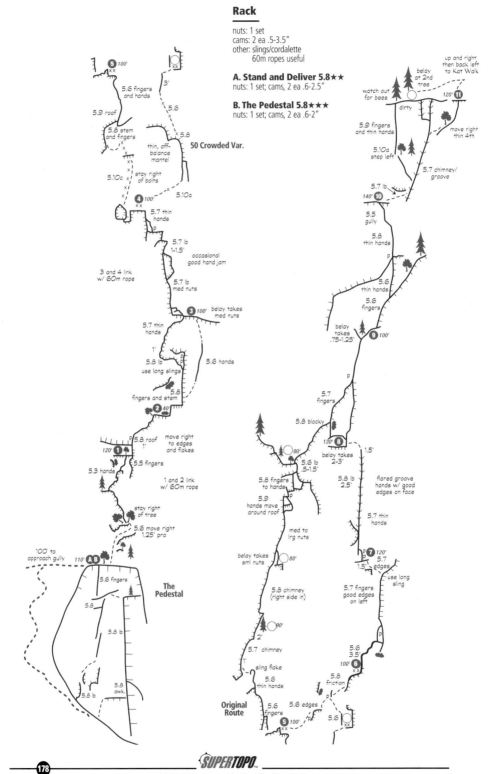

5 100'
xx

5.6 fingers
and hands

5.9 roof

3'

5.6

5.8 stem
and fingers

X 5.8

50 Crowded Var.

thin, off-
balance
mantel

stay right
of bolts

5.10c

5.10a

4 100'
xx

5.7 thin
hands

5.7 lb
1-1.5'

occasional
good hand jam

3 and 4 link
w/ 60m rope

5.7 lb
med nuts

3 100'   belay takes
med nuts

5.7 thin
hands

1'

5.8 lb
use long slings

5.6 hands

5.8
fingers and stem

2 40'

P 5.8 roof
1'

move right
to edges
and flakes

1 120'

5.5 fingers

5.3 hands

1 and 2 link
w/ 60m rope

stay right
of tree

5.6 move right
1.25' pro

100' to
approach gully   110' **A B**

5.6 fingers

**The
Pedestal**

5.8

5.8 lb

5.8
awk.

5.8 lb

up and right
then back left
to Kat Walk

belay
at 2nd
tree

watch out
for bees

dirty

11 120'

5.9 fingers
and thin hands

move right
thin 4th

5.10a
step left

5.7 chimney/
groove

5.7 lb

10 140'

5.5
gully

5.8
thin hands

p

5.6
thin hands

5.6
fingers

belay
takes
.75-1.25'   **9** 100'

p

5.7
fingers

5.8 blocky

8 130'

belay takes
2-3'

1.5'

90'

5.6 lb
.5-1.5'

5.8 lb
2.5'

flared groove
hands w/ good
edges on face

5.8 fingers
to hands

5.9
hands move
around roof

p

5.7 thin
hands

med to
lrg nuts

belay takes
sml nuts   80'

5.8 chimney
(right side in)

5.7 fingers
good edges
on left

7 120'
5.7
edges

1.5'

use long
sling

90'

2'

5.7 chimney

5.6
3.5'

p

6 100'
xx

1'

sling flake

5.8
friction

5.8
thin hands

p

5.6 edges

**Original
Route**

5.6
fingers

5 100'
xx

5.6

xx

Kor-Beck 5.9★★★

Time to climb route:	**4-5 hours**
Approach time:	**20 minutes**
Descent time:	**1 hour**
Sun exposure:	**morning**
Height of route:	**600'**

This stout 5.9 is slightly awkward and technical in that classic Yosemite way. Most of the moves are in well-protected clean grooves and leaning corners. It's harder than the East Buttress of Middle Cathedral and Central Pillar of Frenzy and a good alternative if those climbs are too crowded. Most climbers rappel after Pitch 6. The original route continues to the Kat Walk on dirty and wandering terrain. You can pull through most cruxes on gear.

Strategy

The 5.8 standard start climbs broken rock and is not that classic. The 5.10a variation is awesome and intimidating with just enough protection. Use many slings for either start or bad rope drag will immobilize you. The next two pitches ascend a clean groove that involves everything from fingers to chimney. If you want a close belay for the tricky 5.9 move on Pitch 4, then set the anchor up slightly left to the broken ledge. Pitch 5 climbs sustained jams to your choice of two improbable face traverses right. After the traverse, run it out a little or the follower will face a nasty fall. Belay as high as comfortable. The next pitch is the endurance crux of the route and requires burly lieback moves with polished feet into a wild chimney and stemming corner. Rappel here with two 50m or 60m ropes.

Kor-Beck	Pitch	1	2	3	4	5	6	7
Free difficulty	≥5.10							
	5.9				●	●		●
	5.8	●	●	●			●	
	5.7							
	5.6							
	≤5.5							

Retreat

Retreat at any point by rappelling the route with two ropes.

Rack

nuts: 1 set
cams: 2 ea .5-3.5"
      1 ea. 4.5" (optional)

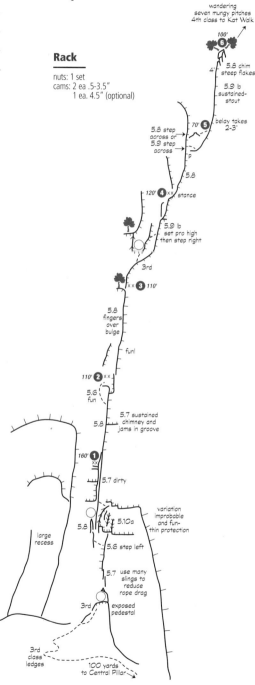

Central Pillar of Frenzy

5.9★★★★★

Time to climb route: **4-6 hours**

Approach time: **15 minutes**

Descent time: **1-1.5 hours**

Sun exposure: **morning**

Height of route: **550'**

Rising from the heart of Middle Cathedral Rock, Central Pillar of Frenzy is one of the most popular 5.9 crack climbs in Yosemite. The route offers five pitches of excellent jamming with everything from fingers to chimney. The views of El Capitan (climbers are often visible) and the gentle emerald oxbows of the Merced River are spectacular. You can pull through most cruxes on gear.

History

Although Frenzy is a great name in itself, this route can be even better appreciated if one knows a little alpine history. On the Italian side of Mont Blanc lie some huge and intimidating buttresses, one of which is called the Central Pillar of Frêney—for a short while the hardest climb in the Alps. It's admittedly a bit of a jump from Frêney to Frenzy, and from the Alps to the Valley, but that's the way the name came about, courtesy of Jim Bridwell, a fellow with a consuming passion for the history of climbing.

Middle Cathedral Rock's beautiful northeast face has many fine routes, but if you want to learn crack climbing, Frenzy is the place to go. Bridwell is responsible for this classic, and in 1973 he, Roger Breedlove, and Ed Barry did the first eight pitches. Two years later Bridwell returned with John Long and Billy Westbay to finish the route.

Central Pillar of Frenzy		Pitch 1	2	3	4	5
Free difficulty	≥5.10					●
	5.9	●	●			●
	5.8			●	●	
	5.7					
	5.6					
	≤5.5					

The route is famous now for its first five pitches, all of which involve 5.8 and 5.9 cracks. Liebacks, fist cracks, hand cracks, squeeze chimneys—you name it, you've got it.

– *Steve Roper*

Strategy

Prepare to wait in line unless you begin extremely early in the morning. Be ready for uncomfortable belay stances and hanging belays. Do not leave food at the base as squirrels lurk in the talus waiting to scavenge through backpacks.

The first pitch is slippery and awkward but protects well. The sustained wide section on Pitch 3 can be challenging, but a few extra 3.5-4" cams will enable those unaccustomed to wide cracks to protect it perfectly. Although most people rappel after Pitch 5, the route continues for another four pitches of less enjoyable 5.9 and hard 5.10. From Pitch 5, use the noted rappel route marked by Metolius hangers. Rappelling the climbing route is not recommended as it creates a danger for climbers below. In addition, ropes often get stuck on Pitch 3.

The route gets morning sun from late May through July, otherwise it is mostly shaded. In the summer, the route is less crowded and can have pleasant temperatures in the afternoon.

Retreat

Carry two 50m or 60m ropes for retreating from the route. Rappel from any point. From Pitch 5, follow the rap route shown on the topo.

A. Pee Pee Pillar   5.10a★★★

If the route is too crowded, but you want to get in a pitch of climbing, walk 400 feet west to Pee Pee Pillar. This 100-foot-long 5.10a climb is great for improving your finger crack, lieback, and stemming technique.

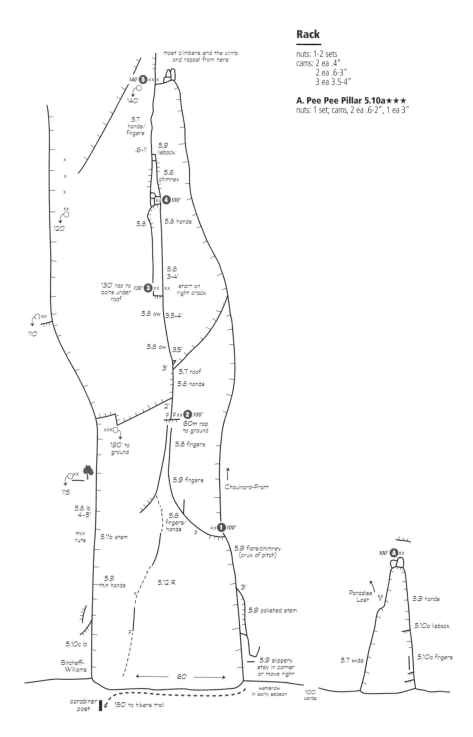

Rack

nuts: 1-2 sets
cams: 2 ea .4"
        2 ea .6-3"
        3 ea 3.5-4"

A. Pee Pee Pillar 5.10a★★★
nuts: 1 set; cams, 2 ea .6-2", 1 ea 3"

most climbers end the climb
and rappel from here

140' ⑤ xx x

140

5.7
hands/
fingers

.6-1'

5.9
lieback

5.6
chimney

xx ④ 100'

120'

5.8   5.8 hands

5.6
3-4"

130' rap to   130' ③ xx   xx   start on
bolts under   right crack
roof

110'

5.8 ow   3.5-4"

5.8 ow   3.5'

3'   5.7 roof

5.8 hands

2' P xx ② 100'
p   60m rap
                to ground

xxx○   5.8 fingers

190' to
ground

5.9 fingers

115'

Chouinard-Pratt

5.8 lb
4-5'

x   5.8
          fingers/
          hands
thin   p
nuts   5.11b stem   xx ① 100'

5.9 flare/chimney
(crux of pitch)

5.9
thin hands   5.12 R

3'

5.9 polished stem

5.10c lb

Bircheff-
Williams

60'   5.9 slippery
                                stay in corner
                                or move right

wet/snow
in early season

carabiner
post   150' to hikers' trail   100
                                            yards

100' Ⓐ xx

Paradise
Lost   xx   5.9 hands

                    5.10a lieback

5.7 wide   5.10a fingers

Direct North Buttress (DNB)

5.11a or 5.10 A0 R★★★★★

Time to climb route:	**10-15 hours**
Approach time:	**10 minutes**
Descent time:	**1 hour**
Sun exposure:	**morning**
Height of route:	**2000'**

The Direct North Buttress of Middle Cathedral was one of the most difficult rock climbs in the world when it was freed in 1965, and remains a burly testpiece. Climbing the DNB is quite an endeavor and many strong parties are forced to bivy on the route or at the top prior to the extremely exposed Kat Walk descent.

Most of the pitches consist of runout 5.10 face climbing or burly 5.6-5.8 chimneys/flares. Beware of one pitch of polished 5.8 offwidth, and one pitch with a dangerous, huge, loose flake that slid down 10 feet and stopped on a ledge in the late 1990s.

The route is generally not popular and retreat from various points in the first five pitches is common.

History

One lazy Camp 4 afternoon in September 1961, Yvon Chouinard forced me into his car and drove down to El Cap Meadow without telling me what was up. This sort of thing had happened before, so I steeled myself for another rave. After we parked I was relieved when he looked south toward the Cathedral Rocks rather than north to El Cap, because I was terrified of the latter and only mildly scared of the more benevolent Cathedrals. "Look!" Chouinard exclaimed, pointing to the far right side of the wide northeast face of Middle. I wasn't too good at picking out new lines, but I pretended to agree before confessing that I certainly couldn't see what the hell he was talking about. "No route there, man," I said (this being before the days of "no route there, dude.").

Of course a few days later we were up there, wandering between thin flakes and nubbly footholds, half the time unsure of where to go next. "No route here, man," I often proclaimed, hoping Chouinard would believe me and we could retreat with honor. Actually, I was enjoying myself quite a lot, pounding pitons behind door-sized flakes, ignoring the monotone sound as the iron hilted way too easily (the classic sound of a well-driven piton, for those who have never driven one, is a rising pitch with each blow, almost orgiastic in tone). At one dicey spot in the early afternoon I popped an aid pin and a few below and tumbled 35 feet, my record at the time. We used lots of aid, too smart and too scared to head upward on possible 5.9 above poor placements. Yet we moved as smartly as coyotes on the hunt, and by dusk we had climbed 900 feet of brand-new terrain, complex and never easy. Relaxing onto big ledges, I unpacked my only bivy gear: a sweater and a down jacket. After a few munchies and philosophical discussions about the newest waitress in the coffee shop, we curled into fetal positions and actually went to sleep.

Not for long, though. The rain was totally unexpected, and to our surprise it didn't let up. Soaked and shivering by morning, we looked up at the prominent crack system above us. Our projected route had become a waterfall. Luckily, we were able to move left on roomy, connected ledges and, after a few easy pitches, reached the Kat Walk, a familiar descent route.

DNB		Pitch 1	2	3	4	5	6	7	8	9	10	11	12	13	14	15	16	17	18	19
Free difficulty	≥5.10			●	●	●	●	●				●								
	5.9								●				●							
	5.8									●							●			
	5.7	●									●				●					
	5.6													●	●					
	≤5.5		●															●	●	

Nine months later in June 1962, Chouinard and I were back at our high point by early afternoon, in perfect weather. About 400 feet higher we bivied. Then at midnight, rain struck once again, and we howled at the gods. By dawn this storm had become a mere drizzle, and we decided that up was better than down. The flared cracks that rose above us would have been hard in dry weather, but now they were slippery nightmares. As a master chimney expert, Chouinard led more than his share and did a superb job in the pitter-patter of rain. Much higher, as we passed abeam the previously named Thirsty Spire (what a misnomer now!), we knew the route was ours and gave it the unimaginative but accurate name: Direct North Buttress. By late afternoon we topped out and staggered back to the valley floor. Stalking the store for groceries, we weighed my down jacket on a scale. Seven and a half pounds!

The route was soon repeated, and typical improvements came immediately. Better variations were jumped upon. The number of aid pitons went down as fast as the 1929 stock market, and the route was soon done in a day. Then came that inevitable moment that Chouinard and I knew would happen. In May 1965 the route, by this time known simply as the DNB, was free climbed. We had used probably 100 points of aid—many due to the wet rock on the second day—but better climbers came along. Frank Sacherer and Eric Beck, speedy as cheetahs, roared up the route in a mere 12 hours, rating six of the pitches 5.9 (some are now rated 10b). That Sacherer was wholeheartedly committed to a free ascent was reflected in Beck's comment to me later: "On one pitch high up I was jamming a well-protected thin section and I called down to Frank, 'I don't know if I can do this.' Among other things, I was getting tired. Frank immediately yelled up, 'Don't grab the pin.'"

– *Steve Roper*

Strategy

Start early, move fast, and be prepared if you are forced to bivy. Bring water and a lighter in case you must build a tiny fire for warmth in a bivy. Do not underestimate the cumulative effects of hot weather, draining leads, and the endless chimneying on the top half of the route.

Pay attention to routefinding on the traverse of Pitch 6, the climbing on Pitches 7 and 8, and the corner transfer of Pitch 12. Be careful with the large loose blocks on Pitch 9; climb and set pro to the right and make sure your rope is not near the blocks that you must stand on for a few moves.

Mid-summer temps and the sun's position (directly in your face) make for unpleasant and potentially dangerously dehydrating conditions. However, the few long, cool days of mid-summer can be the perfect time to climb the DNB. During the early season there may be wet patches, especially near the top. In a storm, the upper 500 feet is a huge chimney system—or a huge raingutter. Regardless of your position, storm runoff from the slabs will soak the route.

If you find yourself on top at dark or if you are tired or dehydrated, spend the night there rather than attempting the extremely exposed and somewhat inconspicuous 4th class Kat Walk, which has claimed climbers' lives in the past.

Retreat

Retreat is simple from the first five pitches and can even be done with a single 60m rope if you are careful. From higher on the route, retreat becomes problematic. From the top of Pitch 6 (slings around a large block) a double-rope rap to the right will gain the Pitch 5 bolted anchor. From the bolted anchor on the top of Pitch 7 you will most likely not be able to reach Pitch 6; however, from the slings on top of Pitch 8 (again around a large loose block) a double-rope rap will probably gain the Pitch 6 anchor. If stuck on top of Pitch 7, you may be able to rap down Paradise Lost (unknown anchor conditions). Above Pitch 8 you will need to leave gear except at a few trees (slings may be necessary). If for some reason you decide to retreat high on the route, consider bivying and finishing the following day, since retreat may be more dangerous.

Rack

nuts: 1 set, including thin;
    might get micro placements here and there
cams: 1 set to 3", bigger if you want more pro
    in chimneys, especially 3-5"
other: many slings

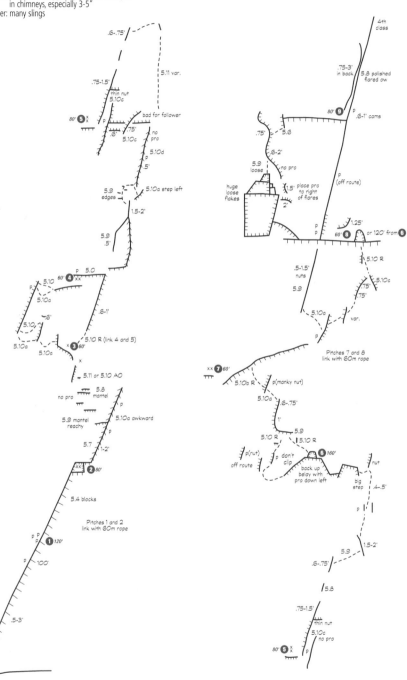

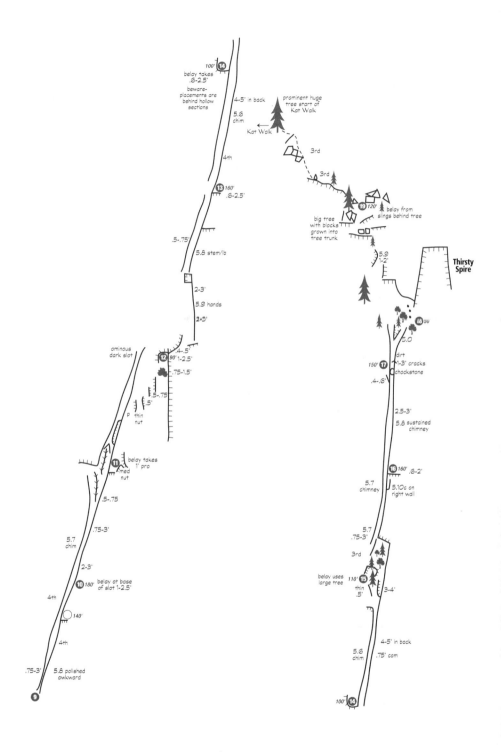

100' 14
belay takes
.6-2.5'
beware-
placements are
behind hollow
sections

4-5' in back

5.6
chim

prominent huge
tree start of
Kat Walk

Kat Walk

3rd

4th

3rd

13 160'
.6-2.5'

19 120'   belay from
slings behind tree

big tree
with blocks
grown into
tree trunk

.5-.75

5.8 stem/lb

5.9
1-2'

Thirsty
Spire

2-3'

5.9 hands

2-5'

ominous
dark slot

4-5'
12 90' 1-2.5'

.75-1.5'

18 90'

5.0

dirt
1-3' cracks
chockstone

150' 17

.4-.6'

.5-.75

.5'

P   thin
      nut

2.5-3'

5.8 sustained
chimney

belay takes
1' pro

11
  med
  nut

16 160' .6-2'

5.7
chimney

5.10c on
right wall

.5-.75

.75-3'

5.7
chim

5.7
.75-3'

3rd

2-3'

belay uses
large tree

110' 15
thin
.5'

3-4'

10 180' belay at base
of slot 1-2.5'

4th

140'

4-5' in back

4th

5.6
chim

.75' cam

.75-3'   5.8 polished
         awkward

100' 14

9

Lower Cathedral Rock, North Buttress Base

Approach time: **5 minutes**

Sun exposure: **none**

Height of routes: **up to 120'**

This north-facing crag gets all day shade and is great in the summer and during warmer weather. All climbs are well-protected and have both bolts and gear placements. The routes have a mixture of positive edges and cracks, and are relatively moderate considering their steepness and length. Most climbs are easy to toprope after leading.

Approach

Park 0.3 miles east of the Southside Drive/Highway 41 junction at the very east end of the long paved pullout. Hike the Valley Loop Trail east for 5 minutes until the trail comes within 150 feet of the base and passes under a talus field with a giant square-cut boulder. Hike up to the wall on a faint climbers' trail. The routes start just right of the toe of the buttress.

Descent

Rappel most routes with one 60m rope. Descend End of the Line with two ropes.

A. Mac Daddy   5.11a★★★

FA: Dan and Sue McDevitt, Jerry, Sigrid, and Lynnea Anderson, Fall 2001.

Sustained and delicate liebacking. Well-protected at the cruxes.

B. Unnamed but Beautiful   5.10c★★★

FA: Dan and Sue McDevitt, Jerry, Sigrid, and Lynnea Anderson, Fall 2001.

Fun liebacking and jamming with a mantel or two. Gear only needed to the second bolt. Joins Mac Daddy for the last three bolts.

C. End of the Line   5.10c★★★★

FA: Jerry, Sigrid, and Lynnea Anderson, Fall 2001.

Mostly 5.8 to 5.9 fingers and hands with a few short 5.10 cruxes. The climbing is varied, the rock is clean, and the rests are big. Requires every technique from fingers to a short offwidth, liebacks to underclings, often complemented with positive face holds. Well-protected with natural gear and one bolt. Bring extra cams if you want to sew it up. Rappel with two ropes.

D. 76 Degrees in the Shade   5.10c★★

FA: Jerry, Sigrid, and Lynnea Anderson, Fall 2001.

A moderate bolted face with good rests leads to two sections of 5.10 liebacking. The crux protects with tiny cams and seems easier for shorter people. The second pitch follows an ever-widening lieback. Descend each pitch with one 60m rope.

186

SUPERTOPO

YOSEMITE VALLEY FREE CLIMBS

A. Mac Daddy 5.11a★★★ cams: 1 ea 2"; 10 quickdraws

B. Unnamed but Beautiful 5.10c★★★ nuts: 1 set; cams: 1 ea .5-1.25"; 8 quickdraws

C. End of the Line 5.10c★★★★ nuts: 1 set; cams: 2 ea .5-3.5"

D. 76 Degrees in the Shade 5.10c★★ nuts: 1 set; cams: 1 ea .4-.6"; 6 quickdraws

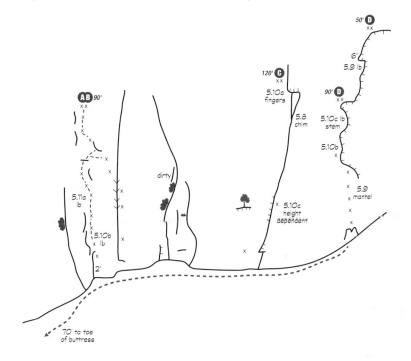

The Rostrum

It is hard to imagine a more perfect pillar of rock than The Rostrum. The face averages dead vertical, the cracks are laser-cut splitters, and all the climbs end on a spire-like summit block. If that were not enough, The Rostrum has the best approach/descent combination of any big feature in Yosemite.

Approach

From the junction of Southside Drive and Highway 41, take Highway 41 west. From the west end of the Wawona Tunnel, drive 0.9 miles and park on the right side of the road at the end of the long stone wall. From the end of the stone wall, hike down dirt, then slabs, then westerly into the trees following a climbers' trail. Once at the rim, continue down steep dirt and boulders skirting the west side of The Rostrum. Two 120-foot or four 70-foot rappels reach the valley floor. From the last rappel, walk east along the base 200 feet to the start.

To begin the climb at the 5.11c finger crack, look for a ledge about 75 feet above the rappel point. Some 4th class and one 5.6 section lead to a comfy ledge at the base of the 5.11c finger crack.

During times of low water, the route can be accessed by parking near the generator station and crossing the river. Be aware of water levels and poison oak as hazards for this variation.

Descent

From the top of The Rostrum, rappel into the notch off bolts or downclimb exposed 5.4. Climb up a 5.2 ramp to the rim and walk south back to the approach trail.

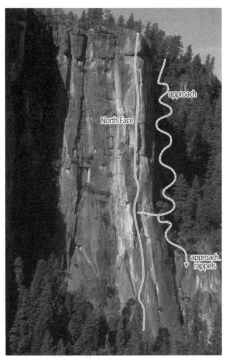

North Face

approach

approach rappels

Mark Kroese

North Face 5.11c★★★★★

Time to climb route:	**6-8 hours**
Approach time:	**40 minutes**
Descent time:	**15 minutes**
Sun exposure:	**morning to afternoon**
Height of route:	**800'**

The Rostrum features the best eight-pitch crack collection in the Valley and is considered to be just as good as Astroman. The wall is steep and all the cracks are perfect splitters. In addition, the Rostrum has one of the best approach/descent combinations: you park near the top, descend to the base and then climb your way back to the rim. Your performance on The Rostrum will indicate whether you are ready to tackle the far more challenging Astroman. You should be proficient at 5.10 offwidth before attempting this climb. You can pull through most cruxes on gear.

History

Although the Rostrum lured the Valley pioneers, it certainly wasn't the preposterously steep north face that attracted them. Rather, the wonderfully-named formation was marginally detached from the main cliff and therefore afforded that wonderful goal impossible to find in Yosemite now: a summit trodden only by ravens and chipmunks. In October 1941 Dave Brower, Ken Adam, Dick Leonard, and Rolf Pundt made short work of the relatively easy 40-foot pitch to the top. Brower described the climb: "Because a fall would end up either on [the Rostrum] or on the jagged blocks of the notch, one piton was used for safety, but the ascent is so short that it is hardly justifiable to place it in class 5 as a 'severe' climb." The climb was quickly and deservedly forgotten by most, although I remember doing it in 1959, on a rest day, simply to touch a new cliff.

The 750-foot north face caught the eye of Warren Harding and Glen Denny, and in July of 1962 they spent two days on the wall, nailing virtually every pitch. Bob Kamps and I were able to make the second ascent two months later, in a respectable 10 hours, but we nailed every pitch also. As I wrote in my 1964 guide, "This is an excellent, strenuous, and predominately direct-aid climb." I would have bet a thousand dollars that the route could not be climbed free.

However, in 1977 those magnificent climbers Ron Kauk and John Yablonski managed to free all but the final pitch, a horrendous roof (they finished 10 feet to the right on Blind Faith, which today is the standard North Face finish). The pair climbed about eight pitches of 5.10 and 5.11, most of it involving extremely strenuous crack climbing. A tremendous accomplishment.

Then, in 1985 Kim Carrigan, Australia's best cragsman, managed to turn the summit roof. Soon Valley regulars were running up this completed free route. Almost literally running, in some cases. For instance, in 1987 Peter Croft climbed the route three times in succession one morning—laps on a Grade IV! What one wag called "Croft's Disease" soon spread: John Bachar soloed the route a short time later, and he was immediately followed by Dave Schultz.

In a mere quarter-century the North Face had gone from an all-day strenuous aid climb to a before-breakfast romp.

— *Steve Roper*

		Pitch							
North Face		**1**	**2**	**3**	**4**	**5**	**6**	**7**	**8**
Free difficulty	≥5.10	●	●	●	●	●	●	●	●
	5.9	●							
	5.8								
	5.7								
	5.6								
	≤5.5								

Strategy

While North Face of The Rostrum is an awesome climb, the 5.11c rating keeps people away. You can usually tell from the parking area if anyone is in front of you. For those unaccustomed to offwidths, the two pitches of offwidth cracks high on the route will prove the crux of the climb. Large cams can adequately protect the first. However, using such cams on the last pitch will likely result in losing them, as the rope will drag them into the crack. Peer deep inside the last pitch offwidth to see two #5 camalots, biners, and slings, all tangled with long sticks from unsuccessful retrieval attempts. Most leaders simply run the last pitch offwidth out or slide a large cam up in front of them. Medium big bros can also be used (#3, maybe #2, not #4). Using a 60m rope will allow linking a long pitch low on the climb and will also allow retreat from the upper half back to the midway ledge.

The North Face is north facing (obviously) and shady, making it one of the few lines that is usually good even on hot summer days. In early season the rock tends to be damp and mossy, but even as colder fall days approach the climb is usually fine as long as there is no wind.

Be aware that occasionally the Rostrum is closed to climbing to protect nesting Peregrine Falcons. Check the SuperTopo Route Beta section to make sure there are no closures. Falcon closures typically begin in January and last until August 1st.

For those who are not fully worked upon reaching the top, simply lower down and toprope either of the 5.12 variations to the last pitch. In addition, two half-rope length killer cracks, the first of Blind Faith (5.11d) and Kaukulator (5.11c) are found to the right of the crux pitch on the midway ledge.

The anchors were recently replaced by the ASCA and are bomber.

Retreat

The route can be rappelled from any pitch using one 60m rope. If retreating from below the 3rd pitch, you must leave gear and cross the river to Highway 140.

Tate Rees cranks through the 5.12b Alien finish with all seven relentlessly steep pitches below.

190

Rack

nuts: 1 set, esp. thin
cams: 2 ea .4-3"
      1 ea 3.5, 4"
optional: 4.5-7" gear

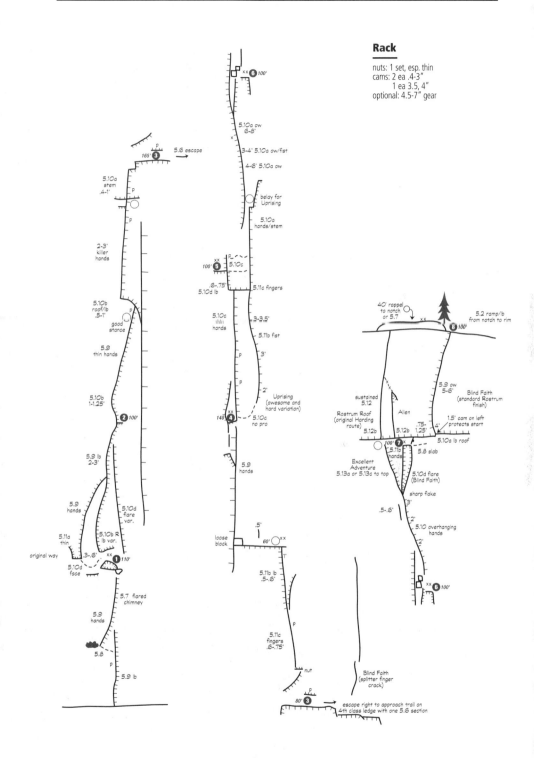

165' **3**   5.6 escape →

5.10a
stem
.4-1"

2-3'
killer
hands

5.10b
roof/lb
.5-1"

good
stance

5.9
thin hands

5.10b
1-1.25"

2 100'

5.9 lb
2-3'

5.9
hands

5.10d
flare
var.

5.11a
thin

5.10b R
lb var.

original way

5.10d
face

3-.6"
xx **1** 110'

5.7 flared
chimney

5.9
hands

5.8

5.9 lb

xx **6** 100'

5.10a ow
6-8'

3-4' 5.10a ow/fist

4-6' 5.10a ow

belay for
Uprising

5.10a
hands/stem

100' xx **5**   5.10c

.6-.75"
5.10d lb   5.11c fingers

5.10c
thin
hands

3-3.5"

5.11b fist

3'

2'

Uprising
(awesome and
hard variation)

140' xx **4**   5.10c
              no pro

5.9
hands

.5'

loose
block   60' xx

1'

5.11b lb
.5-.6"

5.11c
fingers
.6-.75"

nut

80' **3**   escape right to approach trail on
           4th class ledge with one 5.6 section

40' rappel
to notch   xx   **8** 100'   5.2 ramp/lb
or 5.7   from notch to rim

5.9 ow
5-6'

sustained   Blind Faith
5.12   (standard Rostrum
                 finish)

Rostrum Roof   Alien   1.5' cam on left
(original Harding   protects start
route)   5.12b .75- 4"
5.12b   1.25"

100' **7** x   5.10a lb roof

Excellent   5.11b
Adventure   hands   5.8 slab
5.13a or 5.13c to top

            5.10d flare
            (Blind Faith)

            sharp flake

            3'

.5-.6"

            2'

            5.10 overhanging
            hands

            2'

            xx **6** 100'

Blind Faith
(splitter finger
crack)

Crag Comparison

Crag	page	Number of routes at each grade								Topropes	Cracks or Face?	Winter Crag?	Summary
		5.0-5.5	5.6	5.7	5.8	5.9	5.10	5.11	5.12				
Swan Slab	96	2	5	5	3	3	5	1		18	mostly cracks	yes	The best intro to Yosemite climbing. Topropes galore.
Knob Hill	57			3	1	1	1			3	face and cracks	yes	Great intro to Yosemite 5.7. The next stop after Swan Slab.
Sunnyside Bench	108	1		2	2	2	2			4	all cracks	yes	Mixture of easy, moderate, and hard pitches. Crowded.
Church Bowl	116	1	1	1	3		3	2		6	mostly cracks	yes	Great crack training. Opportunity to practice wide cracks.
Glacier Point Apron	150	3	4	2	3	2	3			4	mostly cracks	no	Great friction and intro crack area. Cooler summer temps.
Manure Pile Buttress	88		1	1	3	2	2			4	mostly cracks	yes	5.8 multi-pitch playground. Convenient and crowded.
Five Open Books	100				4	1	1			0	all cracks	yes	Valley mecca of 3-4 pitch climbs.
El Capitan Base	74	1		2	3	2	8	4		9	all cracks	no	Sunny cragging in an awesome location.
Royal Arches Area	120				2	2	3			0	mostly cracks	yes/no	Good intro to Valley 5.10.
Pat and Jack Pinnacle	47				2	2	9	2	1	0	face and cracks	yes	Cool knob climbs on near-vertical faces. Some cracks.
Reed's Pinnacle Area	60			1	2	1	3			0	all cracks	yes	Ultra Classic 5.10 cracks and a few easier ones as well.
Five and Dime Cliff	66				2		3	2		3	face and cracks	yes	Mixture of sport climbs and burly cracks.
New Diversions Cliff	54					2	1	1		0	face and cracks	yes	Wild huge knobs and splitter cracks.
Camp 4 Wall	94					2	3			2	all cracks	yes	Convenient and burly classic Yosemite cracks.
Schultz's Ridge Base	84					1	8	1	1	0	mostly cracks	yes	Highest concentration of well-bolted 5.10s in the Valley.
North Buttress Base	186						3	1		0	face and cracks	no	Well-protected and shaded. Great summer spot.
Generator Station	53				1		2			2	all cracks	yes/no	Stout 5.10 crack training next to the road.
Cookie Cliff	40				1	1	5	9	1	0	mostly cracks	yes	Some of the most classic 5.10 and 5.11 Yosemite cracks.
Arch Rock	37					1	4	3	2	0	mostly cracks	yes	Hard crack training area. Warmest Yosemite crag.

NOTE: Crags are listed from easiest to hardest.

Leo Holding free climbing the West Face of Leaning Tower. (Corey Rich)

Yosemite Topropes

Chris McNamara

Yosemite has few easy routes and the polished granite and smooth cracks demand unfamiliar technique. Immediately jumping on a multi-pitch climb is generally a bad idea. Instead, spend a day or two at one of Yosemite's few toprope crags to get a feel for the rock and climbing style.

This guidebook contains enough topropes (listed below) for you to become acquainted with every technique—from steep hand jams to delicate friction slabs. Be aware that you can walk to few toprope anchors in Yosemite. Instead, you need to either lead an easier route to the side or the route itself to gain the anchors. Ideally, bring a ropegun—a confident climber who can lead the routes and set up the topropes.

In the table below, we have listed the toprope climbs contained in this guidebook along with key beta so you can plan which areas to visit.

Area	Route	Rating	Anchor Access	Technique
Swan Slab	Unnamed gully	5.1	walk	face
Church Bowl	Aunt Fanny's Pantry	5.5	climb route	chimney
Swan Slab	Swan Slab Chimney	5.5	climb route	chimney
Swan Slab	Hanging Flake	5.6	climb route	hands
Swan Slab	Oak Tree Flake	5.6	climb 5.5	lieback
Swan Slab	Swan Slab Gully	5.6	climb route	face, fingers, hands
Glacier Point Apron	Goblet	5.5-5.6	climb 5.6	face
Swan Slab	West Slabs	5.5-5.8	walk	face
Church Bowl	Uncle Fanny	5.7	climb route	chimney
El Capitan Base	La Cosita Left	5.7	climb route	chimney, face
El Capitan Base	Pine Line	5.7	climb route	fingers
Knob Hill	Chicken Pie	5.7	walk then 5.5 move	fists, hands, lieback
Knob Hill	Potbelly	5.7	walk	fingers, hands
Sunnyside Bench	Jamcrack (first pitch)	5.7	climb route	hands
Swan Slab	Penelope's Problem	5.7	climb 5.6	hands
Swan Slab	Swan Slab Squeeze	5.7	climb 5.3	chimney
Swan Slab	Unnamed crack	5.7	climb 5.3	fingers, lieback
Swan Slab	Unnamed face	5.7	climb 5.6	face
Swan Slab	Claude's Delight	5.7	climb route	fingers, hands, lieback
Camp 4 Wall	Doggie Diversions (1st pitch)	5.7	walk	chimney
Church Bowl	Church Bowl Lieback	5.8	climb route	lieback
El Capitan Base	Little John, Left	5.8	climb 5.8	fists, offwidth
El Capitan Base	Little John, Right	5.8	climb route	fingers, hands, chimney
Manure Pile Buttress	C.S. Concerto	5.8	scramble 4th class	face, fingers
Five and Dime	Mockery	5.8	rappel 20 feet	face
Swan Slab	Penthouse cracks	5.8-5.11a	walk	fingers, hands, lieback
El Capitan Base	La Cosita Right	5.9	climb 5.7	hands, lieback
El Capitan Base	Simulkrime	5.9	scramble 3rd class	face
Knob Hill	Unnamed	5.9	walk	fingers

Continued...

Area	Route	Rating	Anchor Access	Technique
Manure Pile Buttress	Fecophelia	5.9	scramble 4th class	face, fists, hands
Manure Pile Buttress	Jump for Joy (1st pitch)	5.9	rappel	face
Sunnyside Bench	Lemon	5.9	climb 5.9	lieback
Swan Slab	Grants Crack	5.9	climb 5.5	fingers
Swan Slab	Unnamed crack	5.9	climb 5.3	fingers, lieback
Swan Slab	Lena's Lieback	5.9	climb 5.7	lieback
Church Bowl	Deja Thorus	5.10a	climb 5.7	lieback
Church Bowl	Pole Position	5.10a	climb 5.7	face
Church Bowl	Revival	5.10a	climb 5.5	face, fingers
Manure Pile Buttress	Hayley's Comet	5.10a	rappel	face
Swan Slab	Unnamed thin crack	5.10a	climb 5.5	face, fingers
Swan Slab	Goat For It	5.10a	climb 5.7	face
Highway Star	Highway Star	5.10a	walk	fingers, hands, lieback
Camp 4 Wall	Doggie Do	5.10a	walk	offwidth
Glacier Point Apron	Variation on a Theme	5.10b	climb 5.8	face
Sunnyside Bench	Bummer	5.10c	climb 5.7	face, fingers, hands
Swan Slab	Unnamed seam	5.10c	climb 5.5	face, lieback
Generator Station	Generator Crack	5.10c	walk	chimney, offwidth
Five and Dime	Bijou	5.10c	walk	face
Sunnyside Bench	Lazy Bum	5.10d	climb 5.7	fingers
Generator Station	Conductor Crack	5.10d	walk	fingers, hands
El Capitan Base	Sparkling Give-away	5.11a	climb 5.7	face, fingers
El Capitan Base	Short But Thin	5.11b	climb 5.7	fingers
El Capitan Base	The Bluffer	5.11d	scramble 4th class	face
Five and Dime	Nickel Bag	5.11d	walk	face

Justin Bailie

Climbs by Rating

5.1 – 5.5

- ☐ Unnamed gully 5.1★ (96)
- ☐ Aunt Fanny's Pantry 5.4★ (117)
- ☐ Monday Morning Slab, Right 5.4★ (150)
- ☐ Sunnyside Bench, Regular Route 5.4★★★ (109)
- ☐ The Footstool, Right 5.4★★ (80)
- ☐ Goblet, Left 5.5★★ (151)
- ☐ The Cow, Center 5.5 R★★★ (154)
- ☐ Swan Slab Chimney 5.5★ (96)
- ☐ West Slabs 5.6-5.8★★ (96)

5.6

- ☐ Arrowhead Spire 5.6★★ (113)
- ☐ Bay Tree Flake 5.6★★★ (97)
- ☐ Church Bowl Chimney 5.6★★ (117)
- ☐ Goblet, Center 5.6★★ (151)
- ☐ Goblet, Right 5.6★★ (151)
- ☐ Hanging Flake 5.6★★ (97)
- ☐ Munginella 5.6★★★★ (101)
- ☐ Oak Tree Flake 5.6★★★ (97)
- ☐ Swan Slab Gully 5.6★★ (97)
- ☐ The Grack, Center 5.6★★★★★ (154)

5.7

- ☐ After Six 5.7★★★★ (89)
- ☐ Anti Ego Crack 5.7★★★ (58)
- ☐ Claude's Delight 5.7★★★ (99)
- ☐ The Cow, Right 5.7★★★ (154)
- ☐ La Cosita Left 5.7★★★★ (76)
- ☐ The Grack, Left 5.7★★★ (154)
- ☐ Penelope's Problem 5.7★★ (97)
- ☐ Pine Line 5.7★★★ (77)
- ☐ Reed's Pinnacle, Center Route 5.7★★ (63)
- ☐ Sloth Wall 5.7★★★★ (58)
- ☐ Snake Dike 5.7 R★★★★★★ (147)
- ☐ Swan Slab Squeeze 5.7★★ (96)
- ☐ Turkey Pie 5.7★★ (58)
- ☐ Uncle Fanny 5.7★★ (117)
- ☐ Unnamed crack 5.7★★ (96)
- ☐ Unnamed face 5.7★★★ (97)

5.8

- ☐ After Seven 5.8★★★★ (90)
- ☐ Arches Terrace 5.8 R★★★ (134)
- ☐ Bishop's Terrace 5.8★★★★★ (117)
- ☐ Black Brown 5.8★★ (117)
- ☐ Bongs Away, Left 5.8★★★ (62)
- ☐ Braille Book 5.8★★★★ (169)
- ☐ The Caverns 5.8★★★★ (102)
- ☐ C.S. Concerto 5.8★★★ (90)
- ☐ Chouinard Crack 5.8★★★ (151)
- ☐ Church Bowl Lieback 5.8★★★★ (117)
- ☐ The Cow, Left 5.8 R★★★ (154)
- ☐ Ejesta 5.8★★★ (63)
- ☐ Elevator Shaft 5.8 R★★ (41)
- ☐ Golden Needles 5.8★★★ (49)
- ☐ Gollum, Right 5.8★★★ (80)
- ☐ Hanging Teeth 5.8★★ (103)
- ☐ Harry Daley 5.8★★★★★ (151)
- ☐ Keystone Corner 5.8★★★ (66)
- ☐ Little John, Left 5.8★★★ (76)
- ☐ Little John, Right 5.8★★★★★ (77)
- ☐ Mockery 5.8★★★★ (66)
- ☐ North Dome, South Face 5.8★★★★ (136)
- ☐ Nurdle 5.8★★★★ (47)
- ☐ Nutcracker 5.8★★★★★ (92)
- ☐ The Pedestal 5.8★★★ (177)
- ☐ Potbelly 5.8★★★ (58)
- ☐ Selaginella 5.8★★★ (103)
- ☐ Stand and Deliver 5.8★★ (177)
- ☐ Trial by Fire 5.8★★★ (122)
- ☐ Try Again Ledge 5.8★★★ (103)
- ☐ Unnamed flared crack 5.8★★ (96)
- ☐ Penthouse cracks 5.8-5.11a★★ (96)

5.9

- ☐ Arrowhead Arête 5.9★★★ (113)
- ☐ Central Pillar of Frenzy 5.9★★★★★ (180)
- ☐ Chicken Pie 5.9★★★★ (55)
- ☐ Commitment 5.9★★★★ (101)
- ☐ The Cookie, Right Side 5.9★★★★ (43)
- ☐ Doggie Deviations 5.9★★★ (94)
- ☐ Doggie Diversions 5.9★★★ (94)

❏ Entrance Exam 5.9★★★ (38)
❏ Fecophilia 5.9 R★★ (90)
❏ Gidget Goes to Yosemite 5.9★★★★ (86)
❏ Goodrich Pinnacle, Right
  5.9 R★★★★★ (151)
❏ Grant's Crack 5.9★★★ (97)
❏ Higher Cathedral Spire, Regular Route
  5.9★★★★ (165)
❏ Higher Cathedral, Northeast Buttress
  5.9★★★★★ (171)
❏ Jamcrack 5.9★★★ (109)
❏ Jump for Joy (1st pitch) 5.9 R★★★ (90)
❏ Kor-Beck 5.9★★★ (179)
❏ La Cosita, Right 5.9★★★★ (76)
❏ Lemon 5.9★★ (109)
❏ Lena's Lieback 5.9★★★ (99)
❏ Lower Cathedral Spire, Regular Route
  5.9 or 5.7 A0★★ (162)
❏ Makayla's Climb 5.9★★ (48)
❏ Marginal 5.9 R★★★★★ (154)
❏ New Deviations 5.9★★★★ (54)
❏ Reed's Pinnacle, Regular Route
  5.9★★★★ (62)
❏ Simulkrime 5.9 R★★★ (80)
❏ Suds 5.9★★★ (49)
❏ Super Slide 5.9★★★ (122)
❏ Unnamed 5.9★★ (58)
❏ Unnamed crack 5.9★★ (96)

5.10a

❏ Arête Butler 5.10a★★★ (129)
❏ Babble On 5.10a★★ (48)
❏ Beverly's Tower 5.10a★★★ (42)
❏ Bikini Beach Party 5.10a R★★★ (86)
❏ Copper Penny 5.10a★★★ (66)
❏ Crest Jewel 5.10a★★★★★ (138)
❏ Deja Thorus 5.10a★ (117)
❏ Doggie Do 5.10a★★ (94)
❏ Goat For It 5.10a★★★ (99)
❏ Gollum, Left 5.10a★★ (80)
❏ Hayley's Comet 5.10a★★★ (90)
❏ Highway Star 5.10a★★★★ (68)
❏ Just Do-do It 5.10a★★★ (90)
❏ Just for Starters 5.10a★★★ (58)
❏ Maxine's Wall 5.10a★★★ (129)
❏ Moby Dick, Center 5.10a★★★★★ (77)
❏ New Diversions 5.10a★★★★★ (54)

❏ Pee Pee Pillar 5.10a★★★ (180)
❏ Peruvian Flake 5.10a★★★ (126)
❏ Pole Position 5.10a★★ (117)
❏ Reed's Pinnacle, Direct Route
  5.10a★★★★★ (62)
❏ Revival 5.10a★★ (117)
❏ Sacherer Cracker 5.10a★★★★★ (75)
❏ Second Thoughts 5.10a★★ (84)
❏ Sons of Yesterday 5.10a★★★★★ (126)
❏ The Surprise 5.10a★★★ (102)
❏ Unnamed thin crack 5.10a★★ (97)
❏ Warm up Crack 5.10a★★ (84)
❏ Y Crack 5.10a★★★ (129)

5.10b

❏ Ahab 5.10b★★★ (77)
❏ Boneheads 5.10b★★★★ (48)
❏ Church Bowl Tree 5.10b★★★ (117)
❏ Crystalline Passage 5.10b★★★★ (86)
❏ El Capitan, East Buttress
  5.10b★★★★★ (69)
❏ Gripper 5.10b★★★★★ (38)
❏ Henley Quits 5.10b★★★ (94)
❏ Knob Job 5.10b★★★ (47)
❏ Knuckleheads 5.10b★★★★ (48)
❏ Midterm 5.10b★★★★★ (38)
❏ Proud Snapper 5.10b★★★★ (84)
❏ Royal Arches
  5.10b or 5.7 A0★★★★★ (128)
❏ Steck Salathé 5.10b★★★★ (157)
❏ Stone Groove 5.10b★★★★ (63)
❏ Trough of Justice 5.10b★★ (48)
❏ Variation on a Theme
  5.10b R★★★ (151)

5.10c

❏ 76 Degrees in the Shade
  5.10c★★ (186)
❏ Bijou 5.10c★★★ (66)
❏ Bummer 5.10c★★★ (109)
❏ End of the Line 5.10c★★★★ (186)
❏ English Breakfast Crack
  5.10c★★★★★ (38)
❏ Generator Crack 5.10c★★★★ (53)
❏ Hooter Alert 5.10c★★★ (84)
❏ Lunatic Fringe 5.10c★★★★★ (62)
❏ Meat Grinder 5.10c★★★★ (42)

Middle Cathedral Rock, East Buttress 5.10c or 5.9 A0★★★★★ (176)

New Suede Shoes 5.10c★★★ (84)

Salathé Wall 5.10c★★★★★ (77)

Sherrie's Crack 5.10c★★★ (47)

Supplication 5.10c★★★ (38)

Unnamed but Beautiful 5.10c★★★ (186)

Unnamed seam 5.10c★★ (97)

Wheat Thin 5.10c★★★★★ (43)

5.10d

Are You Hard Enough? 5.10d★★★ (84)

Book 'em, Dano 5.10d★★★★ (48)

Catchy 5.10d★★★★★ (43)

Conductor Crack 5.10d★★ (53)

Crest Jewel Direct 5.10d★★★★★ (138)

Five and Dime 5.10d★★★★★ (66)

Hardly Pinnacle 5.10d★★★★ (76)

Just Do Me 5.10d★★★★ (84)

Lazy Bum 5.10d★★★ (109)

The Mark of Art 5.10d★★★★★ (76)

Polymastia 5.10d★★★★ (48)

Serenity Crack 5.10d★★★★★ (125)

Skinheads 5.10d★★★ (48)

The Slack, Left 5.10d★★ (75)

Twilight Zone 5.10d★★★★ (42)

5.11a

Bitches' Terror 5.11a★★★ (117)

Book of Revelations 5.11a★★★★ (117)

Butterfingers 5.11a★★★★★ (43)

Catchy Corner 5.11a★★★★★ (43)

Caught at The Lip 5.11a★★★ (86)

Mac Daddy 5.11a★★★ (186)

Middle Cathedral, Direct North Buttress 5.11a or 5.10 A0 R★★★★★ (182)

New Dimensions 5.11a★★★★★ (38)

Outer Limits 5.11a★★★★★ (41)

South by Southwest 5.11a★★★★ (162)

Sparkling Give-away 5.11a★★ (76)

The Tube 5.11a★★★★ (48)

Waverly Wafer 5.11a★★★★★ (42)

5.11b

Adrenaline 5.11b★★★ (127)

Aftershock 5.11b★★★ (42)

Aid Route 5.11b or 5.10a A0★★★★ (99)

Anticipation 5.11b★★★★ (38)

Burst of Brilliance 5.11b★★★ (55)

Cristina 5.11b★★★ (94)

Energizer 5.11b★★★ (117)

G-Man 5.11b R★★ (48)

Hardd 5.11b★★★★ (41)

La Escuela 5.11b★★★★ (75)

Leanie Meanie 5.11b★★★★ (38)

The Moratorium 5.11b★★★★ (83)

Short But Thin 5.11b★★★ (76)

The Enema 5.11b★★★★★ (43)

Whack and Dangle 5.11b★★★ (66)

5.11c

Astroman 5.11c★★★★★ (141)

Butterballs 5.11c★★★★★ (42)

Crack A-Go-Go 5.11c★★★★★ (41)

Demimonde 5.11c★★★ (122)

The Rostrum, North Face 5.11c★★★★★ (189)

5.11d

Dreams of Thailand 5.11d★★★ (84)

Nickel Bag 5.11d★★ (66)

Red Zinger 5.11d★★★★★ (42)

The Bluffer 5.11d★★★ (80)

5.12a – 5.12c

Cookie Monster (Pitch 1) 5.12a★★★★ (42)

Goldilocks 5.12a★★★ (38)

Underclingon 5.12a★★★ (48)

The Principle 5.12b/c★★★★ (38)

Highlander 5.12c★★★ (54)

Climbs by Technique

Almost all Yosemite climbs involve more than one technique. Here we list the technique required for the crux moves of each climb.

Face Climbs

Unnamed gully 5.1★ (96)
The Footstool, Right 5.4★★ (80)
The Cow, Center 5.5 R★★★ (154)
Goblet, Left 5.5★★ (151)
Goblet, Center 5.6★★ (151)
Sloth Wall 5.7★★★★ (58)
Snake Dike 5.7 R★★★★★ (147)
Unnamed face 5.7★★★ (97)
After Seven 5.8★★★★ (90)
Arches Terrace 5.8 R★★★ (134)
The Cow, Left 5.8 R★★★ (154)
Mockery 5.8★★★★ (66)
West Slabs 5.6-5.8★★ (96)
Fecophilia 5.9 R★★ (90)
Gidget Goes to Yosemite 5.9★★★★ (86)
Jump for Joy (1st pitch) 5.9 R★★★ (90)
Lower Cathedral Spire, Regular Route
    5.9 or 5.7 A0★★ (162)
Makayla's Climb 5.9★★ (48)
Marginal 5.9 R★★★★★ (154)
New Deviations 5.9★★★★ (54)
Simulkrime 5.9 R★★★ (80)
Arête Butler 5.10a★★★ (129)
Crest Jewel 5.10a★★★★★ (138)
Goat For It 5.10a★★★ (99)
Bikini Beach Party 5.10a R★★★ (86)
Hayley's Comet 5.10a★★★ (90)
Just for Starters 5.10a★★★ (58)
Maxine's Wall 5.10a★★★ (129)
Pole Position 5.10a★★ (117)
Second Thoughts 5.10a★★ (84)
Boneheads 5.10b★★★ (48)
Crystalline Passage 5.10b★★★★ (86)
Knuckleheads 5.10b★★★★ (48)
Trough of Justice 5.10b★★ (48)
Variation on a Theme 5.10b R★★★ (151)
Bijou 5.10c★★★ (66)
Hooter Alert 5.10c★★★ (84)
New Suede Shoes 5.10c★★★ (84)

Are You Hard Enough? 5.10d★★★ (84)
Book 'em, Dano 5.10d★★★★ (48)
Crest Jewel Direct 5.10d★★★★★ (138)
Just Do Me 5.10d★★★★ (84)
Polymastia 5.10d★★★★ (48)
Skinheads 5.10d★★★ (48)
Bitches' Terror 5.11a★★★ (117)
Caught at The Lip 5.11a★★★ (86)
Sparkling Give-away 5.11a★★ (76)
Adrenaline 5.11b★★★ (127)
Energizer 5.11b★★★ (117)
G-Man 5.11b R★★ (48)
Demimonde 5.11c★★★ (122)
The Bluffer 5.11d★★★ (80)
Dreams of Thailand 5.11d★★★ (84)
Nickel Bag 5.11d★★ (66)
Underclingon 5.12a★★★ (48)
The Principle 5.12b/c★★★★ (38)
Highlander 5.12c★★★ (54)

Lieback Cracks

Munginella 5.6★★★★ (101)
Oak Tree Flake 5.6★★★ (97)
The Grack, Left 5.7★★★ (154)
Unnamed crack 5.7★★ (96)
The Caverns 5.8★★★★ (102)
Church Bowl Lieback 5.8★★★★ (117)
Golden Needles 5.8★★★ (49)
Hanging Teeth 5.8★★ (103)
The Pedestal 5.8★★★ (177)
Commitment 5.9★★★★ (101)
La Cosita, Right 5.9★★★★★ (76)
Lemon 5.9★★ (109)
Lena's Lieback 5.9★★★ (99)
Unnamed crack 5.9★★ (96)
Babble On 5.10a★★ (48)
Deja Thorus 5.10a★ (117)
Proud Snapper 5.10b★★★★ (84)
Supplication 5.10c★★★ (38)
Unnamed seam 5.10c★★ (97)
Wheat Thin 5.10c★★★★★ (43)
The Mark of Art 5.10d★★★★★ (76)
Mac Daddy 5.11a★★★ (186)
The Tube 5.11a★★★★ (48)
Aftershock 5.11b★★★ (42)
Burst of Brilliance 5.11b★★★ (55)
Cristina 5.11b★★★ (94)
La Escuela 5.11b★★★★ (75)
The Moratorium 5.11b★★★★ (83)
Whack and Dangle 5.11b★★★ (66)
Cookie Monster (Pitch 1) 5.12a★★★★ (42)
Goldilocks 5.12a★★★ (38)

Finger Cracks

Bay Tree Flake 5.6★★★ (97)
Goblet, Right 5.6★★ (151)
Pine Line 5.7★★★ (77)
C.S. Concerto 5.8★★★ (90)
Potbelly 5.8★★ (58)
Grant's Crack 5.9★★★ (97)
Unnamed 5.9★★ (58)
Beverly's Tower 5.10a★★★ (42)
Just Do-do It 5.10a★★★ (90)
Pee Pee Pillar 5.10a★★★ (180)
Peruvian Flake 5.10a★★★ (126)
Revival 5.10a★★ (117)
The Surprise 5.10a★★★ (102)
Unnamed thin crack 5.10a★★ (97)
Y Crack 5.10a★★★ (129)
Church Bowl Tree 5.10b★★★ (117)
Stone Groove 5.10b★★★★ (63)
English Breakfast Crack 5.10c★★★★★ (38)
Lunatic Fringe 5.10c★★★★★ (62)
Salathé Wall 5.10c★★★★★ (77)
Sherrie's Crack 5.10c★★★ (47)
Conductor Crack 5.10d★★ (53)
Hardly Pinnacle 5.10d★★★★ (76)
Lazy Bum 5.10d★★★ (109)
Serenity Crack 5.10d★★★★★ (125)
Butterfingers 5.11a★★★★ (43)
Catchy Corner 5.11a★★★★★ (43)
Waverly Wafer 5.11a★★★★★ (42)
Anticipation 5.11b★★★★ (38)
Hardd 5.11b★★★★ (41)
Short But Thin 5.11b★★★ (76)
Butterballs 5.11c★★★★★ (42)
Crack A-Go-Go 5.11c★★★★★ (41)
Red Zinger 5.11d★★★★★ (42)
Penthouse cracks 5.8-5.11a★★ (96)

Hand Cracks

The Grack, Center 5.6★★★★★ (154)
Hanging Flake 5.6★★ (97)
After Six 5.7★★★★ (89)
Claude's Delight 5.7★★★ (99)
Penelope's Problem 5.7★★ (97)
Bishop's Terrace 5.8★★★★★ (117)
Chouinard Crack 5.8★★★ (151)
Ejesta 5.8★★★ (63)
Gollum, Right 5.8★★★ (80)
Nurdle 5.8★★★★ (47)
Unnamed flared crack 5.8★★ (96)
Jamcrack 5.9★★★ (109)
Suds 5.9★★★ (49)

Highway Star 5.10a★★★★ (68)
Reed's Pinnacle, Direct Route
 5.10a★★★★★ (62)
Sons of Yesterday 5.10a★★★★★ (126)
Gripper 5.10b★★★★★ (38)
Knob Job 5.10b★★★ (47)
Meat Grinder 5.10c★★★★ (42)
Catchy 5.10d★★★★★ (43)
Five and Dime 5.10d★★★★★ (66)
Outer Limits 5.11a★★★★★ (41)
South by Southwest 5.11a★★★★ (162)
The Enema 5.11b★★★★★ (43)

Fist Cracks, Offwidths, and Chimneys

Aunt Fanny's Pantry 5.4★ (117)
Swan Slab Chimney 5.5★ (96)
Arrowhead Spire 5.6★★ (113)
Church Bowl Chimney 5.6★★ (117)
Anti Ego Crack 5.7★★★ (58)
La Cosita, Left 5.7★★★★ (76)
Reed's Pinnacle, Center Route (Pitch 1)
 5.7★★ (63)
Swan Slab Squeeze 5.7★★ (96)
Turkey Pie 5.7★★ (58)
Uncle Fanny 5.7★★ (117)
Bongs Away, Left 5.8★★★ (62)
Elevator Shaft 5.8 R★★ (41)
Keystone Corner 5.8★★★ (66)
Little John, Left 5.8★★★ (76)
Trial by Fire 5.8★★★ (122)
Doggie Diversions 5.9★★★ (94)
Entrance Exam 5.9★★★ (38)
Copper Penny 5.10a★★★ (66)
Doggie Do 5.10a★★★ (94)
Gollum, Left 5.10a★★ (80)
Ahab 5.10b★★★ (77)
Generator Crack 5.10c★★★★ (53)
The Slack, Left 5.10d★★ (75)
Twilight Zone 5.10d★★★★ (42)

All techniques required

Monday Morning Slab, Right 5.4★ (150)
Sunnyside Bench, Regular Route
 5.4★★★ (109)
Swan Slab Gully 5.6★★ (97)
The Cow, Right 5.7★★★ (154)
Black is Brown 5.8★★ (117)
Braille Book 5.8★★★★ (169)
Harry Daley 5.8★★★★★ (151)
Little John, Right 5.8★★★★ (77)
North Dome, South Face 5.8★★★★ (136)

Nutcracker 5.8★★★★★ (92)
Selaginella 5.8★★★ (103)
Stand and Deliver 5.8★★ (177)
Try Again Ledge 5.8★★★ (103)
Arrowhead Arête 5.9★★★ (113)
Central Pillar of Frenzy 5.9★★★★★ (180)
Chicken Pie 5.9★★★★ (55)
The Cookie, Right Side 5.9★★★★ (43)
Doggie Deviations 5.9★★★ (94)
Goodrich Pinnacle, Right
    5.9 R★★★★★ (151)
Higher Cathedral Spire, Regular Route
    5.9★★★★ (165)
Higher Cathedral, Northeast Buttress
    5.9★★★★★ (171)
Kor-Beck 5.9★★★ (179)
Reed's Pinnacle, Regular Route
    5.9★★★★ (62)
Super Slide 5.9★★★ (122)
Moby Dick, Center 5.10a★★★★★ (77)
New Diversions 5.10a★★★★★ (54)
Sacherer Cracker 5.10a★★★★★ (75)
El Capitan, East Buttress 5.10b★★★★★ (69)
Henley Quits 5.10b★★★ (94)
Midterm 5.10b★★★★★ (38)
Royal Arches 5.10b or 5.7 A0★★★★★ (128)
Steck Salathé 5.10b★★★★ (157)
76 Degrees in the Shade 5.10c★★ (186)
Bummer 5.10c★★★ (109)
End of the Line 5.10c★★★★ (186)
Middle Cathedral Rock, East Buttress
    5.10c or 5.9 A0★★★★★ (176)
Unnamed but Beautiful 5.10c★★★ (186)
Book of Revelations 5.11a★★★★ (117)
Middle Cathedral Rock, Direct North Buttress
    5.11a or 5.10 A0★★★★★ (182)
New Dimensions 5.11a★★★★★ (38)
Aid Route 5.11b or 5.10a A0★★★★★ (99)
Leanie Meanie 5.11b★★★★ (38)
Astroman 5.11c★★★★★ (141)
The Rostrum , North Face
    5.11c★★★★★ (189)

Climbs by Name

76 Degrees in the Shade 5.10c★★ (186)
Adrenaline 5.11b★★★ (127)
After Seven 5.8★★★★ (90)
After Six 5.7★★★★ (89)
Aftershock 5.11b★★★ (42)
Ahab 5.10b★★★ (77)
Aid Route 5.11b or 5.10a A0★★★★ (99)
Anti Ego Crack 5.7★★★ (58)
Anticipation 5.11b★★★★ (38)
Arches Terrace 5.8 R★★★ (134)
Are You Hard Enough? 5.10d★★★ (84)
Arête Butler 5.10a★★★ (129)
Arrowhead Arête 5.9★★★ (113)
Arrowhead Spire 5.6★★ (113)
Astroman 5.11c★★★★★ (141)
Aunt Fanny's Pantry 5.4★ (117)
Babble On 5.10a★★ (48)
Bay Tree Flake 5.6★★★ (97)
Beverly's Tower 5.10a★★★ (42)
Bijou 5.10c★★★ (66)
Bikini Beach Party 5.10a R★★★ (86)
Bishop's Terrace 5.8★★★★★ (117)
Bitches' Terror 5.11a★★★ (117)
Black is Brown 5.8★★ (117)
The Bluffer 5.11d★★★ (80)
Boneheads 5.10b★★★★ (48)
Bongs Away, Left 5.8★★★ (62)
Book 'em, Dano 5.10d★★★★ (48)
Book of Revelations 5.11a★★★★ (117)
Braille Book 5.8★★★★ (169)
Bummer 5.10c★★★ (109)
Burst of Brilliance 5.11b★★★ (55)
Butterballs 5.11c★★★★★ (42)
Butterfingers 5.11a★★★★★ (43)
C.S. Concerto 5.8★★★ (90)
Catchy 5.10d★★★★ (43)
Catchy Corner 5.11a★★★★★ (43)
Caught at The Lip 5.11a★★★ (86)
The Caverns 5.8★★★★ (102)
Central Pillar of Frenzy 5.9★★★★★ (180)

Chicken Pie 5.9★★★★ (55)
Chouinard Crack 5.8★★★ (151)
Church Bowl Chimney 5.6★★ (117)
Church Bowl Lieback 5.8★★★★ (117)
Church Bowl Tree 5.10b★★★ (117)
Claude's Delight 5.7★★★ (99)
Commitment 5.9★★★★ (101)
Conductor Crack 5.10d★★ (53)
Cookie Monster (Pitch 1) 5.12a★★★★ (42)
The Cookie, Right Side 5.9★★★★ (43)
Copper Penny 5.10a★★★ (66)
The Cow, Center 5.5 R★★★ (154)
The Cow, Left 5.8 R★★★ (154)
The Cow, Right 5.7★★★ (154)
Crack A-Go-Go 5.11c★★★★★ (41)
Crest Jewel 5.10a★★★★★ (138)
Crest Jewel Direct 5.10d★★★★★ (138)
Cristina 5.11b★★★ (94)
Crystalline Passage 5.10b★★★★ (86)
Deja Thorus 5.10a★ (117)
Demimonde 5.11c★★★ (122)
Doggie Deviations 5.9★★★ (94)
Doggie Diversions 5.9★★★ (94)
Doggie Do 5.10a★★★ (94)
Dreams of Thailand 5.11d★★★ (84)
Ejesta 5.8★★★ (63)
El Capitan, East Buttress
    5.10b★★★★★ (69)
Elevator Shaft 5.8 R★★ (41)
End of the Line 5.10c★★★★ (186)
The Enema 5.11b★★★★★ (43)
Energizer 5.11b★★★ (117)
English Breakfast Crack 5.10c★★★★★ (38)
Entrance Exam 5.9★★★ (38)
Fecophilia 5.9 R★★ (90)
Five and Dime 5.10d★★★★★ (66)
The Footstool, Right 5.4★★ (80)
Generator Crack 5.10c★★★★ (53)
Gidget Goes to Yosemite 5.9★★★★ (86)
G-Man 5.11b R★★ (48)
Goat For It 5.10a★★★ (99)
Goblet, Center 5.6★★ (151)
Goblet, Left 5.5★★ (151)
Goblet, Right 5.6★★ (151)
Golden Needles 5.8★★★ (49)
Goldilocks 5.12a★★★ (38)
Gollum, Left 5.10a★★ (80)

Gollum, Right 5.8★★★ (80)
Goodrich Pinnacle, Right
    5.9 R★★★★★ (151)
The Grack, Center 5.6★★★★★ (154)
The Grack, Left 5.7★★★ (154)
Grant's Crack 5.9★★★ (97)
Gripper 5.10b★★★★★ (38)
Hanging Flake 5.6★★ (97)
Hanging Teeth 5.8★★ (103)
Hardd 5.11b★★★★ (41)
Hardly Pinnacle 5.10d★★★★ (76)
Harry Daley 5.8★★★★★ (151)
Hayley's Comet 5.10a★★★ (90)
Henley Quits 5.10b★★★ (94)
Higher Cathedral Spire, Regular Route
    5.9★★★★ (165)
Higher Cathedral, Northeast Buttress
    5.9★★★★★ (171)
Highlander 5.12c★★★ (54)
Highway Star 5.10a★★★★ (68)
Hooter Alert 5.10c★★★ (84)
Jamcrack 5.9★★★ (109)
Jump for Joy (1st pitch) 5.9 R★★★ (90)
Just Do Me 5.10d★★★★ (84)
Just Do-do It 5.10a★★★ (90)
Just for Starters 5.10a★★★ (58)
Keystone Corner 5.8★★★ (66)
Knob Job 5.10b★★★ (47)
Knuckleheads 5.10b★★★★ (48)
Kor-Beck 5.9★★★ (179)
La Cosita, Left 5.7★★★★ (76)
La Cosita, Right 5.9★★★★★ (76)
La Escuela 5.11b★★★★ (75)
Lazy Bum 5.10d★★★ (109)
Leanie Meanie 5.11b★★★★ (38)
Lemon 5.9★★ (109)
Lena's Lieback 5.9★★★ (99)
Little John, Left 5.8★★★ (76)
Little John, Right 5.8★★★★ (77)
Lower Cathedral Spire, Regular Route
    5.9 or 5.7 A0★★ (162)
Lunatic Fringe 5.10c★★★★★ (62)
Mac Daddy 5.11a★★★ (186)
Makayla's Climb 5.9★★ (48)
Marginal 5.9 R★★★★★ (154)
The Mark of Art 5.10d★★★★★ (76)
Maxine's Wall 5.10a★★★ (129)
Meat Grinder 5.10c★★★★ (42)

Middle Cathedral Rock, Direct North Buttress
    5.11a or 5.10 A0★★★★★ (182)
Middle Cathedral Rock, East Buttress
    5.10c or 5.9 A0★★★★★ (176)
Midterm 5.10b★★★★★ (38)
Moby Dick, Center 5.10a★★★★★ (77)
Mockery 5.8★★★★ (66)
Monday Morning Slab, Right 5.4★ (150)
The Moratorium 5.11b★★★★ (83)
Munginella 5.6★★★★ (101)
New Deviations 5.9★★★★ (54)
New Dimensions 5.11a★★★★★ (38)
New Diversions 5.10a★★★★★ (54)
New Suede Shoes 5.10c★★★ (84)
Nickel Bag 5.11d★★ (66)
North Dome, South Face 5.8★★★★ (136)
Nurdle 5.8★★★★ (47)
Nutcracker 5.8★★★★★★ (92)
Oak Tree Flake 5.6★★★ (97)
Outer Limits 5.11a★★★★★ (41)
The Pedestal 5.8★★★ (177)
Pee Pee Pillar 5.10a★★★ (180)
Penelope's Problem 5.7★★ (97)
Penthouse cracks 5.8-5.11a★★ (96)
Peruvian Flake 5.10a★★★ (126)
Pine Line 5.7★★★ (77)
Pole Position 5.10a★★ (117)
Polymastia 5.10d★★★★ (48)
Potbelly 5.8★★★ (58)
The Principle 5.12b/c★★★★ (38)
Proud Snapper 5.10b★★★★ (84)
Red Zinger 5.11d★★★★★ (42)
Reed's Pinnacle, Center Route (Pitch 1)
    5.7★★ (63)
Reed's Pinnacle, Direct Route
    5.10a★★★★★ (62)
Reed's Pinnacle, Regular Route
    5.9★★★★ (62)
Revival 5.10a★★ (117)
The Rostrum , North Face
    5.11c★★★★★ (189)
Royal Arches
    5.10b or 5.7 A0★★★★★ (128)
Sacherer Cracker 5.10a★★★★★ (75)
Salathé Wall 5.10c★★★★ (77)
Second Thoughts 5.10a★★ (84)
Selaginella 5.8★★★ (103)
Serenity Crack 5.10d★★★★★ (125)

Sherrie's Crack 5.10c★★★ (47)
Short But Thin 5.11b★★★ (76)
Simulkrime 5.9 R★★★ (80)
Skinheads 5.10d★★★ (48)
The Slack, Left 5.10d★★ (75)
Sloth Wall 5.7★★★★ (58)
Snake Dike 5.7 R★★★★★ (147)
Sons of Yesterday 5.10a★★★★★ (126)
South by Southwest 5.11a★★★★ (162)
Sparkling Give-away 5.11a★★ (76)
Stand and Deliver 5.8★★ (177)
Steck Salathé 5.10b★★★★ (157)
Stone Groove 5.10b★★★★ (63)
Suds 5.9★★★ (49)
Sunnyside Bench, Regular Route
    5.4★★★ (109)
Super Slide 5.9★★★ (122)
Supplication 5.10c★★★ (38)
The Surprise 5.10a★★★ (102)
Swan Slab Chimney 5.5★ (96)
Swan Slab Gully 5.6★★ (97)
Swan Slab Squeeze 5.7★★ (96)
Trial by Fire 5.8★★★ (122)
Trough of Justice 5.10b★★ (48)
Try Again Ledge 5.8★★★ (103)
The Tube 5.11a★★★★ (48)
Turkey Pie 5.7★★ (58)
Twilight Zone 5.10d★★★★ (42)
Uncle Fanny 5.7★★ (117)
Underclingon 5.12a★★★ (48)
Unnamed 5.9★★ (58)
Unnamed but Beautiful 5.10c★★★ (186)
Unnamed crack 5.7★★ (96)
Unnamed crack 5.9★★ (96)
Unnamed face 5.7★★★ (97)
Unnamed flared crack 5.8★★ (96)
Unnamed gully 5.1★ (96)
Unnamed seam 5.10c★★ (97)
Unnamed thin crack 5.10a★★ (97)
Variations on a Theme 5.10b R★★★ (151)
Waverly Wafer 5.11a★★★★★ (42)
West Slabs 5.6-5.8★★ (96)
Whack and Dangle 5.11b★★★ (66)
Wheat Thin 5.10c★★★★★ (43)
Y Crack 5.10a★★★ (129)

We need YOUR feedback

I love getting feedback on SuperTopos. The reason for we make SuperTopos is so that you and other climbers can have an incredible experience on the rock. If there is any way I can make this experience better I want to know.

Every time you climb a route you will come away with a unique familiarity about each pitch. I want to hear what you thought of the climb and what you think can be improved on our topos. This information will help us make better topos and enhance other people's climbing experience.

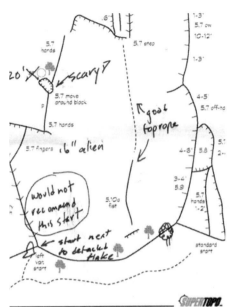

Mail us your topo corrections and help make SuperTopos even better.

Subject: Some feedback on the SuperTopos
From: run@itout.com
To: chris@supertopo.com

The topos ruled. here is some feedback

Jam Crack ...
* Although the topo is very clear, you might want to add the words "15' left" after ".... either belay 15' left at the bolted anchor or continue ....". The reason I say that is the first time I led the climb I just kept climbing up the very thin, maybe .10d section between the top of the 5.7 crack section and the bolts. It looked really hard so I down climbed and realized I was supposed to be further left.

After Six ...
* 1st Pitch ... You might (or not) want to repeat a comment I've heard several times that the 1st pitch is the "hardest 5.6 in the valley". It's awkward after the dead tree and on the polished section in the middle of the pitch ... gravity wants to pull you out of the crack to the right. It's OK after starting the traverse to the right.
* I've always belay at the ledge in the Manzanita bushes just to the left of where the 5.6 variation 2nd pitch goes up. It's solid using the bushes

---

You will greatly help us if after your climb you do one of two things:

- Visit the web site's Climber Beta section (www.supertopo.com/route_beta) and tell SuperTopo users about the climb. What were the conditions like? Is there any extra beta? What did you think of the route?

- If you have any suggestions please email me at chris@supertopo.com or send snail mail to 2 Bradford Way, Mill Valley, CA 94941. Let me know if we got a pitch length wrong, if you disagreed with a rating, or if you think the topo could be better in any way.

Thank you for helping us improve SuperTopo,

Chris McNamara
Founder and CEO
SuperTopo

MORE FROM SUPERTOPO

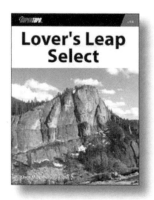

LAKE TAHOE'S CLIMBING GEM
LOVERS LEAP SELECT (eBook)
List Price: $9.95 Available at www.supertopo.com

This guide includes virtually all the moderate classic routes at Lover's Leap. Most of these climbs are well-protected, two to four pitches long, and ascend the incredible granite that Lover's Leap is known for. Because these routes have so many face holds and good rests, they are the perfect introduction to granite trad climbing and outdoor climbing in general.

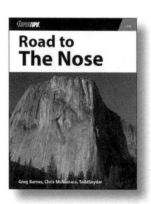

EVER WANTED TO CLIMB A BIG WALL?
ROAD TO THE NOSE (eBook)
List Price: $14.95 Available at www.supertopo.com

Many climbers consider The Nose of El Capitan the crowning achievement of a climbing career. In the *Road to The Nose*, big wall master Chris McNamara takes you through 14 climbs of increasing difficulty to help you build skills, speed, endurance, and comfort with big wall climbing. This guide includes special tips and beta specific to The Nose as well as more general information on getting ready for your first big wall.

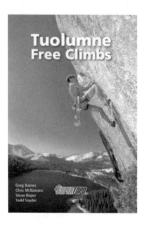

OUTSTANDING PEAKS AND DOMES IN THE HIGH SIERRA
TUOLUMNE FREE CLIMBS (Print Book)
List Price: $24.95 Available at www.supertopo.com

Tuolumne Free Climbs includes over 110 of the best routes in Tuolumne Meadows from 14-pitch trad climbs to one-pitch sport routes. This book focuses on topropes, crags, and multi-pitch climbs in the 5.4-5.9 range. Includes formerly obscure climbs to provide more options for avoiding crowds. As in all SuperTopo books, the authors personally climbed and documented each climb with meticulous care to create the most detailed and accurate topos ever published.v

MORE FROM SUPERTOPO

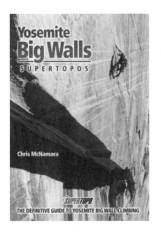

UNPRECEDENTED BIG WALL BETA
YOSEMITE BIG WALLS (Print Book)
List Price: $29.95 Available at www.supertopo.com

Written by Chris McNamara who personally climbed and painstakingly documented every route, this book includes essential route details such as climbing strategy, retreat information, descent topos, pitch lengths, and gear recommendations for each pitch. Yosemite Big Walls covers the 41 best big wall routes on El Capitan, Half Dome, Washington Column, and Leaning Tower.

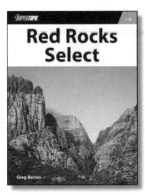

THE BEST WINTER TRAD CLIMBING
RED ROCKS SELECT (eBook)
List Price: $9.95 Available at www.supertopo.com

This book covers the best Red Rocks climbs—most in the 5.4 to 5.11 range. While the guidebook focuses on the most classic multi-pitch routes such as Crimson Chrysalis and Epinepherine, cragging routes are also included. Most of the climbs are on the highest quality sandstone Red Rocks has to offer and are well-protected with bolts or natural gear. This guide is perfect for climbers making their first trip to Red Rocks or returning climbers who want to tick off all the classics.

ALPINE ROCK CLIMBING PARADISE
HIGH SIERRA SELECT (eBook)
List Price: $14.95 Available at www.supertopo.com

Included here are 14 classic High Sierra rock climbs ranging in difficulty from 3rd class to 5.10b. Most of these are well-protected, 10 to 15 pitches long, and ascend some of the best alpine granite anywhere. Whether you plan to scramble up the 3rd class East Ridge of Mt. Russell, climb the 5.7 East Face of Mt. Whitney, or ascend the epic 18-pitch Sun Ribbon Arête, this guidebook will ensure you spend minimum time getting off route and maximum time enjoying the climbing.

About the Authors

Greg Barnes

Greg has been climbing since 1994, and he can tell you every move on every route he's done, draw a topo from memory, give you his opinion on the rating of any pitch, repeat anything written in any guidebook, and tell you about the weather that day. He is Director of the American Safe Climbing Association. From 1998 to June 2002, Greg replaced 121 bolts in Yosemite Valley by hand drilling, which takes 20-30 minutes of pounding per bolt. From Central Pillar of Frenzy to Stoner's Highway to Astroman to the Nose, Greg has worked hard to make climbing safer for all of us. Please support him and the other volunteers of the ASCA by visiting www.safeclimbing.org and donating! Greg lives in Bishop, Yosemite, Tuolumne, Joshua Tree, and Red Rocks and develops SuperTopos for these areas.

Chris McNamara

Climbing Magazine once computed that three percent of Chris McNamara's life on earth has been spent on the face of El Capitan—an accomplishment that has left friends and family pondering Chris' sanity. He's climbed El Capitan over 50 times and holds nine big wall speed climbing records. In 1998 Chris did the first Girdle Traverse of El Capitan, an epic 75-pitch route that begs the question, "Why?" Outside Magazine has called Chris one of "the world's finest aid climbers." He's the winner of the 1999 Bates Award from the American Alpine Club and founder of the American Safe Climbing Association, a nonprofit group that has replaced over 3,000 dangerous anchor bolts. He also serves on the board of directors of the Access Fund.

Steve Roper

Roper was never much of a fan of topos until now. "Routes were vague back in the old days," he says, "and by using vague words we guidebook writers could ensure that climbers would get just as lost as we did." Later, when topos first appeared, he saw their usefulness but was disgusted by their crude appearance. And a wordless description meant that the history of the route was also lost, perhaps forever. In Roper's many books about climbing and backpacking, he stresses history, feeling it's an integral part of the overall experience. "Think of doing the Nose without knowing the name Warren Harding!" The skeptic Roper is now at peace with SuperTopos, feeling that a few hundred well-chosen words placed next to a beautifully drawn topo is the best of all worlds.

Todd Snyder

Todd's impressive credentials include Yosemite Search and Rescue, guiding for Yosemite Mountaineering School and structural engineering work on top-secret supersonic aircraft somewhere in the California desert. He has been climbing for over 15 years and has climbed and/or guided climbers on nearly every great climb in Yosemite Valley. In 1998 he was featured in the climbing instructional video, "Introduction to Aid Climbing." He is currently Operations Manager for Corey Rich's photo business, Coreyography. You can see some of Todd's outstanding work by downloading our free SuperTopo of Half Dome's classic Snake Dike.

The Final Pitch

Chris McNamara

Thanks for buying this SuperTopo guidebook. We hope you enjoy it and the climbing adventure it may help you experience.

Your purchase means a lot to us. We here at SuperTopo are climbers who have set out to create a small business dedicated to giving you, and climbers like you, immediate access to the kind of detailed information you can normally only get by talking with a local expert. It takes a lot of work to create each SuperTopo and we are committed to making sure it's done right.

We are on a mission to develop SuperTopos for the best routes in the best climbing areas in North America. We hold ourselves strictly accountable to a high standard, namely that each of our SuperTopos offers the very finest quality route information obtainable anywhere on each and every route we cover. If you find any shortcoming in our SuperTopos, we ask that you drop us a line at: feedback@supertopo.com and let us know how we can improve. We're dedicated to offering the best information about every route available.

If you found this SuperTopo guidebook useful, we'd like to ask you two favors:

- Please post a message about your experience climbing these routes for the benefit of other climbers at: www.supertopo.com/routebeta

- Tell your friends about SuperTopo. We are about as grassroots an organization as you can imagine, and are entirely dependent on word-of-mouth referrals to keep producing quality SuperTopos.

On behalf of myself and the rest of the crew here at SuperTopo, I want to thank you for your support. Keep climbing and please tell a friend about SuperTopo!

Thanks again,

Chris McNamara

Founder and CEO
SuperTopo